Brewing the Burg

Miamisburg and its Brewers
in Ohio's Canal Era

Timothy R. Gaffney

Library of Congress Control Number: 2025921811

ISBN number: 9798993409603

Cover design: author.

Typography: IM Fell English by Igino Marini; Libre Franklin by
Impallari Type, Libre Franklin Project Authors; Crimson Text by
Sebastian Kosch, Crimson Text Project Authors.

No artificial intelligence tools were used
in the research or writing of this book.

Buried Valley Media
Miamisburg, Ohio
brewingtheburg.com

Dedication

To Brooke

Table of Contents

Acknowledgments.. 7

Introduction 9

Prologue: The Tavern on the River 11

1. The Brewer's Son 15

2. "The Arts and Mysteries of Brewing" 19

3. Henry Emde's Brewery... 27

4. The Basin and the Brewer...41

5. "One Blind Horse"...51

6. Beer on Water Street 65

7. Copperheads and Squirrel Hunters 73

8. A Brewer's Family in the Civil War................................ 83

9. New Brewery for New Beer 101

10. "Mr. Nusz was Largely Known".................................. 113

11. "These 'Tippling Houses' are a Sore Evil".................. 119

12. A. Kuehn's Brewery...129

13. "Order out of Chaos" 143

14. Miamisburg's "Ice War" 151

15. End of an Era 161

16. A New Century..169

Notes 177

Bibliography 195

Picture Credits...215

Index...217

About the Author.. 225

Acknowledgments

The story of Miamisburg's early brewers would not have been possible without help from many people and institutions. I am most grateful to my wife Jean and my family for tolerating my years-long obsession with this project. I am also grateful to Tina S. Ratcliff and her helpful staff at the Montgomery County Records Center and Archives, where I spent many days poring over massive volumes of handwritten documents. The staffs of the Warren County Records Center & Archives and Dayton Metro Library's Dayton Room were similarly helpful. Many volunteers for the Miamisburg Historical Society helped in innumerable ways, especially Ken Ballinger, Martha Ballinger, Laurel Benner, Kim Izor, Susan Johnson, Gary Petticrew and Teri Skudlarek. Nusz family descendants Erin Oldford, Whitney Engle and Jeff Shutz—all siblings—were a great help in sorting out

Nusz family history and sharing family pictures, and their uncle Jeff Moore graciously allowed me to photograph his rare John Nusz beer bottle. Justin Kohnen, owner of Star City Brewing, generously hosted and publicized my speaker series about local brewing history. Gina and Donald Miller, owners of Miami Valley Newspapers, granted me rare access to extremely fragile copies of early issues of the *Miamisburg News*. The Internet's vast, ever-growing and free body of digitized documents and publications was an essential resource. Two genealogical databases I found particularly valuable were Family Search and Find A Grave. Google Books made it possible for me to search countless historical publications. My research also depended heavily on the digitized collections of two vitally important guardians of American history, the Library of Congress and the National Archives.

Introduction

Miamisburg's early brewers never became legendary figures. The names of Emde, Hoover, Kuehn and Nusz, for instance, do not resonate in brewing history like Budweiser, Coors, Pabst or Schlitz. They led modest lives and their fame, if any, did not spread beyond their surrounding counties. When they passed from life they faded from memory, and they left few records to tell of their time in the world. Very few diaries, correspondence, business records or photographs have surfaced in public archives. Until the last third of the nineteenth century, they had no local newspaper to publicize their breweries or chronicle their activities. Historical accounts about the town and township pay them scant attention at most.

In writing this book, I was struck by the notion that trying to learn about the brewers, their breweries and their families seemed like trying to learn about ancient people from scraps of scrolls and shards of pottery scattered across the remains of a buried village. The image of an archaeologist, squinting through a magnifying glass at some relic half-sunk in the sand, often came to mind as I scoured birth, death and marriage records, census reports, court cases, deeds, mortgages, tax duplicates and gravestones for any fragment of information about them. Often, what fragments I found only made sense when I stepped back and examined them in a broader historical context. Slowly—painstakingly—I pieced them together until they resolved into people I could recognize and, to some degree, know.

Putting them in context also helped me see how their lives reflected great events and trends that shaped Miamisburg, Ohio and America in the course of the nineteenth century. They witnessed the coming of the Miami and Erie Canal, the rise of manufacturing, the advent of the railroads, the great cataclysm of the American Civil War and the growth of the temperance movement. They were not the instigators of great changes, but they and their families participated in their community and influenced it in their own ways—ways that were mainly minor, but occasionally consequential.

This book you now hold is not the last word on Miamisburg's early brewers. Rather, it is the first account that brings these individuals together and tells their long-forgotten stories in the context of their times.

Heritage Village in 2025, viewed from the levee of the Great Miami River. Left to right: Kercher House, smokehouse, Gebhart Tavern.

PROLOGUE

The Tavern on the River

Nestled on the east bank of the Great Miami River in southwestern Ohio, Gebhart Tavern stands as an ambassador of the past. Early pioneers hewed massive logs more than two centuries ago to build the sturdy, two-story structure. Its west-facing windows gaze across a grassy lot toward the river, as if expecting to see a Cincinnati-bound flatboat drift into view and its weary crew pull ashore for the night. Today Gebhart Tavern stands on its original spot as the centerpiece of Miamisburg's city-owned Heritage Village—a small square on the north side of West Lock Street between Miami Avenue and Old Main Street.

Gebhart Tavern was the first commercial building in a frontier settlement that was yet to become a village. It bears the name of its builder, Daniel Gebhart. He was one of many early Gebharts in the

Heritage Village Coordinator Susan Johnson and volunteers Dana Gagnon and Eileen O'Connor Book at Gebhart Tavern in 2025.

region and a son of Valentine Gebhart, who brought his family in 1805 from Berks County, Pennsylvania. They were in the vanguard of a great wave of migration that flowed out of the eastern states as a young nation expanded beyond the Allegheny Mountains.[1]

Historical accounts date the tavern to 1810 or 1811. Long covered with siding and used as a dwelling, the tavern was rediscovered in connection with America's celebration of the U.S. Bicentennial in 1976. The tavern was restored as faithfully as possible to its original form and furnishings, and today the Miamisburg Historical Society regularly opens it to the public.[2]

Built before the levee that now protects it—and downtown Miamisburg—from periodic floods, the tavern marked a landing on the river where travelers could stop for rest and refreshment. "Boats plying the river would land at this point and at low water, the river could be forded," Esther Light wrote in *Miamisburg: The Story of Our Town*, a collection of anecdotal essays. The tavern also stood near the primitive road between Dayton and Cincinnati. Besides boatmen and wayfarers, she wrote, "settlers from scattered farms might come for news of the old home back east and get their portion of 'schnapps.' "[3]

Light did not claim the tavern made its own schnapps or any other alcoholic beverage. But in the quest for Miamisburg's brewing roots, the association of taverns with drink, together with the strong German heritage the city's early settlers brought with them, begs the question of whether the tavern also harbored the first local brewery. Architect Marlin Heist, who oversaw the tavern's restoration, asserted as much in a 1982 newspaper interview. Heist, who was also a lifelong Miamisburger, said Gebhart stored beer for the tavern in tunnels dug into the back of the big hill that overlooks the town.[4]

The hill is a prominent landform rising more than two hundred feet from the river. Before the age of refrigeration, cellars or

Ohio historical marker at Heritage Village.

hand-dug caves were a common way to store beer, just as root cellars stored fruits and vegetables. A cave in the foot of the hill would have stored the beer on higher ground, safe from the river's periodic floods. The hill stands about a third of a mile southeast of the tavern, an inconvenient distance at a time when roads were no more than rough trails. As it happened, one of Daniel's brothers, Phillip (also spelled Philip,) owned a large farm that included part of the hill. Later chapters describe how a portion of Phillip Gebhart's farm became the location of choice for Miamisburg's biggest brewery.

A small brewery associated with the tavern is not an unreasonable notion. Up in Dayton, George Newcom added a brewery to his own pioneer tavern at about the same time Gebhart was building his. But alcohol was not a precondition to operating such a business. The word "tavern" today implies a place with alcohol, but in the nineteenth century it could have meant any house for the entertainment or lodging of travelers, whether it served alcohol or not.[5]

At this writing, no evidence of a brewery in association with Gebhart Tavern has surfaced. Heist's belief in a beer cave for the tavern may have been inspired by the later brewery's beer cellars, or he might have been thinking of a brick-faced burrow that once penetrated the south side of the Miamisburg Mound itself. But it is remembered as a root cellar, not a beer cave.

If the tavern had a brewery, it was most likely just large enough to meet the needs of the Gebharts and their clientele, in contrast to an independent operation serving local saloons and the general public. In the tavern's first years, no local market existed to support a brewery: the tavern stood nearly alone for several years before Miamisburg's establishment.

Barring some new discovery, the distinction of Miamisburg's first commercial brewery must go to a man whose accomplishment would have been lost to history but for a brief news article published more than a century ago.

Miamisburg in 1850, looking north on Main Street with the Miami House hotel (now Jayne's on Main) at right.

CHAPTER ONE

The Brewer's Son

Henry Emdee Junior was nearing his eightieth birthday when he returned to Miamisburg for a visit in August 1893. He stayed with his younger sister Sophia, the wife of local merchant John R. Beachler. Their home stood on the east side of South Main Street, a few doors north of Linden Avenue. Sophia was a lifelong resident of Miamisburg. Henry himself had not lived there since 1852, when he had moved his own family to St. Paul, Indiana. What he brought with him on this visit is not known except for one thing: his memories.[6]

Just a few weeks earlier, Emdee had lost his wife of more than fifty years. She was the former Elizabeth Longsdorff, a Pennsylvania native whom he had married in Miamisburg in 1839. Advanced in age and widowed, he was no doubt reflecting on his earlier years in Miamisburg. Now he was back in town—perhaps for the last time—to

Pioneer Reminiscences.

Mr. Henry Emde, of St. Paul. Ind , is the guest of his sister, Mrs John R Brachler, of south Main street Mr. Emde was born in Franklin, Warren County, O, October 3rd, 1813 Came to Miamisburg with his parents when 8 years of age His father, Henry Emde, sr, emigrated to America from Sweden, prior to the war of 1812, and located at Burlington, N. J , where he acquired the arts and mysteries of brewing He established the first brewery in Miamis burg The output of the brewery was about 8 barrels per week, brew ing twice a week, 4 barrels at each brewing. Henry Emde, jr, remembers delivering beer at Alexandersville. West Carrolton, Germantown and Franklin, when a boy about 16 years of age. The brewery was located on south Race (Canal) street, on the premises now accupied by the widow Gebhart. Henry Emde, Jr, removed to Decatur County, Ind, in 1852 About 21 years ago he visited this city to at tend the funeral of his brother, Mr. Geo. Emde About two weeks ago Mr Emde was bereaved of his beloved wife, by the grim reaper, and he is here to visit relatives, after which he will pass the remainder of his life among his children. He is in prosperous circum-tances and a well preserved looking man.

This *Miamisburg Bulletin* article claimed Henry Emde's brewery was the town's first.

reconnect with kinfolk who still lived there.[7]

Miamisburg had changed dramatically in his absence. A proper downtown had grown up around Main Street. A railroad ran through the village with a depot in the heart of town. Factories had sprouted everywhere. Hotels, restaurants and Charles Baum's opulent opera house glowed at night with electric lamps, as did the busiest street corners. Streets were still graveled, but paved sidewalks were spreading along them. New houses reflected prosperity, and a few mansions boasted of wealth.

But every familiar feature in town surely triggered memories. Emdee could remember the town in earlier times. He could even recall when it got its first bridge. It was a covered, wooden span that fostered the small settlement of Bridgeport across the river. It was a dry, time-saving alternative to the ferry at the north end of town or the ford to the south. If he had used the bridge, as was likely, Emdee could have remembered paying the toll and crossing it as a teenager— its tunnel-like span echoing the clop of horses' hooves and the thump of wagon wheels on wooden planks as he delivered kegs of his father's beer to Germantown.[8]

If memories did not spring up with every familiar sight, then surely they did in his conversation with a correspondent for the *Miamisburg Bulletin*, the older of the village's two weekly newspapers. The unnamed correspondent—likely one of the three Blossom brothers who published the paper—was writing a series of columns titled "Pioneer Reminiscences," and he took advantage of Emdee's visit to plumb his memory for recollections of his father's brewery. They met and talked sometime in early September.

Henry Junior ended his surname with two "e"s, and that is how his gravestone has it. But most records ended his father's name with just one "e." The *Bulletin's* editors chose that spelling for both men in the story that appeared in its September fifteenth issue.

The story offered a rare glimpse of an early Miami Valley brewery. But Emde's was especially noteworthy because—so the *Bulletin* asserted—it was Miamisburg's first.

The story described an impressive operation for its time and place. It said Henry Senior brewed eight barrels each week in two batches, or four barrels in a batch. A standard U.S. beer barrel is thirty-one gallons, so Emde was turning out the equivalent of more than thirty-five gallons a day, or 283 pints. It was a substantial amount, in the same range of a neighborhood brewpub today, while only a few hundred people lived in Miamisburg at the time. Emde was likely brewing for a wider market, and Henry Junior recalled delivering beer to Alexandersville, West Carrollton, Germantown and Franklin.

The story only hinted at when Emde started brewing. Born in 1813, Henry Junior recalled moving to Miamisburg from Franklin with his family when he was eight years of age. He also recalled driving the beer wagon when he was sixteen, which would have been about 1829. Was that when his father started brewing, or simply when he decided he could trust his son to roll out of town with a wagonload of beer? The *Bulletin* did not say.

At just over two hundred words, the story was a relatively generous feature for the *Bulletin*, a four-page weekly broadsheet. Still, it left much unsaid about Emde's brewery and the man himself. What it did provide were several key facts that a deep dive into public records could corroborate and which led to other records with more details. Together they make a convincing case that the *Bulletin* was correct. The story of Miamisburg's early brewers starts with Henry Emde.

William Penn's brew house as depicted in an 1882 illustration.

CHAPTER TWO

"The Arts and Mysteries
of Brewing"

T he Emdes—Henry, his wife Eve, Henry Junior and at least one younger sibling—were in Miamisburg by 1824, only six years after the town was laid out. It is likely they arrived a few years earlier.

Officially, Miamisburg was an unincorporated village in western Washington Township (Miami Township was not formed until 1829.) What the Emdes found was little more than a platted site, hugging the east bank of the Great Miami River and dotted with cabins. Daniel Gebhart's tavern was not more than fourteen years old. All around, pioneer farms were pushing back the wilderness. It was only two decades since Congress had carved it out of the vast Northwest Territory to make it the nation's seventeenth state. Except for small boats that could navigate the river, a rough wagon road was all that connected Miamisburg to other Miami River settlements between Dayton and Cincinnati. Another road led eastward, up the slope of the valley and over to Centerville, and one ran through the hills southeast to Springboro in Warren County. But any travelers heading west would have had to cross the river by ferry or ford. The Miami and Erie Canal was still a concept. Settlers would not hear the piercing whistle of a railroad locomotive for a generation.[9]

Entering town, the Emdes might have wondered if they had strayed into an enclave of some distant German kingdom. They would not have been far wrong. Anyone they met on a street might well have greeted them in German. If church goers, they would have found their two most prominent choices either Lutheran or German Reformed. Both congregations shared the same rough log church on the bank of Sycamore Creek east of town, and both heard their sermons given in German. This was so because most of Miamisburg's pioneers, while American-born, came from Pennsylvania Dutch country. That was the part of eastern and central Pennsylvania where immigrants from Germany's Palatinate region had begun settling in the 1600s, and they had faithfully preserved their old ways.[10]

The same was true elsewhere in the valley. In 1804 Philip Gunckel led a large group of German-speaking settlers from Pennsylvania's Berks County to Twin Valley, a picturesque dale about four miles west of Miamisburg. The group's German heritage was so strong that county officials named the area German Township. Likewise, the new village that Gunckel platted in 1814 took the name Germantown.[11]

The four men who recorded the plat of Miamisburg in 1818 also came from Pennsylvania Dutch country. Emanuel Gebhart was born in Lancaster County. Jacob Kercher came from Berks County. So did Dr. John Treon and his uncle Peter. The original plat map and many early records show the town spelled "Miamisburgh"—ending with an "h"—similar to Pittsburgh in their home state.[12]

But Henry Emde was not Pennsylvania Dutch. He was not of

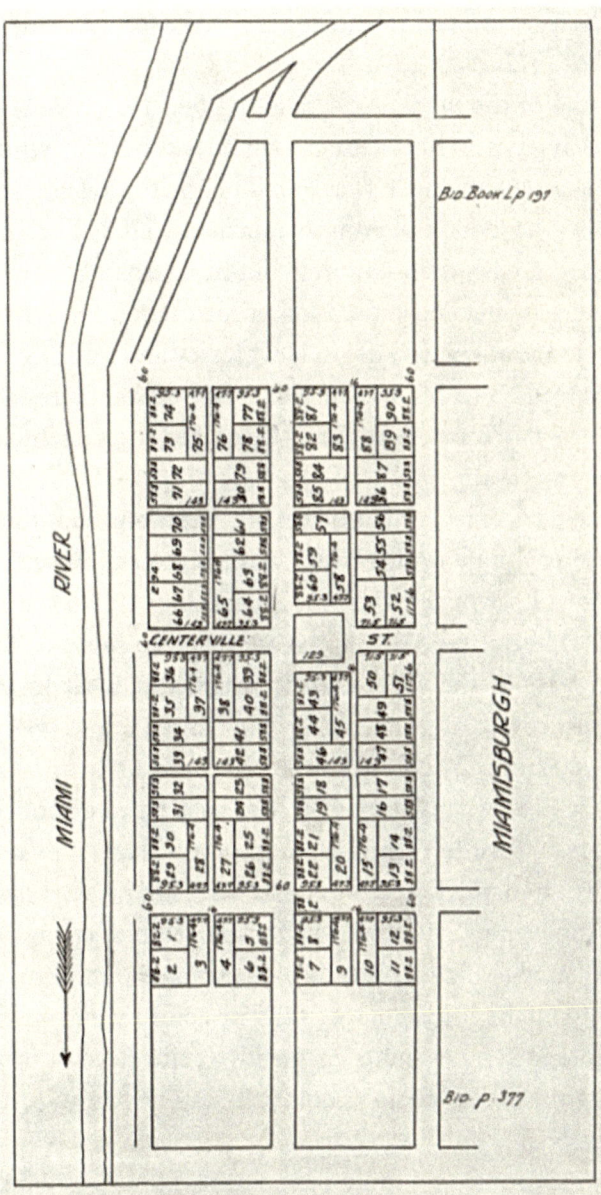

A transcribed copy of the original plat of "Miamisburgh." Note: "Centerville" Street is now Central Avenue.

German descent at all, according to the *Miamisburg Bulletin*: the paper gave Sweden as his homeland. Exactly when he emigrated, it did not say—only that he arrived in Burlington, New Jersey, sometime prior to the War of 1812.

It was one of the very few details the *Bulletin* gave about Emde's background. It gave no hint about when he was born or when he died. Public records identify his wife as Eve—her birth surname eluded discovery—who was born in Pennsylvania about 1788. The 1850 census shows her living with their children, but her husband's name does not appear—a sign he may have died sometime earlier. Likewise, the *Bulletin* said little about Henry's life in New Jersey and nothing about how or why he relocated to Miamisburg. But one detail it gave about Burlington was key: it was where Emde "acquired the arts and mysteries of brewing."

The *Bulletin* also left unanswered big questions about the beer itself. What kind did he brew? What was his recipe? How did it taste? Without direct knowledge, the best general idea comes from learning what kinds of beer Emde would have learned to brew in Burlington in the first years of the nineteenth century. But what kinds of beer *could* he have brewed at a time when the United States was not many years removed from the colonial era?

Just what is beer, anyway? The beer section in a modern supermarket offers a bewildering assortment of ales, lagers, pilsners, porters and stouts, to name but a few styles. They are brewed mainly with barley, but sometimes also with any combination of corn, rice, rye or wheat. They may be flavored with lime, orange, pumpkin, chocolate or even coffee. They flow out of taps in colors running the gamut from pale gold to black—sometimes with a thick head of froth, sometimes just a thin film of foam. Their taste can be sweet, bitter or lip-puckeringly sour.

All are variations on a basic recipe of just four ingredients: malt, hops, yeast and water. Malt is grain—usually barley—crushed and soaked in water. It is allowed to germinate, releasing sugars and enzymes, then dried. The malt can be roasted immediately for brewing or stored for later use. Hops are green, cone-shaped flowers that grow on climbing stems called bines. The pungent fruits contribute bitterness, aroma and flavor, and their acids add a natural preservative. Yeast is a single-cell fungus that feeds on the malt's sugars, releasing alcohol and carbon dioxide in the process.

Although brewing involves many steps, the basic recipe combines the malt and hops in water and brings it to a boil to create a mixture called wort (pronounced "wert.") The wort is allowed to cool to a point where yeast can be added, then set aside for several days while the yeast transforms the wort into beer—the magical process of fermentation. A brewer can produce different flavors and styles by tweaking the recipe with lighter or darker malt, using different varieties of hops, and adding fruits, spices or other flavorings. Frederick William Salem described the basic recipe in his 1880 book *Beer, its History, and its Economic Value as a National Beverage,* but it's one that European brewers have followed for centuries. Native Americans fermented beverages since ancient times, but Europeans arriving on the continent had their own notions of how beer should be brewed.[13]

Beer was aboard the ships of the first English colonists. The Jamestown colony in Virginia is said to have served beer at its first feast in 1607. *Mourt's Relation*, a detailed account of the *Mayflower's* arrival at Plymouth in 1622, said the Pilgrims reached land with "our victuals being much spent especially our beere." A belief widely shared in popular media is that the colonists, and Europeans in general, considered beer a safer alternative to water. The idea makes sense, especially on long sea voyages where water stored in wooden casks can become tainted. Making beer involves boiling water, and the alcohol in it has some preservative value. But the Pilgrims did not shun fresh water. On the same page it chronicled the beer shortage, *Mourt's Relation* described their going ashore to find "a very sweet brooke" and "many delicate springs of as good water as can be drunke ... " The *Mayflower's* Pilgrims may have favored the grain-based beverage for its nutritional value, not just for slaking their thirst.[14]

Early colonists struggled to survive in a world that was rich in resources, but not always the resources they knew. They needed barley and hops to make beer as they knew it, but barley was not native to

North America, and native hops were not the same as European varieties. Resourceful people substituted what was at hand. An early colonial ballad put it this way:

> If barley be wanting to make into malt,
> We must be content, and think it no fault;
> For we can make liquor to sweeten our lips,
> Of pumpkins and parsnips and walnut tree chips.[15]

Pumpkin, parsnip and other fruits could stand in for barley as a source of sugar. Walnut could also be used as a flavoring.[16]

Colonial soldiers often had to live off the land. If they wanted beer, they had to make it. Long before the American Revolution, George Washington had a recipe for "Small Beer"—meaning weak. The future first president was a young Virginia militia colonel at Fort Loudoun in Pennsylvania when he wrote it down about 1757. Preserved at the New York Public Library, Washington's handwritten recipe details the process for brewing beer over a campfire from bran, molasses, yeast and water. In cold weather, the soldier-brewer was to insulate the wort with blankets during a hasty, one-day fermentation.[17]

Another substitute for barley was maize, commonly called Indian corn. Native Americans created corn through thousands of years of cultivation and introduced it to early colonists, who found it a wonderfully versatile crop. In 1668 John Winthrop the Younger, governor of the Connecticut colony, gave a report to the Royal Society of London about the many uses of corn. It described how corn could be grown and malted to make "a very good beer." Malting maize required care, but in a pinch one could use fist-size chunks of cornbread instead.[18]

Even crushing corn stalks could yield a syrup adequate to make a kind of weak beer. But making beer that way could literally cost you an arm. A Cincinnati physician, Daniel Drake, described a graphic case in an 1852 publication. In 1792, he recounted, a colleague named

Richard Allison was stationed at a frontier Army post near Louisville, Kentucky, when word came of a terrible accident at a tiny settlement about six miles away. There, "one of the settlers had constructed a sort of mill for crushing Indian corn stalks from the juice of which the people made molasses and also a kind of beer." A young teen named John Pope was feeding corn stalks into the mill when somehow "his hand was caught, and his arm crushed nearly to the shoulder." The injury was so severe that Allison had to amputate the limb. The story might have ended there as another frontier tragedy, but Allison's operation succeeded. Pope not only survived to live another fifty-three years, but he also enjoyed a high-profile career as a lawyer, member of Congress, senator and governor of the Arkansas Territory. The loss earned him the enduring nickname "One-Arm Pope." In explaining his missing limb, most accounts only vaguely allude to some mishap. One could imagine him losing it in a battle or a duel. That a cornstalk mill took it while he was trying to make beer seems blissfully forgotten.[19]

As resourceful as they were, colonists preferred their traditional beer made of malted barley and hops—so much so that in early years they imported the ingredients from Europe. Ships bound for New England as early as 1629 included hops and malt on their manifests. They also cultivated the plants. The climate along the Atlantic seaboard was not favorable to barley, but it grew well in western New York, making it the early barley capital of the country. The story is similar for European hops.[20]

George Ehret's *Twenty-five Years of Brewing* named beer production as one of the earliest industries in colonial America, especially in the northern colonies. Beginning in the early 1600s, breweries popped up across New England. William Penn, founder of his namesake Pennsylvania, built the colony's first brewery and promoted brewing as an industry. Breweries were present in New Jersey at least by the early 1640s, when a Dutch settler named Aert Teunissen built one in Hoboken.[21]

Residents of Burlington, where the *Bulletin* said Emde learned to brew, lived clear across the state from Hoboken—about a hundred miles as the crow flies. But it was close to the biggest brewing center in the country. Burlington was right across the border from Pennsylvania, and Philadelphia was only about fifteen miles down the Delaware River. In a 1698 description of Philadelphia, local resident Gabriel Thomas wrote that it boasted "Three or Four Spacious Malt-Houses, as many Brew-Houses, and many handsome Bake-Houses for Public Use." *A History of American Manufactures* credits the city with an early reputation for the quality of its beer. Its porter beer, an innovation of the eighteenth century, "was considered scarcely inferior to the English, and was in repute throughout the country."[22]

The same history noted Burlington had breweries of its own by at least 1698, and in 1757 the *Pennsylvania Gazette* advertised for sale "A Large convenient Dwelling-house, with a Brew-house, and all necessary Utensils for Brewing, a large Malt-house adjoining the same, and a Hop-Yard."[23]

In 1810 the first U.S. census surveyed the state of America's manufacturing industry, including brewing. It found commercial breweries in ten of the nation's seventeen states and the District of Columbia. Altogether that year they rolled out nearly 183 thousand barrels of beer, ale and porter. Pennsylvania led with forty-eight breweries filling 71,263 barrels. In Philadelphia alone, eleven breweries filled forty-eight thousand barrels. New Jersey's six breweries produced far less, just 2,170 barrels. But more than half of it, or 1,238 barrels, came from a single brewery in Burlington.[24]

So, even in the new nation's first decades, the U.S. brewing industry was well established with many prodigious breweries. Pennsylvania was America's biggest beer-producing state, and it enjoyed a reputation for top quality. New Jersey trailed distantly overall, but Burlington had a powerhouse brewery and was close to the biggest brewing center in the country. The record of Emde's time in Burlington is blank, but it is clear he had access to the biggest American breweries of his day and, by extension, some of their most experienced brewers. He was well situated to learn the "arts and mysteries of brewing." He had no need for pumpkins, parsnips or walnut tree chips.

Old mill buildings still stand across South First Street from the site of Henry Emde's brewery.

CHAPTER THREE

Henry Emde's Brewery

When it comes to tracing Henry Emde's life, the *Miamisburg Bulletin* story is the only information tying him to New Jersey. He first surfaced in Ohio records in March 1813. They show him living in Franklin, five miles below Miamisburg in Warren County. He was already married to Eve, a Pennsylvania native who was about twenty-five years of age. The *Bulletin* story and other records indicate she was pregnant with Henry Junior, as he was born on October third. Several more children followed.

Like so much else about the Emdes, how they migrated from Burlington to Franklin is unknown. A route many westward-bound migrants traveled in those days was overland to Pittsburgh, then down the Ohio River to Cincinnati. From there the Emdes could have

Franklin's 1802 plat map shows the Emdes' lots, 29 and 30 (lower left,) on the east side of Front Street between First and Second.

followed other settlers up the Miami Valley to Franklin. Whatever their route, the trip was a journey of more than five hundred miles from Burlington to what was then America's western frontier.

As distant as they were from their old home, they may have found some familiar faces in their new neighborhood. The opening years of the nineteenth century saw many migrants from New Jersey settling on the border between Warren and Montgomery counties—so many that the area around the village of Carlisle, which straddles the county line next to Franklin, became known as the "Jersey Settlement."[25]

The migration began after the American Revolution with the opening of the Northwest Territory. This was a region northwest of the Ohio River that included present-day Ohio, Indiana, Illinois, Michigan, Wisconsin and part of Minnesota. With little hard currency but a lot of land, the federal government paid war veterans with certificates called military bounty land warrants. Veterans could redeem the warrants for land in the new territories or trade them. It also

allowed speculators to form companies to buy vast tracts and subdi-
vide them for resale to settlers. One such speculator was John Cleves
Symmes of New Jersey. Beverley W. Bond, Jr., who edited the collection of Symmes' official letters in *The Correspondence of John Cleves
Symmes*, described him as a respected Revolutionary War officer, a
delegate to the Continental Congress and a senior state justice. En-
thused by stories of the Ohio country and his own exploration along
the Ohio River, Symmes organized a group of investors in what was
known as the Miami Purchase (also the Symmes Purchase) to buy an
enormous tract running north from the Ohio River between the
Great and Little Miamis.[26]

By all accounts, the Miami Purchase was an ambitious venture
with deeply flawed execution. Bond faulted Symmes for careless sur-
vey work, "slipshod" record-keeping and other failures which led to
boundary disputes and "endless confusion" over land ownership. Settlers bombarded Symmes with lawsuits, and Congress enacted a series
of laws in an effort to straighten out the mess. Wrote Bond, "In view
of his long legal experience it is difficult to explain the utter disregard
for legal technicalities which he displayed. Perhaps with his dream of
a Western colony before him, such trifles as a legal title to his lands
seemed mere quibbling." Symmes died in "great poverty" in 1814 in his
namesake Cleves, Ohio, but he triggered a wave of migration from
New Jersey and Pennsylvania into the Miami Valley. Henry and Eve
were in that wave.[27]

Franklin was the creation of another New Jerseyan, William C.
Schenck. A highly educated surveyor, Schenck arrived in Cincinnati
in the early 1790s with other surveyors who worked across western
and central Ohio. He laid out Franklin in the winter of 1796 and platted
Newark, in Licking County, in the winter of 1801-1802. He made Franklin
his permanent home in 1803. Schenck served in the territorial and Ohio
legislatures and in the Ohio militia for some time, gaining the rank of
brigadier general. He was "highly esteemed" by the public for his "unim-
peachable integrity" among other virtues, wrote W. H. Shinn in *Memoirs
of the Miami Valley*. Schenck's reputation may have been a factor in
drawing New Jersey migrants like the Emdes to Franklin.[28]

On the thirtieth of March in 1813, Emde bought two adjoining lots, 29 and 30, from John and Elizabeth Sellman of Hamilton County. The parcels occupied the northeast corner of Second and Front (now River) streets. The deed is the earliest record of their presence in Ohio, but it indicates the Emdes arrived sometime earlier. It describes the parcels as "the same lots on which Henry Emde now resides."

Seven months after buying their homesite, Eve gave birth to Henry Junior, their first child. Five months later, Henry Senior took part in setting up Franklin's local government. Beers's *History of Warren County* lists him among twenty-three men who gathered in March 1814 to elect the first town council. Schenck himself was among them. The council comprised eleven officers and trustees, and electors chose nine from among themselves. One, of course, was Schenck. If Emde himself wanted to serve, he must have been disappointed: Beers never listed him on a council roster.[29]

The Emdes' livelihood in Franklin is another blank chapter. It is tempting to think it involved brewing. It was the only business his son ascribed to him, and it would have been a commercial skill of some value in a budding community. But no evidence surfaced that Emde started a brewery in Franklin or worked in one during his time there. Indeed, nothing was found to suggest Franklin even had a brewery while the Emdes lived there.

What history shows is that the Emdes were sailing into uncharted financial waters. Writing a century later in his doctoral thesis *A History of Banking and Currency in Ohio Before the Civil War*, Ohio State University Professor Charles Clifford Huntington found that Ohio after the War of 1812 witnessed a surge in population and unbridled growth in economic activity, spurred by a proliferation of banknotes without regard to gold or silver reserves:

> "... speculation in land, in town sites, in everything of
> which the new-comers stood in need was carried to a
> ruinous excess. Banks increased in all parts of the state
> and supplied an abundant circulating medium. This

removed the one obstacle to the wild speculation in
which the community wished to join, — it overcame
the scarcity of money, — and speculation ran riot."[30]

Ohio was experiencing a national trend, influenced by myriad factors
worldwide that would depress the economy for years. Looking back,
some historians and journalists have dubbed it the Panic of 1819.
("Panic" is an old label for a sudden financial downturn.) In his book
of the same title—with the subtitle *The First Great Depression*—historian Andrew H. Browning acknowledged there was no panic in a lit-
eral sense, in contrast to the "Black Tuesday" stock market crash of
1929 that triggered the Great Depression. Instead, it began as early as
1815 with a regional depression in the east that spread westward until
it became "a full-blown national depression" that lingered into the
mid-1820s. A later episode, the Panic of 1837, has been widely regarded as America's first great depression, but in Browning's view this
ignominious title should belong to 1819.[31]

Emde paid one thousand dollars for the property he bought in
Franklin. Exactly what served for money is not recorded, but the next
day he used the parcels to secure a 750-dollar loan from three Cincinnati men. He was to repay the loan "with lawful interest" in three in-
stallments over the next eighteen months. If his situation was typical,
Emde saw little in the way of "hard money"—gold or silver coin. Paper
notes stood in for currency—not just bank notes, Huntington wrote,
but the even more plentiful "shinplasters" with values as small as three
cents. They were issued by local governments and businesses, even
"private tavern keepers, and shoeblacks." Emde may well have bought
his parcels with such notes and taken his loan in notes as well.[32]

The record of Emde's life to the end of the decade is nearly blank,
but the times were not uneventful. "The speculation and high prices
promoted by the several years of commercial expansion and excessive
banking," Huntington wrote, "were succeeded by a contraction of
credits and a fall in prices when the banks endeavored to return to a
specie basis [gold or silver bullion or coin] in 1817." He called the wild

expansion of credit an "unnatural state of things [which] could not last long. Men who contracted debts found, when called upon for payment, that the means were wanting. Banks that had made excessive issues found themselves unable at times to redeem their paper on demand, and the currency of course began to depreciate." In Ohio, "the stagnation and distress following the Crisis of 1818-19 continued without relief through 1820 and 1821 and well into 1822." Across the state, food and land prices fell, hurting farmers and landowners.[33]

Local history books written in the 1800s said little about the financial downturn. They did not recognize it as a "panic," as they labeled later ones. But they noted a period of hardship in those years. Beers's *History of Montgomery County* observed that Dayton's rapid growth halted in 1820 "when the depression in business put a stop to all improvement." Beers also noted this: "Money was so scarce in 1820, 1821 and 1822, that trade of all kinds was carried on by barter. Wolf-scalp certificates"—notes issued by counties as bounty payments for wolf scalps—"were the 'log cabin currency.'" Augustus Drury's *History of the City of Dayton and Montgomery County* used the label "Hard Times" for the period from 1820 to 1827. But Browning argued the availability of more records in recent decades show the period was not just a financial bump in the road but "one of the great traumas of our nation's history." Specific examples of the impact in Ohio are scarce, but Browning found one in Cincinnati. The depression arrived there in 1818, he wrote, "and soon half of Cincinnati, which had been the country's fastest growing city, was in receivership."[34]

The Emdes could not have been immune to all this, and records of their financial activities hint as much. On October twenty-eighth, 1819, Emde gave neighbor Philip Rossman a promissory note—essentially an IOU—for 150 dollars. The note included a promise to pay it within twelve months, plus some amount of interest. Emde secured the note on November third by signing over one of his two parcels—Lot 30—for one dollar. The deal included the condition that Emde could keep the parcel if he repaid the note on time. Emde and Rossman had known each other for years. They had been among the electors who formed the first town council in 1814, and Rossman served on the council himself in the early 1820s and 1830s. But any good terms they were on must have vanished in 1820 when Emde's note came due. He failed to pay, and Rossman sued him in Warren County Common Pleas Court in Lebanon, the county seat. The court decided in Rossman's favor in August 1821, and Emde lost Lot 30 to him.[35]

In the meantime, Emde's situation went from bad to worse. One month before his note to Rossman was due, he wrote another note to Frederick Fox for 713 dollars. He secured it with Lot 29—the one his family lived on. Again he defaulted, and again he got hauled into court.[36]

The Emdes' woes did not end there. Even before their home was at risk, an obscure lawsuit from 1813 by Joseph Russell somehow came to a head in 1821. In October the "Sheriff's Sales" notices in the *Western Star* of Lebanon began advertising an auction of the Emdes' household belongings in relation to Russell's lawsuit. It was apparently the third attempt to execute the sale, and another—the last one found—was made the following February. Sad as it must have been for the Emde family, the notices give a glimpse of their household at the time. The February notice, in its original spelling, listed "2 milch cows, one horse saddle and bridle, 9 head of sheep, one ten plate stove with its pipe, one kitchen cupboard, two dozen chairs, one breakfast table, one bureau, and clock and case." The house itself went in November when the Fox lawsuit led to an order for the sheriff to auction off Lot 29. Fox himself made the winning bid.[37]

Again the record is blank until 1824, when the Emdes somehow resurfaced in Miamisburg. The *Bulletin*'s 1893 story only reported Henry Junior was eight years of age when his family relocated. That would have put the move sometime in 1821 or 1822, when Emde was still embroiled in lawsuits down in Warren County. At least one deed in 1822 identified the Emdes as still "of Franklin." The earliest record of Emde's presence in Montgomery County is a January 1824 deed for Lot 18, which he bought from Daniel and Polly Gebhart for twenty-five dollars. The deed described "Emdee" as a current resident, indicating he was already living in Montgomery County, if not Miamisburg itself. The parcel, now addressed as 48 South Main Street, is where the A. R. Stocker building has stood since 1890.[38]

By this time, Ohio and the nation had begun to recover from the aftermath of the panic. Huntington credited two major infrastructure projects, or "internal improvements" as they were known then: the opening of the Erie Canal between Lake Erie and the Hudson River, and the beginning of Ohio's own canal system. The Erie Canal gave Ohio "access at once to the markets of New York City and the Atlantic coast region," he wrote, while Ohio's canals connected the state's interior with Lake Erie and the Ohio River. Together, they put Ohio "well on the way to prosperity."[39]

The Main Street property may have been where the Emdes lived, or they may have used it for some other purpose—but not for the brewery. That establishment the *Bulletin* placed about a block east and south: "The brewery was located on south Race street, on the premises now occupied by the widow Gebhart."

Such a description might have been clear to readers in 1893, but it offers little help today. A stroll among the gravestones in the hilly, older sections of Hillgrove Union Cemetery might give you the impression that Miamisburg's nineteenth century population consisted almost entirely of Gebharts and Gepharts. Indeed there were many, and not a few of their descendants still live in the area. Any number of women named Gebhart might have been widowed at the time of the *Bulletin's* story. But the description offered a breadcrumb trail of clues that led to more information on old maps, deeds, census records, city directories and tax duplicates.

In 1869 Ellen Gebhart bought the south halves of two parcels. They included, the deed said, "all that part of Lots 10 and 11 of which Henry Emde died seized"—meaning Emde once owned the property. Lot 11 faces First Street just south of Linden Avenue, with Lot 10 adjoining it on the west. First Street originally was Race and later Canal, just as the *Bulletin* described and as nineteenth century maps show.

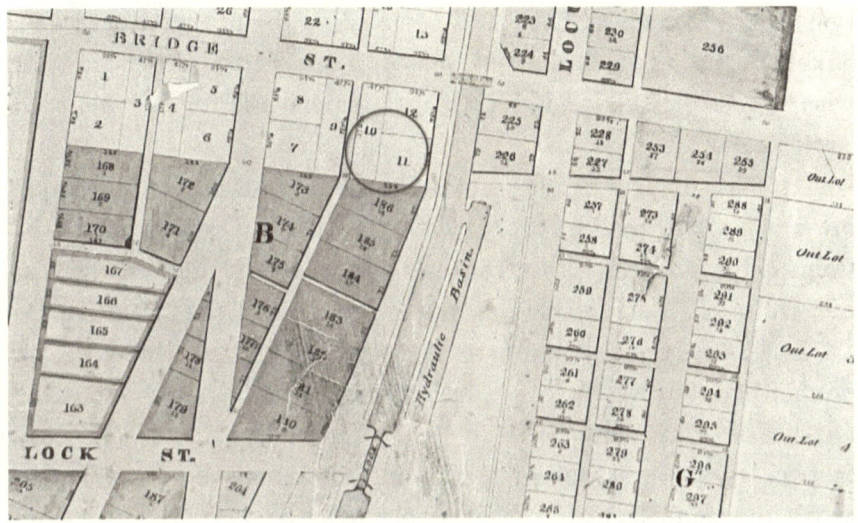

Henry Emde's brewery occupied the south halves of lots 10 and 11 (top center,) south of Bridge (Linden) and west of the canal.

Likewise, the 1880 census shows Ellen Gebhart living alone on Canal Street, and an 1880-81 directory placed her on Canal Street south of Bridge (Linden.) Finally, an 1898 issue of the *Miamisburg News* carried the obituary of Ellen "Gephart" ("Gebhart" in all other records.) She was eighty, of South First Street, and the widow of a Daniel Gebhart (not the pioneer tavern owner.) Today the brewery site is under a parking lot on the south side of the Masters Insurance building at the southwest corner of East Linden and South First.[40]

How Emde bought property and built a brewery in Miamisburg, after all his financial troubles in Franklin, is another missing piece of the puzzle, as is the exact year when he opened it. The first public record tying his name to a brewery is an 1832 real estate tax assessment. He may have been brewing earlier: 1832 was simply the first year Ohio levied property taxes on breweries, distilleries and several other types of business. Henry Junior's memory of delivering beer when he was sixteen indicates his father was brewing at least by 1829. Property records offer no more clues. Emde did not sign the parcels' deeds until March 1835, and they were not recorded until 1864. As in

Franklin, he may have been using or renting the property before he bought it. Or, as sometimes happened, he may have closed the deal with a handshake, leaving the legal paperwork for his heirs to straighten out.[41]

An even more difficult question is, what kinds of beer did Emde brew? The *Bulletin* did not say, but he most likely brewed the traditional choices: common beer, ale and porter. By the mid-1820s, all of the traditional ingredients for beer were available in the Miami Valley.

Barley was not native, but farmers in the region started growing it when early breweries "created a demand for barley which increased rapidly," W. C. Culkins wrote in *Memoirs of the Miami Valley*. As early as 1815, two prodigious breweries in Cincinnati consumed up to thirty thousand bushels of barley per year between them. Wrote Cincinnati physician Daniel Drake in his book *Picture of Cincinnati*, they produced "beer, porter and ale, of a quality at least equal to that of the Atlantic states."[42]

One of those breweries might have been the one owned by Daniel Symmes, another New Jersey transplant and nephew of John Cleves Symmes. Daniel Symmes died in May 1817, but new owners kept the brewery going. To do so, they shopped the region for barley. In July they began advertising in the *Western Star* that "ten thousand bushels of Barley will be wanted yearly for a number of years."[43]

Other breweries were opening between Cincinnati and Dayton. While smaller than Cincinnati's big plants, they all needed barley to make traditional beer. In 1822 John Doray let *Western Star* readers know his Lebanon Brewery "wishes to purchase a quantity of barley for which he will give a fair price." If Emde could not find a local farmer to sell him barley, he might have found one not far away in Warren County. Beers's *History of Warren County* found that by 1830, the fertile land between Lebanon and Middletown was "producing vast quantities of corn, wheat, oats, barley and pork."[44]

Less information is available about hops, but Drake listed "humulus lupulus"—the plant's botanical name—in a catalog of flora found growing in the Cincinnati area. Some breweries grew their own hops on small plots. In 1883 the *Bulletin* serialized a memoir by a "B. Day," who wrote about a hop yard in connection with a brewery where he apprenticed in 1822. He placed the operation "on the east fork of the Little Miami," east of Cincinnati and about thirty miles south of Miamisburg. Although Day's apprenticeship also included working in a blacksmith's shop, one passage he wrote gives a glimpse of what Emde's daily routine might have been like, including the cultivation of hops:

> Still I found time to run a mill, by horse power, to grind the malt for brewing, and during busy times about the brewery I often assisted in making fires under the malt kiln and copper boiler where the crushed malt and hops were boiled together. The malt had to be often turned on the kiln to prevent scorching. Then again we had a hop yard where, during the picking season, all found employment including those from the shop, the parlor and kitchen. This hop gathering season was looked upon more in the light of a little holiday festival than anything else.[45]

Miamisburg's first brewery came at a turning point in the town's history. The change was dramatic and visible. It was a spectacle Emde could have witnessed unfolding right across the street from his brewery, if he had it going on Race Street by 1828.

What he would have seen was an army of mud-streaked laborers, many of them German and Irish immigrants, digging a great trench along the east side of the street from one end of town to the other. Equipped mainly with picks and shovels, workers were excavating the channel of the Miami Canal—one of the two Ohio canals Huntington had credited with changing the state's fortunes after the Panic of 1819. Just down the street, he would have seen them building the massive walls and gates of a canal lock.

From the beginning of statehood, Ohio's leaders had seen that

The *Genl Harrison* at the Johnston Farm and Indian Agency in Piqua, Ohio, is a replica of boats that once plied the Miami Canal.

farmers needed a way to move products from the state's interior to markets on the East Coast and the Gulf of Mexico. In 1820 the state formed a committee to draw up plans for a canal to connect interior regions with ports on Lake Erie and the Ohio River. From the lake, shipments could go through the Erie Canal to the East Coast. The Ohio River gave access to the Mississippi and New Orleans. In 1825 lawmakers approved a plan for two canals. The Ohio and Erie Canal would serve the eastern half of the state. The Miami Canal would serve the western half, following the Great Miami River between Cincinnati and Dayton. (A later extension to Lake Erie caused its name to be changed to the Miami and Erie Canal.) Construction of both canals started in July that year. A groundbreaking ceremony for the Miami Canal took place in Middletown on July twenty-first.[46]

What followed was ditch-digging on an epic scale. Without the advantage of powered earthmoving machines, workers first had to clear trees, stumps, roots and other obstructions from a wide swath of

Miami and Erie Canal Lock 26 at Miamisburg in 1901 with the brick
lock tender's house. The flour mill is behind it and sawmill is at right.

land along the canal's sixty-six mile route. Next they had to dig the
canal itself. By regulation, the channel was to be no less than forty feet
wide at the waterline and four feet deep. It needed six aqueducts to
bridge creeks along its route, including Sycamore Creek just north of
Miamisburg. It also had to deal with an elevation gain of nearly three
hundred feet from the Ohio River to the Mad River in Dayton. The
solution was a series of thirty-two lift locks on the canal to raise or
lower boats as they passed through.[47]

One was Lock 26 in Miamisburg, where the appropriately named
Lock Street now meets First. Besides the walls and gates of the lock
itself, the design included a hydraulic channel or race that skirted the
east side of the lock between the canal and Locust Street (South Second.)[48]

The race helped regulate water flow at the lock, but it also provided an important power source for manufacturing. Over the next
several years, Emde could have watched a line of water-powered mills
rising along the race—first a sawmill and flour mill, and later cotton,
wool and linseed oil mills as well as an iron foundry. Together, they
established a manufacturing district that would boost the town's economy for the rest of the century.

The mills were more than simple buildings, and they produced more than commodities. They housed large machines, and their massive, water-driven parts made a percussion orchestra. Together they created a new soundscape at the south end of town—a mechanical symphony of rumbling water wheels, splashing paddles and chattering gears and grindstones. It was the music of manufactuing, and it was playing in Miamisburg. It informed local residents and travelers passing through that the village was no longer merely a farming community, but a rising industrial town.

Business flourished and Miamisburg grew. The 1830 census found 405 residents in the village, "but [it] has since rapidly increased," the 1833 *Ohio Gazetteer* reported. The same census found a township population of 1,830.[49]

The *Bulletin* did not say how long Emde continued to brew. The last tax record showing the brewery was for 1836, when it was marked "not in use." An 1890 story noted Sophia Beachler owned a small, 102-year-old chest her mother had used as a cash box "when Henry Emde was engaged in brewing on south Canal street, this city, in 1842." Emde himself was hard to trace by then: land and tax records naming Henry Emde might refer either to him or his son. Eve appeared without her husband in the 1850 census. After that, Eve herself disappeared.[50]

It seems a stroke of serendipity that Henry Junior returned to Miamisburg in 1893, just shy of his eightieth birthday and just as the *Bulletin*'s aging publishers were taking an interest in their town's history. Otherwise, the story of Henry Emde and his brewery might well have been lost forever: Henry Junior died seven months later. He is buried in St. Paul, Indiana. When his parents died, and where they rest now, remain to be discovered.

"Kneeling by the Miami," a bronze statue by Marie Barbera, is the centerpiece of a memorial at the Miamisburg Civic Center.

CHAPTER FOUR

The Basin and the Brewer

Near Gebhart Tavern in Heritage Village stands a plain, two-story house. Its gray lap siding might make you wonder how it earned a place there. But the siding covers a surprise. Peek around a corner at the back and you will see an exposed wall of hewn logs much like the tavern's. Another early settler, Jacob Kercher, built the house as early as 1809. He was a pioneer with large landholdings, and he was one of the four men who platted Miamisburg. Local preservationists two centuries later put his home next to Gebhart Tavern to save it from demolition. It originally stood a few blocks north at 14 West Ferry Street.[51]

That is where Jacob and his wife, Anna Margaret (Gebhart,) were living on February eighteenth, 1828, when they sold a portion of their

The Kercher House and a brick smokehouse in Heritage Village.

land for two hundred dollars to a man named Elias Murray. The parcel was a narrow wedge of ground stretching nearly one thousand feet along the east side of Race Street (North First,) from the north side of Market (Central Avenue) up to the south side of present-day Pearl Street. Bordering the east side of the strip was the not-yet-open Miami Canal.[52]

The canal may have been why Murray was in Miamisburg. He was a pioneer with a knack for seizing opportunities. Over his lifetime he opened a frontier store in Ohio with a brother and served in a militia during the War of 1812. He won numerous local elections and government appointments and founded the Indiana city of Huntington, which he named for his grand-uncle Samuel Huntington, a signer of the Declaration of Independence. Murray is an obscure figure in Ohio, but Indiana preserves his name on at least two historical markers: one in Huntington itself, and one in Fort Wayne that marks the place where work started on the Wabash and Erie Canal—of which Murray was a state commissioner. But the few published biographical sketches of Murray miss his time in Miamisburg.[53]

Two sketches describing Murray's early life agree he was born in New York in 1787, but they give slightly different accounts of his arrival in Ohio. In one, he moved to Cleveland with a brother about 1810 and opened the fledgling town's first general store. In the other, he moved to Delaware County and opened the first store in Galena the same year. The accounts agree he served in the War of 1812 as chaplain of a cavalry company with the rank of captain, which made him "Cap-

tain Murray" for life. He also married Dolly Byxbe Messenger, the widowed daughter of Moses Byxbe, a politically connected co-founder of Delaware, Ohio.[54]

Murray enjoyed his own political affiliations. Besides the Huntington he memorialized in Indiana, he was also a distant cousin of another Samuel Huntington. This one became an Ohio supreme court justice and served a term as governor from 1808 through 1810. Murray himself made a

Elias Murray's wedge of land, with basin at upper right on 1848 map.

lifelong career of elected and appointed positions in state and local governments, including three terms as an Ohio state representative—in 1820, 1824 and 1825. His last term put him in the right place at the right time to vote for the bill that created the Ohio canals, and then to benefit from it. The bill tasked the Canal Commission of Ohio with overseeing construction, and the commission's 1830 report shows it paid Murray for work between 1825 and 1829. His name appears several times in long lists of contractors and workers.[55]

Murray's wife Dolly died in 1825. Sometime that year or the next, he left Delaware for Montgomery County, where he married Henrietta Pond in 1826.[56]

Why he moved is not clear, but his canal work may have been a factor. He showed up in Washington Township's 1827 tax duplicate with personal property assessments on a horse and a cow. Miamisburg still lay in Washington Township, and the canal was going right through the village.[57]

The canal was more than a long ditch. It included a variety of features to control the movement of water in the canal and boat traffic on its surface. In addition to a lock and an aqueduct, the Miamisburg section included a basin at each end of town. An 1893 canal map put the northern basin on Murray's parcel, roughly midway between Ferry and Pearl streets. It was a rectangular pool a bit larger than a basketball court. It was just large enough for a canal boat to pull out of the channel to load, turn around, or for any other necessity.[58]

The basin was a significant feature of Murray's parcel, but the record of his purchase did not note it. Murray was surely aware of it, and records suggest he had a hand in planning or even digging it as a part of his canal work. As Murray sold off chunks of his parcel over the next few years, several deeds and mortgages referred to the pool as "Murray's basin" or the basin "formerly made by Elias Murray." (A few early records spelled it "bason.") It was significant because it added value to the adjacent properties. The very same day Murray bought the parcel from the Kerchers, he resold a piece along the south side of the basin—the future Lot 212—to Edwin A. Vickroy for one hundred dollars. It came "together with the privilege free of all charges of shipping, all exports and imports to and from said lot through the bason." That sale alone recouped half of what Murray had paid for the whole parcel. Vickroy built a warehouse on his land, and Murray built one on the north side of the basin, on the future Lot 211.[59]

But Murray did not stick around. He and his family had moved to Indiana by the time he sold off the last lots of his parcel. In the Hoosier state he left a checkered legacy. Indiana recognizes him for founding Huntington and serving in the state legislature. But the Miami Tribe of Oklahoma remembers him for his role in rounding up the Myaamia (Miami Indian) people for their forced removal from the area of Peru, Indiana. In October 1846, five canal boats carried more than 300 Miami people up the Wabash and Erie Canal to Toledo and down the Miami and Erie Canal to Cincinnati. From there, steamboats ferried them to Kansas City for a brutal winter trek to a reservation. (The government later uprooted them again and forced them to resettle in Oklahoma.) The canal boats made a melancholy procession along a river and through places that carried the Miami people's name—including Miamisburg, where today a marker describes their forced relocation. It is part of a memorial located outside the Civic Center on land Murray once owned.[60]

What did Murray's basin have to do with brewing beer? It drew David H. Hoover to the neighborhood. In 1833 Hoover bought Lot 211 in two parts (as Murray had subdivided it.) He paid just twenty-five dollars for the top part, but he shelled out 925 dollars for the bottom— the part whose south side bordered the basin. Similar to Lot 212, it came with "the perpetual privilege of egress and ingress of said basin," as well as the warehouse Murray had built. A year later, Hoover bought two parcels farther down Murray's tract. This was where he opened a brewery, making him Miamisburg's next brewer after Henry Emde.[61]

David H. Hoover was a Pennsylvania transplant, born in 1799 to Frederick Adam Hoover and Frederick's first wife, Magdalena Herrman. He was the eldest of eight siblings, with five brothers and two sisters. His father was of German descent, born in what is now Lebanon County, Pennsylvania. Sometime in the early 1800s, David's family joined the westward migration. A biographical sketch of the family, published in Drury's *History*, described Frederick as "one of the very early settlers of Montgomery county." David, it noted, "was reared to farm life" on the 243-acre farm his father bought in 1817, south of town in the area of Pipestone Creek. County tax records also show Frederick had a distillery at least by 1832, the first year the records listed breweries and distilleries.[62]

Relatively little is known about David's early life. As part of his agrarian tutelage, he may have learned how to make fermented beverages in his father's distillery. He also had another family connection with fermented drink. In 1828 he married Catharine Houtz, a daughter of another farmer-distiller. She too hailed from Pennsylvania Dutch country. Born in 1806 in Lancaster County, she was a daughter of John and Elizabeth Snyder Houtz. Her father was a prominent business and land owner there. According to Drury, he owned about nineteen thousand acres, nearly as much land as present-day Miamisburg and Miami Township combined. He also ran a flour mill, barrel-making shop, store and distillery. Why he gave it all up to take his family west, Drury did not say, but he joined the migration to Montgomery County in 1818. There, John resumed farming and distilling, "sending his products down the Ohio and Mississippi rivers on flat boats to New Orleans"—a standard practice before the canal era. But at some point he pulled up stakes again, settling for good in Miami County. Wrote Drury, Houtz became a "strict Presbyterian" and quit making liquor.[63]

In February 1834, David Hoover paid Peter Richard ("Reichard" or "Reickard" in some records) nine hundred dollars for Lot 215. Another piece of Murray's old parcel, it stretched 127 feet along the east side of Race Street, midway between Ferry and Market.

Hoover soon built his brewery there, either in a new building or by converting the warehouse Richard had built on the northwest corner of the property. In November his brother Martin bought a half-interest in the property for 450 dollars. A month later they jointly bought the next parcel north, Lot 214. Its price, just seventy-five dollars, suggests it was undeveloped, but by 1840 a brick malt house stood on it.[64]

The Hoover brothers had the brewery going by 1836, but its name, if it had one, seems lost to history. That year's county tax duplicates show an assessment on "Hoover D & M" for "1 Brewery." Breweries today often have imaginative names—"Toxic Brew" and "Warped Wing" in Dayton and "Entropy" in Miamisburg come to mind—but at least in this case, no business name was recorded. A few later records, such as an 1843 mortgage, describe the property as "the Miamisburg Brewery," but that simply may have been a way of saying where it was. Any name engraved on the signboard outside the establishment's door—if a signboard it had—is gone with the brewery. With at most one other brewery at the opposite end of town—Emde's, if it was still going—a formal name may have seemed superfluous.[65]

Today, all signs of the brewery and most signs of the canal are long gone. The front lawn of the Miamisburg Civic Center covers the spot where the brewery stood, and the civic center building stands on the old canal bed. From there, vestiges of the canal run northeast, starting with the narrow, leafy lawn of Keelboat Park between Pearl and Sycamore streets. Continuing on, a narrow lane still bears the old name Canal Street until it meets the north end of Fourth at Sycamore Creek. There, a screen of trees and brush hides massive stone walls that line the creek and support a small footbridge. The overgrown stonework marks where the aqueduct once carried canal boats across the creek.

In his time, Hoover could have stood outside his brew house and watched the daily promenade of long, narrow boats—freighters loaded with cargo and packets crowded with passengers—gliding languidly up and down the canal, towed by teams of horses or mules, their hooves beating a slow rhythm on the earthen towpath.

Hoover's brewery stood at the north end of town, but the area around it was burgeoning. Infrastructure projects like the canal boosted the continuing flow of settlers into the region. Just a block west of the canal, the Great Miami Turnpike—forerunner of the Dixie Highway—followed Main Street through Miamisburg to connect river towns from Cincinnati to Dayton. The 1841 edition of Jenkins' *Ohio Gazetteer and Traveller's Guide* listed a wide array of manufacturing and merchandising operations, including "1 brewery"—another hint that Emde's brewery may have closed by then, leaving the local beer market to the Hoover brothers.[66]

How David Hoover used the warehouse on the north side of the

Keelboat Park, looking north from East Pearl Street in 2025 (top,) and remains of Sycamore Creek aqueduct in 2024.

basin is unclear, but Vickroy's old warehouse on the south side became a well-known general store. The basin's time eventually passed. The Bookwalter wagon wheel company filled it in and built over it by the end of the 1860s, but memories of the basin and the store lingered.[67]

Simon Huiet, the store's proprietor, could have been a poster child for Miamisburg's early development. He was a son of one of Miami

Township's noted pioneers. Philip Huiet's mill on the Great Miami River at Sycamore Creek is said to have supplied five hundred barrels of flour to the Army during the War of 1812. A lengthy obituary in the *Miamisburg Bulletin* described Simon as part of a large family—the eleventh child and seventh son, born in 1802—transplanted by his parents from North Carolina when he was about four. The Huiets had journeyed to Utica, Indiana, then to Preble County, Ohio, before finally settling in the Miamisburg area in 1812. The same year, Philip built his mill and operated it until his death in 1816. Simon moved to Warren County in 1823 and ran a sawmill for two years, then returned to rebuild his father's mill. He ran it until 1828, when he took a contract to work on the construction of the canal. Once the canal opened, Huiet launched a career as a canal boat captain. He quit the canal boating business in 1836 to build a distillery along the creek. He operated it until 1842, when he went back to boating, farming and other pursuits—including the store.[68]

In 1887, a decade after Huiet's death, the *Bulletin* nostalgically recalled the old "Huiet Grocery Building on the site of the old basin" as the Bookwalter company tore it down to expand its factory. "It was a famous trading place in early days," the paper reported. "Who has forgotten the conical packages of loaf sugar, in blue paper, suspended from the ceiling—and how many remember the giant frog that roared in the basin, moonlight nights?"[69]

Down at their brewery, the Hoover brothers might have heard the basin's throaty frog. But Martin Hoover and his wife Julia Ann moved to Clark County after a few years, and in 1839 he sold his interest in the brewery for eighteen hundred dollars.[70]

The buyer was Joseph Watson. He was born in Vermont, but he was hardly a stranger when he became David Hoover's partner. He had married Nancy Houtz in 1827, a year before Hoover had married her sister Catharine. Even before they partnered on the brewery, it seems Hoover and Watson shared some other venture. For several years beginning in 1836, county tax duplicates show "Hoover & Watson" assessed on two nonadjacent parcels at the north end of town. The records are silent about what they did there, but as early as 1835 Watson also entered into a budding farm implement business at the south end of town. Hoover would join him there several years later, changing his career and Miamisburg's future.[71]

But by April 1842, David H. Hoover was in trouble. He was about to sign away his brewery, the land where it stood and more—even his own home—for a dollar.

David Hoover's brewery stood about where these trees now grow on the east side of North First, midway between Ferry and Central.

CHAPTER FIVE

"One Blind Horse"

B y the 1830s, Americans had dug themselves out of the Panic of 1819—literally, in the case of the canals, but also with steam technology. Railroads, ships and factories quickly embraced it. "The decade from 1830 to 1840 witnessed the beginning of a new era of progress throughout the civilized world," Huntington wrote in his banking thesis. "The country was in the midst of an era of internal improvements, and the possibilities of the future seemed unlimited." But it also seems the country overcame the depression without learning its lessons. Huntington especially noted the return of land speculation, fueled by cheap government prices combined with a growing demand for money and a proliferation of banks all too eager to print banknotes. Alasdair Roberts, Canadian public policy professor, argued that people in the early 1800s looked at financial times in much the same way they viewed the weather: in hard times, finance could seem "incomprehensible, fickle, and dangerous. In good times, when everyone was making money, this analogy was easily forgotten, and in 1836 the weather still seemed good to many people," Roberts wrote in *America's First Great Depression: Economic Crisis and Political Disorder after the Panic of 1837.* "And yet," he added, "there were signs of trouble on the horizon." Across the country, commodity prices and land values were soaring, and banks once again "became careless" about maintaining reserves to back up their banknotes.[72]

In other words, the same stormy economic weather that swirled around Emde during his time in Franklin was blowing back up nearly two decades later, just as David H. Hoover was taking on debt to buy land and start his brewery.

In May 1835, Hoover mortgaged his property on the north side of the basin to his father for fifteen hundred dollars. The mortgage noted he needed the money to pay off a promissory note he owed to someone else. Ten months later, David and his brother Martin gave John D. Mullison ("Molleson" in some records) a promissory note for 1,650 dollars, securing it with the brewery. Separately, in November 1840, he and Joseph Watson—who had replaced Martin as David's partner—mortgaged the malt house to William Sawyer, a local blacksmith, for 637 dollars and fifty cents.[73]

At the same time, David was essentially buying back his own land at a premium. In 1834 he had sold a half interest in his brewery to his brother Martin for 450 dollars, and together they had paid seventy-five dollars to buy the adjacent parcel for the malt house. In 1839 Joseph Watson had bought Martin's share for eighteen hundred dollars. Fifteen months later, Hoover bought out Watson's interest for twenty-five hundred dollars—five times what he had paid in the first place. The higher price may have reflected significant improvements on the property, but the deed does not note any.[74]

By the 1840s, Hoover's debt problems were mounting. In September 1840, Mullison sued David and Martin for failing to pay off the promissory note they had given him four years earlier—the one secured with the brewery property. In December 1841, a year after buying out Watson's interest, Hoover mortgaged the malt house property again. This time it was to Harry Gardner of Butler County for 350 dollars and fifty cents. But he still owed Sawyer for the same property, which he and Watson had mortgaged to him a year earlier.[75]

In the meantime, America's economy was teetering atop a mountain of credit. It only needed a nudge to tumble it. Alasdair Roberts wrote that the Panic of 1837 started with a viral rumor about a New York bank president's suicide. "It was not true—he had died of a heart attack ... but it was enough to start a run on the bank," Roberts wrote. The immediate impact was limited, but it was the first financial shock that would lead to a years-long depression. Banks across the country suspended operations or folded, business ground to a halt and even state governments defaulted on loans.[76]

The local impact gets scant attention in history books from the nineteenth century. Frank Conover's *Centennial Portrait* noted "the great commercial panic which spread over the country" and a "sudden depression" in pork prices. But newspapers across Ohio were full of articles and advertisements reflecting tough times. Political rhetoric and bombast about banking and monetary policy filled columns on front pages, while inside pages revealed the local impact in grittier terms. In 1839 the *Cleveland Herald* reported, "The *Yazoo Banner* published at Benton [Mississippi], is filled entirely with advertisements— nearly all legal ones. Times are getting worse and worse." The *Clermont Courier* of Batavia had similar news about nearby Cincinnati in September: "The *Cincinnati Gazette* of Friday last, has advertisements of seventy-two Sheriff's sales, the property of some of the most respectable and heretofore the most substantial citizens of the Queen City." In Lebanon, the *Western Star* began publishing eight or more notices of sheriff's sales or public auctions every week.[77]

As the depression ground on, some merchants sought to turn the grim reality of "hard times" into a selling point. In 1840, for example, a Maumee City store offered goods "on terms to correspond with hard times." Likewise, in 1842 the *Hamilton Intelligencer* carried Ebert &

Cummings' ads for cooking stoves "calculated in size and price to suit the present hard times." Numerous ads also made plain the need for hard currency instead of credit—none more so than Lebanon pork packer William Russell's one-sentence notice in the *Western Star* refusing credit in May 1842: "These times are enough to make any man in his senses know that I want money."[78]

Evidence of the depression's impact on Miamisburg itself is thin—the town had no newspaper of its own in those days to chronicle events—but one example brought it a bit of notoriety. It was the so-called Washington Bank, which stemmed from an effort by the area's early settlers to create a public library. In 1810 a group of private investors formed a joint stock company they called the Washington Social Library Company. It received a state charter. "This library was kept up for thirty years and was a source of much intellectual improvement to the township," Joseph Nutt, an early Centerville resident and official, wrote in Beers's *History of Montgomery County*. But a new group of investors in 1839 turned its business to banking and started printing banknotes as the Washington Bank. The state general assembly yanked its charter in 1840, and the next year it lost an appeal to the state supreme court. "Its life was a brief one, but long enough for some persons to lose large amounts of money," Nutt wrote.[79]

The economic swoon pulled Hoover down with it, or so he hinted. On April fourth, 1842, he signed a document called an assignment. In it, he blamed "the misfortunes of trade and change of times" for being unable to pay off debts amounting to some five thousand dollars. The assignment was an agreement to hand over certain properties to an assignee. The assignee's job was to settle Hoover's debts by selling off his property and distributing the proceeds among some thirty-six creditors. The assignment described three parcels he was giving up: two adjoining lots south of the basin, including the brew house and the already twice-mortgaged malt house; and the lot on the north side of the basin, which included the warehouse and "the property on which said Hoover now lives." The land and buildings were not all. Hoover also signed away "all my stock of ale, beer and porter

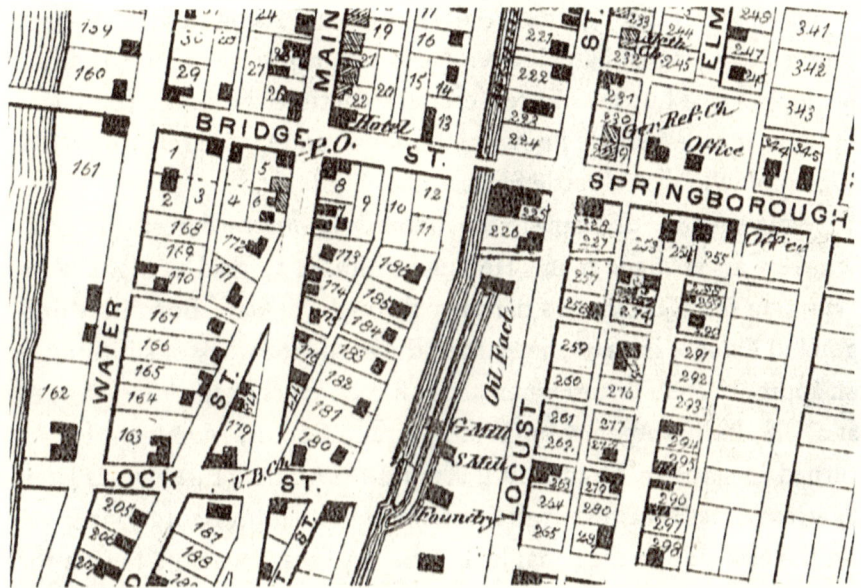

The foundry of McElwee and Sawyer, bottom center on an 1869 map. Note nearby canal lock with mill race and mills.

on hand, & all grain and apparatus belonging to my brew-house," including "one blind horse, one stove, one windmill, all my house hold and kitchen furniture not excepted above, all note book accounts, and judgements in my favor and all other articles which may not now be recollected." The "excepted" items were only the few essentials that the law allowed a family in financial straits to keep.[80]

The assignee was Emanuel Gebhart, one of the signers of the original plat of Miamisburg. Born in Pennsylvania in 1786, he had come to the area in 1808 or 1809. He was politically active, holding local public offices from time to time. A veteran of the War of 1812, he was known as "Colonel" Gebhart. For Hoover's assignment, he was to use "the best of his judgement and discretion" to sell properties and settle debts "after deducting all the necessary expenses."[81]

How lucrative the assignment would have been to Gebhart is not clear, but it soon became moot. Hoover would have to reckon with a preemptive lawsuit by William Sawyer.

Sawyer was a rough-hewn blacksmith and rising politician about four years younger than Hoover. Deed and mortgage records indicate he made a side business in real estate, sometimes holding promissory notes as mortgages. He knew the business, and he did not sound like someone who would settle for less than his due.

Sawyer's 1877 obituary in the *Miamisburg Bulletin* described him as "entirely a self-made man." He taught himself to read at night "after swinging the blacksmith's hammer through the day." Born in Montgomery County in 1803, he learned the hard, hot work of smithing as an apprentice in Dayton when about fifteen years of age, then worked at a U.S. Indian Agency outpost in Grand Rapids, Michigan. He returned to settle in Miamisburg around 1829. Some three years later, Sawyer started Miamisburg's first iron foundry with George McElwee on the east side of the canal lock, where a vacant lot now lies on the south side of Star City Brewing. The same year, Sawyer began serving the first of three annual terms as a state representative. He seemed to love the soapbox as much as the forge: the obituary added, "While actually at hard work at the anvil, he frequently made speeches to listening neighbors who gathered into his shop."[82]

Finishing his run in the state legislature as house speaker, Sawyer aimed higher. He ran for a seat in the U.S. House of Representatives. A Democrat, he ran twice in Montgomery County—in 1838 and 1840—each time failing to unseat Whig incumbent Patrick Gaines Goode. In the 1840 race, Sawyer found himself running during the presidential campaign of William Henry Harrison, a well-heeled Virginia native who had served as secretary of the Northwest Territory and first governor of the Indiana Territory. Democrats suggested the aging Whig should retire to his "hard cider" and "Log Cabin"—an insult Harrison's supporters spun into the successful "Hard Cider and Log Cabin" campaign, burnishing his image as the champion of the common man. In *History of the Maumee Valley*, Horace G. Knapp wrote that Sawyer tried the same idea in his own campaign. He used a stump speech to cast himself as a frontiersman. He also sketched an image of Miamisburg as it was then, or at least as he wanted voters to see it:

"As to myself," continued Sawyer, "I was born in a log cabin, and I yet reside in a log cabin. My blacksmith shop, where, when at home, my circumstances compel me to severe toil about twelve hours out of the twenty four, is a log cabin. My associations, sympathies and hopes have ever been, and now are, identified with pioneers of the country, and the occupants of log cabins."[83]

In 1843, after back-to-back losses in Montgomery County, Sawyer moved sixty miles north to St. Marys. Running in a different congressional district the next year, he found the votes he needed to win the first of two consecutive House terms. In the halls of Congress, Sawyer's western background and unrefined ways made the Democrat an easy target for Whig-leaning newspaper correspondents. The *United States Gazette* of Philadelphia called him a representative "from some backwoods benighted region in Ohio" who had grown up on "hog and hominy." Horace Greeley's *New York Daily Tribune* roasted him for his habit of taking a two o'clock lunch break every day in the House chamber:

About that hour he is seen leaving his seat, and taking a position in the window back of the Speaker's Chair, to the left. He unfolds a greasy paper in which is contained a chunk of bread and a sausage or some other unctuous substance. These he disposes of quite rapidly, wipes his hands with the greasy paper for a napkin, and then throws it out of the window.—What little grease is left on his hands he wipes on his almost bald head which saves any outlay for Pomatum."[84]

No doubt Sawyer could stand the sting of flying sparks all day long, but he was thin-skinned when it came to ridicule. The offended lawmaker aired his complaint in the House and persuaded a majority of its members to revoke the *Tribune* reporter's press privileges. But his actions only drew more attention. "Mr. Sawyer was resolved to go down to posterity in some shape," the *New Bedford Mercury* declared, "and he will henceforth be known in history as 'the man who boarded himself in the Hall of Representatives.'" The *Mercury*'s words were prophetic: the incident lives on today as a post in the House historian's blog.[85]

Sawyer still lived in Miamisburg at the end of 1841 when Hoover filed the assignment. The long list of creditors attached to it included Sawyer, but he was not about to take what likely would have been pennies on the dollar. Sawyer sued both Hoover and his former partner Watson in common pleas court, which found in his favor and ordered the malt house sold at auction. Sawyer was not alone. Mullison also sued Hoover along with his brother Martin, his brewery partner before Watson. This time the court ordered the brewery sold. Both parcels went on the block in February 1843. Both were scooped up by John Swartztrauber, who bid 1,185 dollars for the brewery and six hundred dollars for the malt house. Thus ended Hoover's brief brewing career. The brewery, including the malt house, would continue to operate under other owners. Hoover's failed venture would be forgotten, overwritten by later accomplishments.[86]

Swartztrauber was a recent arrival from Germany, one of the growing number of German immigrants who were swelling the populations of Miamisburg and the Miami Valley. Born in 1804 in either Bavaria or Württemberg—records differ—he arrived in Miamisburg in 1842 or 1843 with his wife, Catharine Albrecht Swartztrauber, and their growing family. Through the rest of the century, public records, directories and newspaper stories frequently connected Swartztrauber and his sons with brewery-related activities, including saloons, a vineyard and an ice business. John and Catharine's name appeared as "Swartztrauber" on deeds and on their grave monument in Hillgrove Union Cemetery, but as "Schwartztrauber" in many other public records and newspaper reports. (Their eldest child, Jacob, has the longer spelling on his gravestone, and he will go by it in this book.) Spelled either way, for a short time Swartztrauber was Miamisburg's only brewer.[87]

Like Hoover, Swartztrauber turned to Sawyer for financial help. In April 1843, he signed a promissory note to Sawyer for five hundred dollars, securing it with the same malt house. When it came due three years later, Swartztrauber failed to pay. Sawyer, just as he had done with Hoover, dragged him into court—or tried to: Swartztrauber defaulted, and his malt house went back on the block in March 1848.[88]

This time the buyer was Jacob Zimmer with a bid of 317 dollars. Born in 1815, Zimmer was another immigrant. He hailed from Bettenhausen, a village in what was then the Kingdom of Bavaria. He arrived in Miami Township in 1835. Zimmer held several occupations over his 86-year lifetime, including hotelier, vintner, county auditor and railroad agent. He is best remembered as a tobacco buyer credited with developing a new variety dubbed "Zimmer Spanish," a well-known leaf in the late 1800s. He also wrote the chapter about Miami Township in Beers's *History of Montgomery County*. His writing was the earliest published source of much that Miamisburg now regards as its early history. One practice for which he was not known was brewing beer. When Zimmer bought the malt house in 1848, he was the proprietor of the Miami House hotel (now home to Jayne's on Main, on the northeast corner of Main and Linden.) Whatever his reason for buying the malt house, Zimmer did not keep it for long. He sold it just two months later to Erhard Duetch for the same price he had paid. The same day, Duetch bought the brew house from Swartztrauber for 2,030 dollars.[89]

Duetch (as spelled on deeds) is a faint figure in Miamisburg's history, and he only owned the brewery for a few months. In November 1848, he sold it to Charles Schrauder for eighteen hundred dollars, a loss of 230 dollars.[90]

Of all Miamisburg's brewers, Schrauder left the faintest record. Similar spellings of his name appear in census and tax records in the mid-1800s, including "Schroeder" and "Schrouder." County tax duplicates spelled it both ways between 1851 and 1853. The 1850 census identified a 26-year-old German immigrant named Charles "Shroider" as a local brewer with a wife named Catharine and a daughter, Eloise. Another brewer named Charles, whose surname is illegible, lived in the same dwelling. But these meager clues led to no other records that might have shed more light on his life. Ironically, he was the first Miamisburg brewer to be identified in a commercial publication, the 1853 issue of *Reilly's Ohio State Business Directory*. He was the only Miamisburg brewer it listed.[91]

It was the same year in which Schrauder sold the brewery. He turned it over to William and Jacob Wenz of Cincinnati for forty-five hundred dollars—more than double what he had paid. Although the brewery was nearly twenty years old by then, the hefty price hike suggests Schrauder may have made improvements to the property. Its value on tax duplicates also rose from 705 to 1,490 dollars. The Wenz men and their wives, Maria Anna and Paulina, must have thought the brewery worth it.

They appeared to suffer a minor setback in 1855 when they filed a claim of 297 dollars with the Aetna Fire Insurance Company for the loss of "brewer's stock." But in 1865 something else, not detailed in any records found, caused the brewery's tax value to plunge to 280 dollars. It barely rose to three hundred dollars two years later. The Wenzes sold the property in 1871 to Simon Huiet, who had bought and sold different parcels of Elias Murray's land over the years as well as other local real estate. Huiet paid just 1,050 dollars, less than a fourth of what the Wenzes had paid for it eighteen years earlier. By then they had parted ways: William and Anna Maria were living in Charleston, Illinois, south of Champaign, and Jacob and Paulina were in Tennessee near Nashville. Exactly when the brewery closed is unknown, but its dramatic drop in assessed value in 1865 suggests its brew kettle had grown cold by that time.[92]

Any number of factors might have shuttered the old Hoover brewery. Miamisburg had gone through great changes by the 1870s. Its population had grown, new buildings had gone up and factories had opened. A railroad, telegraph service and a weekly newspaper connected the town with the world as never before. But the main

EXCELSIOR REAPER AND MOWER.
MANUFACTURED BY D. H. HOOVER & CO., MIAMISBURG, OHIO.
CASE & PARKER, Agents, Indianapolis.

David H. Hoover's company and its Excelsior line of farm machines lived on after his death in 1870.

reason for the brewery's demise might have boiled down to one thing: competition. Just a few blocks away, another brewery had been in business since 1860 or earlier. It may have edged out the Wenzes' brewery, and it is the subject of the next chapter.

In the meantime, what of the old brewery's founder, David H. Hoover? He somehow found a way to buy into a new business opportunity at the south end of town. Once again he joined his former partner, Joseph Watson. Unlike his failed and forgotten brewing venture, this enterprise would change Miamisburg's economy and engrave the Hoover name in local history. It was the genesis of Hoover & Gamble, maker of mowers, reapers, twine binders and twine-making machines. It would become an economic engine for the town through the turn of the century, generating hundreds of jobs, and it would play a significant role in turning what had been mainly an agricultural village into a manufacturing town.

When Hoover is mentioned at all, local history books trace his

success to 1835 when, they say, Watson joined a small business venture making farm machinery. They essentially echo a passage from
Zimmer's chapter on Miami Township in Beers's *History of Montgomery County*. This is what Zimmer wrote:

> In 1835, Allen, Watson & Allen commenced the
> manufacture of grain separators on the northwest cor-
> ner of Bridge and Canal streets. The power employed
> was a one horse tread wheel. This firm was changed in
> 1841 when DH Hoover took the place of the Messrs
> Allen, the firm being thereupon Watson & Hoover.[93]

Neither Beers nor any of his followers described exactly who these Allens were. But public records suggest the story of Hoover's transformation, from a failed brewer to one of Miamisburg's most important
manufacturers, was more complex than Zimmer's brief account
suggests.

Patent reports and other records indicate that what became Hoover
& Gamble had its roots in the inventions of a man named Samuel S.
Allen. They connect him to a series of patent awards and renewals over
two decades. First were two 1835 patents to Samuel S. Allen of Saratoga
Springs, New York—one for a "thrashing" (threshing) and hulling machine, and one for a "horse power"—literally a treadmill for horses,
equipped with gears and shafts to drive threshers or other machinery.
In 1840 Samuel S. Allen of Miamisburg received a new horse power
patent and a patent on a hulling, husking and shelling machine. In 1841
he added another patent for improvements to his hulling machine. Finally, in 1853 Samuel S. Allen of Salem, New Jersey, "formerly of Miamisburg," applied for an extension of his patent on the hulling machine. The same name shows up in tax duplicates for Miami Township
beginning in 1838. The township's 1840 census, which included Miamisburg, listed a Samuel S. Allen, living alone, between thirty and
forty years of age.[94]

While Samuel S. Allen was improving his inventions, another local

EXCELSIOR TWINE BINDER & MOWER WORKS, HOOVER & GAMBLE.

The 1886 lithograph of Miamisburg includes an exaggerated view of Hoover & Gamble Co.'s Excelsior works.

Allen—George F.—teamed up with David B. Groat in 1837 to buy a parcel, Lot 13. It was the same parcel Beers noted as Allen, Watson and Allen's business location, on the northwest corner of Bridge and Canal (Linden and First.) In 1838, Samuel S. Allen bought out Groat's share, making him and George F. Allen partners. They appeared as "Allen S. & G." on tax duplicates for 1839 and 1840. Both Allens show up in public records and disappear at about the same times, suggesting that they were somehow related.[95]

In contrast to Zimmer's reference to "Allen, Watson and Allen" in 1835, public records only include Joseph Watson beginning in 1841. It was the year when he and another partner, John Seibey, bought the parcel at Bridge and Canal from the Allens. Hoover came along in 1845, when he bought Seibey's interest. This appears to mark the start of the Hoover-Watson manufacturing partnership noted in history books. At some point in the next few years, Watson moved to Indianapolis. He was living there by 1850 when he sold his interest to Hoover. In the following years, Hoover and his heirs became known as makers of a growing line of threshers, separators, horse powers, wheat drills, corn shellers and other machinery. But Samuel S. Allen, whose inventions seem to have been the foundation of the enterprise, is forgotten.[96]

A factor in Hoover's success, ironically enough, lay in acquiring what had been the business of the hammer-wielding politician William Sawyer. When he left Miamisburg in 1843, Sawyer turned over his share of the iron foundry to his partner McElwee, who continued to run the business for several years. Hoover eventually took it over. An 1853 business directory listed him as Miamisburg's sole iron founder. The foundry became the ironworking hub of Hoover's company, whose products sold under the brand name Excelsior. The company would prosper and grow throughout the century as it passed from David H. Hoover to his heirs.[97]

The Miamisburg Brewery on Water Street (later Miami) was converted to apartments in the 1880s and stood until the early 2000s.

CHAPTER SIX

Beer on Water Street

I n 1851 a new sound swept across Miamisburg and echoed through the valley. It was the sharp call of a railroad locomotive's steam whistle.

Railroad service was not a new idea. As early as 1831, the Ohio legislature considered a bill to incorporate a railroad company to connect Miamisburg with Wilmington and Chillicothe. That plan never materialized, but two decades later the Cincinnati, Hamilton and Dayton Railroad Company—the CH&D—laid the first tracks through the township. The line included a depot across the river in tiny Bridgeport, a block from the bridge to Miamisburg. On August twentieth, an excursion train filled with local officials chugged down from Dayton to celebrate the line's completion at Miamisburg. Round-trip tickets cost twenty-five cents. Jacob Zimmer served dinner in his Miami

Hotel at Main and Bridge, just a block east of the river. Ever since, the rumble of steel wheels on rails and the cry of locomotive whistles— succeeded by the blast of diesel-engine air horns—have been a prominent part of daily downtown life in the Burg.[98]

The railroad opened a new chapter in Miamisburg's history. The Miami and Erie Canal had brought growth in the 1830s. The railroad accelerated it, while the outpaced canal's traffic dwindled. The 1850s saw Miamisburg's population swell by more than half, from 1,095 in the census of 1850 to 1,639 a decade later. Mills and factories supported ever more manufacturing jobs.[99]

The growing town also gained its share of saloons—more than its share, in the opinion of some. "Grog-shops and drunkenness prevail too extensively here—proving very detrimental to society, morals & religion," Isaac H. "I. H." Reiter wrote in his diary on July twenty-sixth, 1857. A descendant of Palatinate immigrants, Reiter had moved with his family from Pennsylvania's Berks County to Ohio in 1831. He had grown up in a German Reformed household on his parents' farm in Wooster. In 1851 he was among the first students to enter Heidelberg College, a German Reformed-affiliated school in Tiffin. Battling a chronic and sometimes debilitating intestinal ailment that would trouble him all his life, he finished his studies in 1854 to serve Miamisburg's German Reformed and Lutheran congregations, which shared a primitive log cabin in their early years. He also served four other congregations around the area, riding a Sunday circuit on horseback to deliver sermons—usually in German. Young and ardently pious, Reiter strongly opposed drink—not just liquor, but alcohol of any kind. He penned his thoughts in 1857 after attending a gathering at Miamisburg's Town Hall, where he had heard a "very good" temperance lecture by an S. F. Cary—possibly Samuel Fenton Cary, an early prohibitionist from Cincinnati who later won a term in Congress.[100]

Strictly speaking, "grog" is a mixture of rum and water, but Reiter likely used the word more broadly. Several distilleries in the township turned out whiskey, and of course Miamisburg had the Wenzes' brewery.

The general public seems not to have shared Reiter's indignation,

certainly when it came to beer. It was a welcome part of local festivi-
ties. For example, it figured in a celebration when Miamisburg completed the replacement of its first bridge in 1859.

Erected in 1827 by a joint stock company, the old bridge was surely
an impressive feat for its time, when Miamisburg was little more than
a frontier settlement. The all-wood, covered bridge measured ten feet
wide, sixteen feet high and 315 feet long. Its design followed one of the
newest of its day: the Town lattice truss bridge, patented just seven
years earlier by architect Ithiel Town of New Haven, Connecticut. A
Town bridge used a series of diagonal, crisscrossed boards to connect
its upper and lower beams. This allowed builders to erect long, sturdy
spans without iron beams or massive timbers. It was likely the namesake of Bridge Street (Linden Avenue) as well as Bridgeport at the foot
of the bridge across the river. For three decades, the toll bridge gave
Miamisburgers and travelers a drier, easier crossing than the old ford
or ferry.[101]

By 1859 the elements had taken their toll, and the bridge company
deemed it time to replace the weathered structure. "The roof and sides
had been removed some years ago," the *Dayton Daily Empire* reported
in a front-page feature about its removal. But it did not mean the old
bridge was ready to go quietly.[102]

The bridge company laid plans to replace the span with the help of
the county, which would take over the new one. A contractor won the
job of removing the old structure with a two hundred dollar bid. The
demolition plan included salvaging much of the old bridge's wood.
Workers were to split the long span in the middle and draw each half
to shore with ropes, where they could dismantle its remains at their
leisure.

The big split was set for April fifteenth, but spring rains had swollen
the river into a strong, wide current that surged just a few feet below
the bridge deck. This presented a problem: laboriously sawing the span
in half and then scrambling away before the severed ends plunged into
the powerful stream would be dangerous, if not impossible. Someone
hit on the idea of setting a fire in the middle of the bridge—likely on

a mid-stream abutment. When the fire burned through, the ends would fall into the river, which would naturally extinguish the flames. The current would do most of the work of swinging the spans around, aided by workers hauling on ropes from the safety of shore.

A crowd gathered to watch the spectacle. Everything went as planned until the severed halves fell. Instead of swinging them around to shore, the current tore loose the greater parts of each span. Thus freed, the *Empire* reported, the two sections "floated off majestically" until "at distance of half a mile the wreck had the appearance of two immense chicken coops, bound on a voyage of discovery for the sunny south!" The project engineer gave chase in a boat, fearful the massive rafts would damage other bridges downstream. (A search of several Ohio newspapers published over the next two months found no reports of further damage.)

Local residents and travelers resorted to ferry boats until June, when a new covered bridge was completed with no word of trouble. As soon as workers laid the last deck plank on June twenty-second, the *Empire* reported, "The occasion was celebrated with the triumphal entrance of a wheelbarrow from the 'Burg into the 'Port, loaded with beer and ginger cake." More beer and other refreshments likely flowed at a festive "hop" that night in the nearby Miami House.[103]

The beer may have come from the Wenzes' brewery at the north end of town. But another brewery may have been up and running by then as well, and it was much closer to the celebration. This was the Miamisburg Brewery and Malt House, which stood on the east bank of the river just a short stroll north of the bridge. It was there at least by July 1860 and possibly earlier. From then on for a few years, Miamisburg may have had two small breweries going at the same time.

Alas for beer history aficionados, no historical markers identify the sites of Miamisburg's early breweries. Figuring out precisely where the Miamisburg Brewery stood required digging through old, sometimes misleading records and the help of some of the brewer's descendants. The brewery's ads placed it on "Water Street between Market (Central) and Ferry." But George Hawes' 1860 *Ohio State*

Gazetteer placed it at "River," and a deed likewise placed its property on "River Street." Careful examination of old land records and maps revealed the brewery indeed stood on Water Street just as its ads declared, but some mid-nineteenth century records identified Water Street as River. The twentieth century brought another layer of confusion: after the 1913 flood, Water Street was renamed Miami, and the name Water Street was assigned to a previously unnamed lane running north and south between Miami and Main. Most recently, the creation of Riverfront Park remodeled the whole area along the river between Ferry and Linden Avenue. In the simplest terms at this writing, the brewery stood near the east bank of the river in the northern part of Riverfront Park. Its structure was a narrow brick building, later converted into apartments. It stood in front of a low wall until it was demolished in the early 2000s.[104]

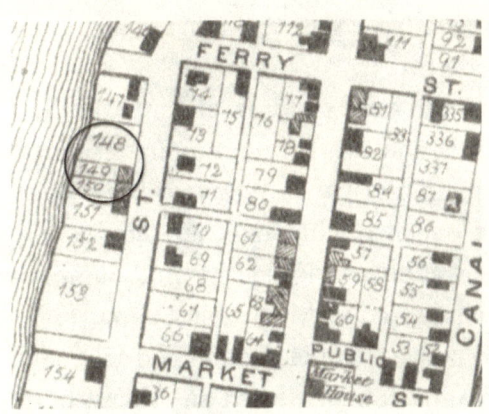

An 1869 map shows the Miamisburg Brewery's lots 148-150, halfway between Ferry and Market (Central.)

Identifying the brewery's proprietors was nearly as difficult as confirming its location. The gazetteer identified them only as "Nutz and Herrmann." One was a mangled reference to George Wilhelm "William" Nusz. The other was either Philip Herrmann or George Herman—one or possibly two surnames also found under various spellings. Nusz was married to Margaret Herrmann, who owned the brewery property jointly with her brother Philip. Very little is known about George, including whether he was related to the Herrmanns. Census records for 1860 and 1870 show him living with William and Margaret. Both records associate George Herman with brewing, while Philip lived separately with his own family. He worked as a tobacconist (1860) and later a farmer

(1870.) Record keepers spelled the names of Nusz and Herrmann in different ways—sometimes more than one way in the same record. On the Herrmann-Nusz family monument in Hillgrove Union Cemetery, Herrmann is spelled with the letters r and n doubled. But it mainly appears in records with one of each letter, and sometimes with an "a" or "o" in place of an "e" or "a." Nusz's name seems to have been especially challenging. "Nusz," as it appears on the same family monument, may have been spelled in German as "Nuß," with an eszett instead of "sz." The English alphabet does not include the eszett, so it may be translated as "sz," as Nusz himself spelled it, or a double "s." But someone hearing it spoken might have settled on "Nutz" or even "Nuiest," as an 1860 census taker wrote it.[105]

Philip and Margaret Herrmann were children of John and Susanna Herrmann. Census records and the family monument dated John's birth to 1810 somewhere in Germany. A *Dayton Daily News* obituary for Susanna "Herrman" (spelled with single and double "r"s in the same article) reported she was born in Heddesheim, about forty miles south of Frankfurt, and emigrated to Miamisburg about 1843. Philip and Margaret were both born in the old country in 1836 and 1839, respectively. The Herrmanns first appeared in Miamisburg records in 1849, when they bought Lot 147, a parcel along the river just south of Ferry Street.[106]

Philip and Margaret moved to Miamisburg in tow of their parents, but what drew Nusz there is something of a mystery. His obituary in the *Miamisburg Bulletin* gave his birthplace as Huechelheim, about thirty miles north of Frankfurt. The article reported he was born there in 1825, emigrated in 1849 and reached Miamisburg in 1852. Nusz accompanied or joined at least two family members. One was a brother, John, who died in Davenport, Iowa, in 1880. A brief report on John's death in the *Bulletin* identified him as William's "only remaining brother." The paper indirectly named a second sibling, Peter Nusz, who died in 1864 at age forty-five and is buried near the family monument. When his son Peter Junior died in 1879, the *Bulletin* identified William as his uncle.[107]

As for the brewery, was it already going before Nusz came on the scene? If so, was George Herman the brewer? He was also from Bavaria and about ten years Nusz's senior. The 1860 census identifies Nusz and "Haman" equally as "brewer"—a possible indication of partnership— but the 1870 census lists Nusz as brewer, while noting "Harman" only "works at brewery." A brewery ad in an 1867 issue of the *Bulletin*—the earliest one found—named Nusz alone as the proprietor.[108]

William and Margaret were married no more than two years after he arrived in Dayton. He was twenty-seven, but she was barely fifteen. A note on their marriage record indicates her parents consented to the union. In 1856, John and Susanna paid 450 dollars for the next parcels south of theirs: lots 148, 149 and the northern nine feet of Lot 150. Taking just a narrow slice off the top of the third parcel seems odd, but a brick building—apparently the brewery—already stood on the north end of Lot 150. The Herrmanns bought just enough land to include it. In September 1859, Nusz bought the remainder of the parcel for 275 dollars.[109]

No record shows who built the brewery or when it was built. The earliest document that specifically mentions it is an 1860 deed. In July of that year, John and Susanna granted the property to Philip and Margaret, including "all personal property belonging to the brewery which stands on the above described real estate." They sold the property for one dollar and the "love and affection" of their children. (Philip sold his share to William in May 1868 for fifteen hundred dollars.) Obviously the brewery was built sometime before then, but possibly not long before: the 1860 county tax duplicate does not list the brewery, but it shows a jump in the property's value from 420 dollars in the previous record to 830 dollars.[110]

Details about the brewery's first years are equally sparse. One reason is simply because Miamisburg had no hometown newspaper then to carry news or advertisements about it. True, a Dayton man named John Anderson tried to start a small paper called the *Gridiron* in 1822, but he only published it for about eighteen months. The next attempt was the *Miamisburg Union* in 1855, which Isaac Pepper and his three sons published from a second-floor shop on the southeast corner of Main and Market. Reiter, the German Reformed pastor, found the paper's debut sufficiently noteworthy to record it in his diary on November thirtieth:

> Today the first number of the *Miamisburg Union* ... was issued by Mr. Isaac Pepper, formerly from Germantown. The paper is an ordinary size and makes a tolerable good appearance. Its mission is politics of the Democratic school, but promises to be a medium of general intelligence, &c. &c.

The Peppers apparently printed at least forty issues. The Miamisburg Historical Society has a full-size photocopy of Issue 40, dated November twenty-eighth, 1856. The four-page, six-column broadsheet carried stories of general interest and some Democratic-leaning political content, but its columns offered no local news. Its advertisers were mainly from Dayton, although Miamisburg business ads appeared on pages three and four. No brewery ads appeared anywhere in the issue. The *Union* soon disappeared, leaving no report of its own demise. Not until the *Bulletin* started publishing in 1867 did the town begin to compile a record of local happenings, and only a few issues are available from before 1872. (The weekly *Miamisburg News* joined the *Bulletin* in 1880 and remains in publication today.) [111]

Whenever the Miamisburg Brewery opened, no doubt it was cheered by beer drinkers and lamented by abstinents like Reiter. Either way, it was another sign of the village's growth.

But by 1860, breweries surely were not uppermost in people's minds. America was in a time of political ferment. Opposing views of the country's future course were dividing states and local communities. In Miamisburg as elsewhere, families faced a growing prospect of civil war.

Undated lithograph of Union troops crossing the Ohio River from Cincinnati on a pontoon bridge.

CHAPTER SEVEN

Copperheads
and Squirrel Hunters

O hio played a major role in the American Civil War. The nation's third most populous state at the time, it contributed more than 310 thousand troops, including at least 219 from Miamisburg and the surrounding township. Ohio produced several of the Union's best-known generals, including Ulysses S. Grant and William T. Sherman. Nobody was immune to the war and its effects, including Miamisburg's brewers and their families.[112]

Although the war started in 1861, the chief issue behind it had been festering since colonial times: the enslavement of African Americans, not expressly prohibited in the United States Constitution and expressly allowed by many states, mainly in the South. It tested the limits of states' rights and the nation's founding principle that all men are created equal.

Abolitionists sought to end slavery across America, or at least prevent it from spreading as the growing nation opened new territories and accepted new states into the Union. But not all who opposed slavery embraced the idea of racial equality. The Northwest Ordinance of 1787 prohibited slavery in the Ohio country, and Ohio kept the provision in its own constitution when it gained statehood. But the fledgling state's population was nearly all white, and many white residents wanted to keep it that way. Nervously eyeing two slave-owning states just across the Ohio River, Kentucky and Virginia (West Virginia was not yet a state) legislators crafted laws to discourage free Black people and those escaping slavery from resettling in Ohio. Some Ohioans fought just as hard to abolish the laws and help freedom seekers make their way through Ohio to Canada, where they could be safe from capture and re-enslavement.

The effort to restrict the rights of Black residents in Ohio began in the state's earliest years and fostered some of its earliest laws, known as the Black Laws of 1804 and 1807. Under an 1804 law, for example, one could face fines of up to one thousand dollars for interfering with the lawful capture and removal of a person fleeing enslavement. Free Black residents had to carry papers certifying their freedom and register them with their local county clerk of courts. An 1807 law made it harder for free Black people to become legal residents. It required them to find two or more property owners who would post a five hundred dollar bond to guarantee their good behavior and welfare. The law also prohibited Black or "mulatto" people— those with one Black parent—from providing testimony against white defendants in court. The Black Laws were designed "to make life for African Americans in Ohio so intolerable" it would never become a sanctuary state, wrote Stephen Middleton in *The Black Laws: Race and the Legal Process in early Ohio*. The state constitution itself restricted voting rights to white men above the age of twenty-one.[113]

The issue of racial equality came up in the Ohio Constitutional

Convention of 1850-1851. It was the first overhaul of the state's governing document. One who rose against it had a familiar name: William Sawyer of St. Marys, the former Miamisburg blacksmith. Following his terms in Congress, Sawyer had been named a delegate to the state convention. He was already on record for tolerating slavery. In January 1849, while still in the House, he had railed against a protracted debate over a bill to abolish slavery in the District of Columbia. His own state had banned slavery at its founding, but Sawyer found the issue a waste of time. He aired his grievance in a floor speech: "Sir, I am heartily tired of this n— business," he complained to the House speaker. It was holding up worthier legislation, he argued, including his own bill to reduce the price of public lands. Abolitionism, he charged, "appropriates to its own use the time which properly belongs to the people—the white people—the people who constitute this great nation." (Congress finally abolished slavery in the nation's capital in 1862.)[114]

True to form, Sawyer showed no shyness at the state convention about opposing equal rights and protections for Black people. Noted a report on the convention, "These United States, he [Sawyer] believed, were designed by the God of Heaven to be governed and inhabited by the Anglo Saxon race and by them alone." When it came time to define just who should be eligible to vote under the new constitution, Sawyer blasted a proposal to strike the word "white" from "every white male citizen." He said he favored allowing free Black people to exercise full rights in Africa, " 'But that negroes have the same rights with white men in this country I utterly deny.' " Sawyer, of course, voted against the amendment, as did Montgomery County's two delegates. The body overwhelmingly rejected it.[115]

Divisions over the issue of slavery deepened as the decade wore on. Doubts grew over the future of the Union, and the prospect of disunion or even civil war increased. But as serious as the legal and moral implications of slavery and racial equality were, the abolition movement may have seemed academic to local folks. Miamisburg and Miami Township were essentially all white, up to and after the Civil

War. Various records indicate Miamisburg's population grew from the *Ohio Gazetteer's* estimate of 405 in 1830 to 1,639 in the 1860 census, but the 1850 census counted only one "free colored" person living there, and the 1860 census found none.[116]

More than a century later, few records survive to give more than a glimpse of how the growing national ferment affected daily life in Miamisburg. The town's only newspaper, the *Miamisburg Union,* seems to have died sometime in the late 1850s, but issues of an out-of-town

paper offer a few clues. The *Dayton Daily Empire* had an unnamed correspondent who kept tabs on Miamisburg. Newspapers then were avowedly partisan, and the *Empire* served up its news from an intensely Democratic perspective. Its Republican counterpart, the *Dayton Journal,* carried less news about Miamisburg. But even the *Empire's* one-sided coverage shows Miamisburgers were not oblivious to the highly charged politics of the time.

Clement Laird Vallandigham.

While Montgomery County generally leaned Republican, the *Empire* found strong support in Miamisburg and the township for Clement Laird Vallandigham. He was a Dayton attorney, anti-abolition Democrat and a leader of the "Copperheads"—northern Democrats who believed the issue of slavery should be left to the states, not the federal government. Vallandigham blamed "the treason and fanaticisms" of abolitionists, not the enslavement of African Americans, for drawing the nation toward war. He served in the Ohio statehouse in the 1840s. In the 1850s, he began running for the third district seat of Congress, which then included Montgomery, Butler and Preble counties. After losing in 1852 and 1854, he narrowly won the 1856 election after contesting the results. He won re-election in 1858.[117]

Vallandigham's next re-election bid coincided with a presidential election year, and one such as America had never seen. The 1860s began as the nation seemed poised for either disunion or war. Stephen A. Douglas spearheaded the Democratic ticket, while Republicans championed Abraham Lincoln. The third district race pitted Vallandigham against Dayton attorney Samuel Craighead.

On July thirteenth, 1860, the *Empire* reported, some four hundred Democratic Party loyalists filled Miamisburg's town hall. It was an organizing meeting chaired by "Colonel" Samuel Mays, a local vintner and militia colonel. After Mays dispensed with business, "Hon. C. L. Vallandigham took the stand, and for an hour held the attention of the crowd," the paper reported.[118]

In the opposing camp, Miamisburg Republicans formed a local arm of the "Wide-Awakes," as grassroots Lincoln supporters had begun calling themselves. (Local Democrats dubbed their group the "Never Sleeps.") On July twenty-eighth the *Empire* correspondent, "not being of the faith," infiltrated the Republicans' private organizing meeting and reported only eighteen "Lincolnites" attended.[119]

Miamisburg Democrats hosted Vallandigham again on September eleventh. This time they held an evening march and rally, bolstered by party faithfuls from Dayton and around the area. The next day's *Empire* gave an openly partisan but entertaining account of the event, devoting more than a full column of local news space to it. "Ground swell in Miami! A Waking Up of Democrats! The 'Burg in a Blaze!" trumpeted the headline.[120]

By the paper's account, Dayton Democrats filled ten cars of a special train that chugged down the valley to the depot at Bridgeport. There, it reported,

> a sight, the grandest we ever beheld, met our vision.
> The depot was surrounded by blazing torches, with
> their red, white and blue globes, and from the depot to

a point beyond the bridge into town, on either side
was a line of torches, through which the Dayton boys
marched, greeted by cheer after cheer, loud and long,
for "Douglas and Vall."

Crossing the river into Miamisburg, the marchers made their way to
the public square, where a battery of three small cannons fired booming salutes and wreathed the crowd in smoke. The report claimed the
crowd numbered 1,160, mainly from Dayton, with 250 from Miamisburg and Miami Township. Vallandigham and other politicians
mounted platforms to speak from ten to eleven. Finally the throng returned to the depot, "and the train left with as enthusiastic a 'good bye'
as was its welcome. ... The loud huzza, which greeted our ears above
the locomotive's shriek, told plainly that the doom of the negro party
is sealed in Montgomery."

Miamisburg Republicans held at least one rally of their own,
drawing their own trainload of supporters from Dayton. How many
attended is unknown, but the *Empire's* September twelfth report dis-
missively noted the Republicans' train to Miamisburg was much
smaller than the Democrats'.

Voters had their say on November sixth. Lincoln defeated Douglas
along with two other presidential hopefuls. He carried Ohio but only
narrowly won in Montgomery County, 4,974 to Douglas's 4,710. Miami Township voters picked Douglas over Lincoln, 456 to 406. Vallandigham faced Craighead in the Third District, which included
Montgomery, Butler and Preble counties. Vallandigham lost in Montgomery, 5,125 to 5,282, as well as in Preble, but strong support in Butler allowed him to keep his seat.[121]

Once the war started, Vallandigham and the Copperheads lost
support in their own party, which turned in favor of "War Democrats"—those who supported the Union in the conflict. The 1862 election saw him unseated by popular Daytonian Robert C. Schenck, a
war-wounded general and Lincoln ally (also, as it happened, a son of
Franklin founder William C. Schenck.) Vallandigham's unceasing

harangues against the Union led, in 1863, to his arrest and conviction on a charge of sympathizing with the enemy. Lincoln banished him to the Confederacy, only for Vallandigham to make his way to Canada. There, he campaigned from exile against Ohio Governor David Tod, a War Democrat. But the party threw its support behind John Brough, another War Democrat from Cuyahoga County. He dealt Vallandigham a crushing defeat, winning sixty-three percent of all 476 thousand votes cast. But Miami Township voters still favored Vallandigham, 480 to four hundred.[122]

The close township vote did not reflect its physical response to the war. Some 219 or more men from the town and township saw military duty at some point during the conflict.

Among the earliest—certainly the youngest—of Miamisburg's volunteers was fourteen-year-old John A. Hall, who signed up for three years in 1861 with his father, Jeremiah Hall, in the Thirty-ninth Regiment, Ohio Volunteer Infantry. John was put in the regimental band as a musician and mustered out a year later, but in May 1864, still young at sixteen, he re-enlisted for one hundred days in the 131st Regiment. Father and son both survived the war. Afterward, Jeremiah resumed his work as a carriage painter, and John followed in his path.[123]

Ohioans worried about the state's southern border. Kentucky allowed slavery and took a neutral stance in the war. It only had weak home guards to deter invasion. Rebel troops moved into southern Kentucky in September 1861. In spring and summer 1862, rebel general John Hunt Morgan led cavalry raids around the state, Ohio journalist and war chronicler Whitelaw Reid wrote in *Ohio in the War*. Morgan struck home guards in several towns and threatened Lexington, just eighty miles south of Cincinnati. Alarmed, Cincinnatians quickly organized militias and sent them to Lexington to bolster its defense.[124]

The excitement in Cincinnati no doubt galvanized the response to Ohio's ongoing efforts to recruit soldiers for federal duty. In July 1862, the Ninety-third Regiment began organizing in Dayton. By August ninth it had drawn nearly a thousand men from around the area, including many from Miamisburg—recruits the *Miamisburg Bulletin*, years later, called "the best bone and sinew of the Third Congressional District." After less than a month of training, the Ninety-Third marched south to join the Army of the Cumberland, where it fought in some of the most brutal battles of the western theater.[125]

Illustration of a squirrel hunter in Whitelaw Reid's *Ohio in the War.*

Fresh alarms came later in the summer when Confederate Major General Edmund Kirby Smith led twelve thousand troops into Kentucky from Tennessee, scattering the Bluegrass State's militias. On September first they marched into Lexington. Smith dispatched a force of several thousand northward to probe defenses approaching Cincinnati. In the Queen City, "The shock was profound," Reid wrote.[126]

Cincinnati officials ordered businesses to close, declared martial law and began bracing for an attack. Governor Tod called for men in southern counties to grab their guns and rush to Cincinnati's defense. Overnight, workers threw together a pontoon bridge between Cincinnati and Covington, speeding equipment across the river to build fortifications in Kentucky. Meanwhile, volunteer defenders began arriving by the thousands. "From every quarter of the State they came, in every form of organization, with every species of arms. The 'Squirrel Hunters' in their homespun, with powder-horn and buckskin pouch," Reid wrote.[127]

Thousands responded, including seventy-six from Miamisburg. Many familiar names were among them, such as Philip Herrmann (listed as "Herrman,") brother-in-law of brewer William Nusz; Philip Schwartztrauber (as spelled in records,) a son of former Race Street brewer John Swartztrauber; Albert H. and Charles E. Blossom, future publishers (with third brother Miles) of the *Miamisburg Bulletin*; prominent attorney Adam Clay and his young son Amos, and William A. Mays, son of Miamisburg's Never Sleeps organizer Samuel Mays. But the dreaded invasion did not come.[128]

Men from Miamisburg were in the thick of the war, especially in its Western Theater. Those in the Ninety-Third experienced harsh conditions with long marches, austere camps and fierce fighting. Several were wounded, captured, or both. Some never saw their families again. John T. Snyder, twenty years of age when he took up arms, was captured in 1863 in the Battle of Chickamauga near Chattanooga, Tennessee. He died a year later in a rebel prison camp in Florence, South Carolina. Nelson Coleman, forty, and Henry Shoup, nineteen, were killed in 1864 in the Battle of Dallas, Georgia. Zebulon Sharrits, twenty-six, survived the war only to die less than three weeks after rebel general Robert E. Lee surrendered. Early on April twenty-seventh, 1865, he was among more than twenty-three hundred soldiers, passengers and crew aboard the overcrowded steamship *Sultana* when its boilers exploded on the Mississippi River near Memphis. The ship caught fire and sank. Estimates of the death toll have ranged widely, but the Sultana Association of Descendants and Friends estimates 1,169 people perished.[129]

By early 1864, the Civil War had been raging for three years. Ulysses S. Grant, by then the Union's top general, was preparing a massive campaign to finish it. Lincoln was pressing the states to furnish ever more troops for Grant's armies. But Ohio Governor Brough worried that taking more men out of the state would leave it vulnerable to attack. Only a year earlier, Morgan's rebel cavalry had made its daring raid across the state's southern counties.

In consultation with the governors of four other western states— Illinois, Indiana, Iowa and Wisconsin—Brough proposed a way to meet the Union's needs while preserving security along the states' borders: activate eighty-five thousand men from all five states for just one hundred days of federal duty. The troops would go east to guard critical points around Washington, D.C. This would free up regular army troops from garrison duty so Grant could send them to the front. Grant's forces would keep Ohio and the other western states safe by pinning down Lee's army in Virginia, while Union General William T. Sherman went after rebel forces in the west. By the time the hundred days were up, the war would be won—or such was the hope. The scheme became known as the Hundred Days' Men plan. Lincoln approved the plan two days after he saw it.[130]

Fourteen weeks or so of garrison duty, out of range of rebel guns, must have sounded like a good way to do one's duty and get paid for it without too much danger. Ohio not only met its pledge but surpassed it: nearly thirty-six thousand men volunteered.[131]

Once again Philip Herrmann's name (this time as "Hermann") appeared on the roster; then twenty-nine, he became a sergeant in the 131st Ohio. His brother-in-law William Nusz apparently stayed out: at thirty-eight, the brewer was not too old for the second-class military draft list, but his name does not appear on any roster of Ohio regiments.[132]

Lincoln provided another way for Nusz to help the cause whether he wanted to or not. Desperate to fund the war, the president did something the federal government had not done since 1791, when Congress briefly levied an excise tax on liquor. It had triggered the infamous "Whiskey Rebellion," the young nation's first serious domestic challenge. The uprising only ended in 1794 when President Washington raised a militia that defused the rebellion. After a few years Congress repealed the tax. Six decades later, in the midst of war, Lincoln urged Congress to pass the Revenue Act of 1862, which taxed liquor and beer in a wide range of other goods, as well as income. The new law levied a tax on every barrel of beer Nusz brewed. But an old Miamisburg brewer's family would be more deeply involved.[133]

Union tents among ruins at White House Landing, Virginia, in 1862.

CHAPTER EIGHT

A Brewer's Family
in the Civil War

Philip Herrmann was not the only member of a Miamisburg brewer's family affected by the Hundred Days' Men plan. Another was Charles R. Allen. He was married to the former Elizabeth Hoover, elder daughter of David H. Hoover, the early brewer turned manufacturer. Charles, thirty-five, and Elizabeth, thirty-three, were a prosperous Miamisburg couple with two young sons, a house in town and a farm down in the township.[134]

Charles had not yet been in the war, but he held a major's rank in the Twelfth Battalion of the state militia—recently reorganized as the Ohio National Guard. In early April, the battalion received orders to report to Camp Chase, just west of Columbus.[135]

During their separation, Charles and Elizabeth corresponded regularly, as Charles found himself at the front and Elizabeth persevered at home. From April through early September 1864, they exchanged at least 37 letters. Their descendants kept them, and more than a century later they gave a carefully edited transcript to the Miamisburg Historical Society, with accompanying materials for background and context. The collection gives a rare, personal glimpse of life in Miamisburg during the Civil War.

Portrait of Charles R. Allen.

The typewritten transcript does not include images of the letters themselves, but an introduction explains it sought to reproduce the original "underlining, punctuation, spelling and spelling errors." It showed Charles's writing was generally more refined than Elizabeth's, but he cared little about punctuation: a short dash typically served in place of a period or comma. His spelling of some words seems to have been his best guess based on how they sounded. Elizabeth's spelling was equally flawed, and she used almost no punctuation. In most cases, only a short dash or an extra space separated sentences. While her letters were less polished than her husband's, Elizabeth's unvarnished style powerfully conveyed her loneliness, anxiety and fear—not only for her husband, but also their family. This chapter presents their words as they appear in the transcript, except for an occasional ellipsis, comma or period as needed for clarity.

The collection begins with Charles's account of his arrival at Camp Chase early on April eleventh. He usually began his letters with "Dear Wife" or "Dear Lib," as she signed her name, but she had a habit of beginning her letters with "Dear Charlie"—despite him signing his own name as "Charley." So he began his first letter as he wrote from the relative comfort of his tent.

> Dear Wife
> we left Dayton last evening 10 o,clock- arrived at
> Columbus 3 o,clock this morning- raining all the
> while- Quartered in cars until this morning-
> regiment marched out to camp- 4 miles- snowing and
> raining at the same time.

Even as Governor Brough was hashing out the details of his Hundred Days' Men plan, the state national guard was organizing regiments for federal duty. On April thirteenth, Charles described Camp Chase as "a vast military camp at present - regiments & Batallians are constantly arriving, consolidating, equipping and departing."[136]

Most of the Twelfth Battalion was consolidated into the 131st Regiment, Ohio Volunteer Infantry. It seems Charles knew its mission already: "The regiment has marching orders tomorrow- their destination is Baltimore." For "several reasons" he left unexplained, Charles passed up a chance to take a major's slot in the new regiment. Because of this, and because "Camp life has brought back the rumatic affection in one of my nees," he expected to be relieved from further duty. "If I hear no bad news from home- I think I shall go with the boys to Baltimore. Spend a week perhaps and return home." But his knee improved, and he discovered the Army had other plans for him.

The 131st Regiment did not complete its consolidation until May fourteenth. Its members included many from Miamisburg and the surrounding area. As Charles expected, its orders were for Baltimore. But one company, Company D, was folded into the 132nd Regiment with the Thirty-Eighth Battalion from Logan County and the Forty-Second

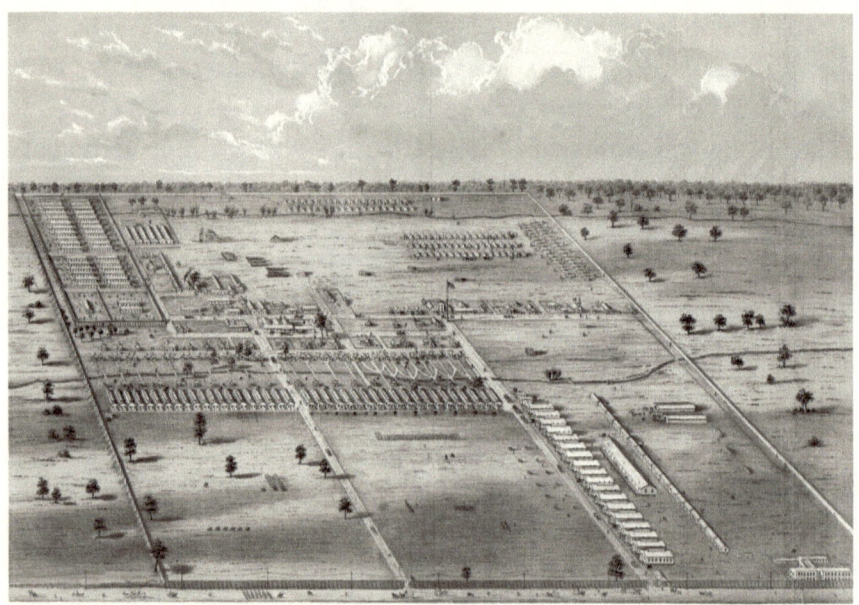

Bird's eye view of Camp Chase near Columbus. Not drawn to scale.

from Paulding County. Company D was Charles's company. "We are under Col. Haines 132nd regiment our destination is Washington," Charles wrote on May sixteenth. He lost his rank of major and mustered into the regiment as a private. He would see one hundred days' duty, after all. But he was to spend his time in a safe location, so he tried to sound upbeat: "we expect to have positions that will be as easy and pay as good as our places in our old regiment."[137]

As late as May eighteenth, Charles doubted his regiment would be sent out of Ohio at all: "The probabilities are that our regiment will be kept at Camp Chase- are not yet positive- as soon as that is determined I will try and make a flying visit home-"

It seems he made a quick trip home with a friend, Germantown physician Joseph E. Donnellan, only to have the regiment depart in their absence. His next letter was dated Tuesday, May twenty-fourth, after his return to camp: "On arriving here I find our regiment left- Sunday afternoon for Washington." They made arrangements to catch up with the regiment by train. But just before mailing the letter,

Charles added a postscript that he had just heard his regiment's final destination was not Washington after all, but somewhere closer to the fighting. Sounding more cautious, he wrote: "The indications are I shall see something in this 100 days."

While the Hundred Days' regiments were supposed to do garrison duty, the 132nd's commander had a different idea. He was Joel Haines, a popular dry goods merchant from West Middleburg (now Middleburg) in Paulding County. He had been in the state militia since about 1855. He was forty-seven when war broke out, but he had recruited a company of volunteers and mustered into the Seventeenth Regiment's Company C as a captain. The regiment had marched into Kentucky, fought in the Battle of Camp Wild Cat near London in October 1861 and then made a hard march to Louisville. The regiment had gone on to Tennessee, but the trek across Kentucky had proved to be too much for Haines. He had been sent home, but he had written to then-governor David Tod, asking for another chance to serve in some position that required less marching. For the next two years he had remained in the national guard. He had been nearly fifty when the Hundred Days' call came, but it had given him his chance to get back in the fight. He and three of his four sons had reported to Camp Chase, leaving his business and his pregnant wife in the hands of their youngest, eighteen-year-old William. Upon taking command of the 132nd with sons of his own in the ranks, Haines promptly volunteered his new regiment for duty at the front. He got his wish.[138]

In the meantime, Grant had launched his massive Overland Campaign, starting on May fourth with the Battle of the Wilderness. But instead of quickly smashing Lee's army, the campaign had devolved into a horrific, more than month-long series of bloody battles that left the Union with some fifty-five thousand killed, wounded or missing soldiers, while Lee's army lost perhaps 33,600.[139]

The end of May found Charles in Arlington Heights, Virginia. Overlooking Washington, D.C., from across the Potomac River, Arlington Heights had been Lee's home until he had turned against the Union. Today it is the site of Arlington National Cemetery, but when

Charles arrived it was the staging ground for Grant's campaign. Charles penned an update about his travel on May 29. He had stopped in Baltimore to "visit the boys of the Old 12th," his former militia unit. He also noted he had been named the regiment's sutler, which would allow him to set up the Civil War equivalent of a base commissary. It was good news, he told Elizabeth, because sutlers could stay behind the lines.

He struck a defensive tone as he reminded Elizabeth of an earlier conversation, perhaps during his brief visit home, about the regiment's gung-ho commander: "I think I told you before I left home that if any Ohio N. G. Regiment got a dangerous place it would be Col. Hains." Then, playing down the risks, he added, "It does not scare me a bit for I dont think I am to be killed in this war- I have something of a desire to hear a rebel bomb-shell whistle- dont want them to come to close however."

Elizabeth was not buying it. On June first she wrote, "I am sorry that you are going to be sent so near the front you say you are not uneasy you dont think you will be killed in this war you are just as liable to be killed as any other man if you are induced to take a hand with the boys in a fight. … I wish you was in Baltimore with the rest of the boys."

She directed her anger at Haines: "May be Col Hains will have a chance to smell a little more gun powder than he desires before the hundred days are up he will not be so brave on the potomack as in Columbus."

She changed the subject to their two young sons, nine-year-old Ellwood and four-year-old David. "The boys are both well and eat as much as ever," she wrote. "I would not know what to do if it was not for Ella he is not much trouble very often does most of the howing in the garden and weeds his tobacco beds which takes up most of his time."

Elizabeth closed her letter by noting she was not feeling well herself: "Well I must stop I feel so sick and fainty I cant set up any longer." The unnamed ailment seemed to dog her. On June eighth she noted,

"My health is tolerable good as long as I am not on my feet," and on June twenty-first she explained her previous letter had been brief because "I was not well."

On May thirtieth, Charles's regiment crowded aboard a riverboat "bound for the front." The others in his regiment "all seem determined to brave their fate- it is the general believe however that we will see the 'Elephant' [a reference to the enemy]- But we started out to serve our country a hundred day- and none bitterly complain," he wrote.

The boat steamed down the Potomac to Chesapeake Bay, then up the York and Pamunkey rivers to White House Landing. Now he was no more than twenty miles east of Richmond, where Grant hoped to trap and destroy Lee's army.

White House was a thousand-acre estate where Martha Custis lived before she married George Washington. Once a picturesque plantation, it was burned nearly to ashes during fighting in 1862. Arriving on May thirty-first, Charles found "nothing but chimneys" standing in the midst of Union tents. He and Donnellan were in time to witness the marshaling of a massive force for the Battle of Cold Harbor, northeast of Richmond. "Grants reinforcements are all landing here-not less than thirty thousand left for the front last evening- it was a great sight to see them filing in to line and moving to the conflict- We can hear the cannonading very distinctly," he wrote on June first.

In a long letter of June fourth, Charles struggled to describe the magnitude of what he was seeing around him:

> This is the place where all the supplies are unloaded
> and halled to the front- all the reinforcements arrive
> here- all the wonded are sent here- all the prisoners
> captured are sent here and shiped to places of safe
> keeping. ... Trains of ambulance arrive daily from the
> front loaded with wonded- a terable sight it is- they
> are placed aboard vesils & put in temperary hospitals.
> ... As I sit in my tent writing I here the booming of

the artilery in the front- Grant is fighting despert-
every day- carnage on our side awfull.

Charles shared his tent with Donnellan, who had been working
steadily in the field hospitals. He walked in as Charles wrote. "Dr Donnellan has returned from the hospitals where he has been assisting- A
long train of ambulances are coming in and being unloded- I lay my
letter aside to go down and see--"
    Charles picked up his pen again sometime later.

> I have returned after having witnessed a heart
> rending scene- Some 2000 wonded are laying around
> on the ground and being carried in the hospital tents
> as they are unloded from the ambulances- the most of
> the amputating has been done on the field- some is
> being done here- it takes some courage to stand by
> the Surgeon and see him cut off a mans legs and arms.

Although Elizabeth continually prayed for any word from her husband, such news was hardly a balm. His absence weighed on her, as
did her fear for his safety. Her letter of June sixth conveyed her anger
and worry: "I do hope you will not engage in a fight. You were not sent
out to fight battles but to protect and garrison forts. The idea of sending Ohio militia to richmond to fight makes me hate Old Brough." She
meant the governor and his Hundred Days' Men plan.
    She had reason to be fearful. Her letter of June eighth carried grim
news from the western theater, where so many Miamisburg men had
gone: "George Grove has been killed in battle Coleman is wounded
and missing." George J. Grove, twenty-six, was a lieutenant in Ohio's
First Regiment. Nelson Coleman had joined the Ninety-third as a private. Both had died in battles in Georgia on the same day, May
twenty-seventh—Grove at Chickamauga and Coleman at Dallas.[140]
    Adding to Elizabeth's worry were rumors of a conspiracy to spark
an insurrection in Ohio and other parts of the northwest. In fact,
rebels operating from Canada schemed with Copperheads in the

A sutler's tent at the Siege of Petersburg.

northern states, including a group called the Sons of Liberty, led by none other than Clement Vallandigham. John Hunt Morgan, scourge of southern Ohio, was said to be plotting an encore to his earlier raid in support of the uprising. The scheme never materialized, but the rumors further frayed Elizabeth's nerves and added to her bitterness toward the governor: "Brough has sent all the union men out of the state and I suppose the rebels are going to take advantage of it."[141]

Besides the dangers of war, she worried Charles would suffer from the South's "unhealthy and unpleasant climate. ... By a dream that I had last night I fear that you are sick I watch my dreams now a days as though there was a reality in them," she confided. "every night I lay and think and go to sleep praying for you."

Also troubling Elizabeth was the vague, persistent ailment that left her feeling weak, and she worried about a spell of hot, dry weather weighing on the region. "The ground is very dry and hard and the tobacco plants are large enough to set out," she wrote. "There will be a great time setting out tobacco if it should rain to night."

At White House, Charles set up his sutlery. "We have got our Sutler 'Chebang' running," he wrote on June ninth. He likely meant "shebang," Civil War-era parlance for a temporary shelter. In his case, it was a tent typical of those used by sutlers in other regiments. Sutlers sold food and personal items the military did not provide, and soldiers could apply to be a regiment's sutler. It seems to have been something Charles had in mind back in May, when he thought he might serve his enlistment at Camp Chase. In his May twenty-fourth letter, as Charles prepared to follow his regiment to Washington, he mentioned that he had "stored my sutler stores in Columbus." He won the appointment as the regiment's sutler at Arlington Heights just as the unit was preparing to go forward, but he learned sutlers were not allowed to take their own supplies. "I have however smuggled some little abord," he confided in a May thirtieth letter.

The 132nd had been building fortifications about a half-mile from the river, and Charles set up his sutlery close behind them. "We have put up our tent about 50 yards from one of the forts," he wrote.

Sales were brisk but barely profitable. "We had considerable stuff but have but little profit- We have to buy of whole sale Sutlers who have whole cargoes on the river- and have to sell at the same that they retail- They allow regimental sutlers but little margins."

Even so, Charles's little shop enjoyed a lively business.

> We have a good place for trade we catch the hungry
> men that came in from the front- Sometimes a squad
> of hungry men will come in and eat us out in short
> time- I am getting pretty handy as a clerk- you should
> see me fly round- cut cheese- count ginger cakes and
> change money ... we might make a nice thing this 100
> days-

What Charles wanted for himself was something no sutler could provide: pictures of his wife and their boys. In the days before digital images and even roll film, photographs of loved ones were rare and precious.

"We both wish so much for pictures of our families," he wrote of himself and Donnellan. "Most of the vetern soldiers who have families- have a family group that they hold more dear than life its self- I have seen the fatally wonded holding the family group befor their eyes, as if to die gazing upon the dear ones at home."

For a mother with two small children, getting pictures made was not an easy task. "I will try and get the children photography taken I do not know about mine I dont look like myself," Elizabeth wrote on June twenty-first. She had only achieved partial success by July sixth. "I sent Ellas Photograph in my last letter … I tried Davie again to day but could not get one … he would always roll his big black eyes around and spoil it." Davie, not quite five, eventually cooperated.

By then, the 132nd had moved again. As the Battle of Cold Harbor ground to a dismal end, Grant took aim at Petersburg, about twenty miles south. With a railroad running straight to Richmond, Petersburg was a vital supply hub for Lee's army. Grant meant to cut it off.

Charles's regiment was among the first to relocate. On Saturday, June eleventh, he was among a thousand or more soldiers who crowded onto a steamer bound for Bermuda Hundred, a colonial-era settlement about eight miles northeast of Petersburg. Their voyage took them back down to the Chesapeake Bay, then up the James to Bermuda Hundred. They arrived Sunday evening and slept on the riverbank. The next morning, they marched to a line of new fortifications that stretched from the James southeast to the Appomattox— some five miles, he estimated in a June eighteenth letter. Peering over the breastwork, Charles could see rebel rifle-pits and pickets. Down at the Appomattox, he wrote on June eighteenth, "I could see the church spires in Petersburg distinctly with the naked eye." From the north end of the Union line, he could just make out the spires of Richmond through a spyglass.

"We are in the front of Butler's army, where we see fighting more or less every day," Charles wrote on June twenty-fourth. "Our regiment has not been in any active engagement as yet. Neither is it the intention of General Butler to put them in—at least, he so says."

Butler never sent the 132nd into battle. Instead, they wielded shovels and axes to build fortifications. But the work still put them within range of rebel guns. Wrote Charles:

> Some of our men have been wonded- some of other
> hundred day regiments have been killed- 8 or ten
> hundred day regiments from Ohio are here- They
> do picket duty where the two lines are not more
> than a hundred yards apart- pickets do not shoot at
> each other much- The rebel works and our works
> are just far enough apart for good shelling distance-
> we have a nice little artilery duel every after-noon.
> the shells burst over and around us- sometimes to
> close to be pleasant-

On one occasion, a rebel ironclad steamed down the James and hurled cannon balls at Union boats. One ball crashed down in the camp, Charles wrote. Recovered by curious soldiers, it weighed in at 120 pounds. "It is strange how soon men become indifferent to danger," Charles mused. Still, at night they slept in the rifle pits.

Despite the danger, Charles understood he occupied a front-row seat to history. On June thirtieth he wrote, "The great struggle that is to decide the fate of this nation- is now going on- And we are as it were- right in the midst of it." But his hope that he was witnessing its final act was fading.

> A desperate battle has been going on all day in the
> neighborhood of Petersburg- commencing very early
> this morning- There has been one continuous roar of
> artilery & musketry all day- and while writing 9
> o,clock this evening the artilery still belches forth-
> know nothing of results at present writing- am sorry
> to say that my confidence in Grants taking Richmond
> has not been strengthened by coming to the front-

Enemy artillery was not the only threat to the Hundred Days' men, or even the deadliest. Laboring in hot summer weather by day, spending chilly nights in open trenches, eating skimpy rations and living in crowded camps with poor sanitation made soldiers easy prey for disease. For all the Civil War's terrible battles, twice as many soldiers are thought to have died from disease as from combat. While Charles remained healthy, he wrote of measles spreading through the ranks as well as "flux"—an old name for dysentery, a severely dehydrating affliction. Even at White House in June, soldiers were falling ill. "Quite a number of our regiment were sick and had to be left behind" when they steamed south, Charles wrote on June eleventh.[142]

By June thirtieth, the regiment had been "considerably thined" by sickness, and on August first Charles reported "much sickness prevailing in the regiment- and among the hundred day men generally- 4 men have died in Cap. Beards Co- About 30 have died out of the regiment-" Captain Jacob Beard commanded Allen's company. "Cap Beard's Co. was 84 men strong- to day 16 men was reported for duty in his Co. Other companies are in the same condition," he wrote. On August tenth, he added, "our regiment has lost about 40 men- other regiments about in the same proportion-"

But the war held no monopoly on illness. After Elizabeth's own undefined ailment, she struggled in the growing summer heat. On a hot July sixth she wrote, "The heat here is as much as a person wants to stand some nights are sultry and suffocating." She explained how she was coping in her letter of July eleventh:

> I am very carful of my health and am getting along as
> well as could be expected I buy all my bread and hire
> my washing done the weather is so warm that I do
> not make a fire only to do a little cooking I try to
> keep the house as cool as I can

As the summer wore on, she more often noted the illness spreading across the area. As early as June sixth she wrote, "Mrs Brittons youngest child was buried yesterday. Molly Halemen is very sick not expected to live had a miscarriage." June twelfth: "Lily Frewn is very sick they did not think she would live a day ... and Ikey has the measles." On June nineteenth, a "Mrs Boche" was "very sick." A month later, "Mrs Ragon was taken very sick last night with congestion chills she is not conscious this morning."

Elizabeth penned her longest, saddest tale of woe on Thursday, August fourth, starting with her own troubles: "I was quite sick for a night and day with choloramobas," or cholera morbus—an old term for acute gastroenteritis. "I am very careful now what I eat," she added. Just days earlier, someone else they knew "took the choloramobas that same night and died she had a babe only two months old."[143]

She was just getting started. "Bill Eagle was buried on tuesday he died of tiphoid fever ... Mrs Shulas mother lay dead the same day. ... Em Jordan buryed her little boy this afternoon there were five children lay dead on Sunday all of the flux Amy Neal buryed her little girl this week Mrs Ragon continues the same."

The worst news of all was about their own family. "Abe and Clara buried little Harry last Sunday," she wrote. She was referring to her brother Abel Hoover and his wife, the former Clara Hoff, and the loss of their first-born child. Harry was also a grandson of David H. Hoover, the early brewer. Born sometime after the 1860 census, Harry was not yet four. Elizabeth wrote he had fallen ill suddenly with "inflammation of the brain" and "died in spasms" after a day and night of suffering.

Even before the family could put Harry to rest, illness struck Elizabeth's sixty-four-year-old father, David H. "Saturday night father was sick very suddenly" with a severe pain in his side, she wrote. A doctor they called was unable to help. "On sunday he had no mind at all ... we had a sorryful day. ... It seems there is nothing but sickness and death in the burg it seems like the church bells are ringing continually."

Elizabeth was not exaggerating. Isaac H. Reiter, Miamisburg's German Reformed pastor, described his own somber experience with a summer of deadly illness in an undated October 1864 entry in his diary:

> The people of my charge, especially the Miamisburg
> congregation, experienced an unusual degree of
> affliction during the summer, and early part of fall.
> For several months my labors were mainly confined
> to the sick, and dying, and bereaved. During the
> worst fatal period, I had 14 funerals in 16 days. ... My
> own health has been much impaired for the last six
> weeks.[144]

The same kind of news was reaching soldiers in the 131st regiment in Baltimore. One was John Evans Kinder, whose son Charles Edward Kinder would become the founder of the *Miamisburg News* in 1880. On the same day Elizabeth was writing her sad news to Charles, Kinder was penning his reply to what must have been a similar letter from his own wife, also named Elizabeth: "Poor Mrs. Simington. It is hard to realize that she is dead. Also Bill Eagle. ... You write to me of a great deal of sickness and death."[145]

Elizabeth Allen's August fourth letter found some solace in the fact that their boys were still "well and harty." Her father David was recovering by then, too: "I was alarmed when I see the Drs uneasy but now he is out of danger and getting along very well he cant wait till he can get a squirel to eat."

Charles thought all the disease and war he had witnessed had hardened his feelings, but on August tenth he admitted Elizabeth's letter had pierced his heart:

> Although I am here surrounded by death- see men die
> every day- and hundreds of once stout men-
> languising on cots from which they will never be
> moved- except after death- all this I can see unmoved
> as it were, so used I have become to it. Yet when I

read of Able and Clary's sad bereavement- I wept like
a child- and there by discovered that I still had a
tender heart ... I have just taken Ella & Davy's
pictures out and looked at them- Dave's is so natural-
I pray <u>God</u> that they may be spared untill I see them
again- This really is the first day of sadness I have
experience in the army-

The Allens' son David as an adult.

Whether by divine intervention or simple coincidence, the answer to Charles's prayer came just hours after he sent off his letter. New orders rousted his regiment at one the next morning. It was time to break camp and go home.

Charles described the scene in his next letter: "In five minutes after the orders came- the camp was aroused- every one busy packing up for the move." The mood among the soldiers must have been joyous, but in the darkness came a somber procession. "At Three o,clock 20 army-wagons- & 20 ambulances drove up to carry the sick and their baggage together with the guns etc. of those that had died-"

Soon a big riverboat crowded with troops was steaming down the James. They reached Norfolk, Virginia, just before sundown. Sick troops were ferried across the bay to an army hospital at Portsmouth, while the others marched to their new camp two miles outside of Norfolk. Charles penned his letter of August thirteenth in the comfort of Norfolk's Atlantic Hotel. "Dr. Donnellan & I and some of the Officers who were not well went to the Hotel where we now are," he explained. With their enlistment ending and only company paperwork to carry out—Charles had been appointed the company's clerk—they favored the cost of a hotel over camp. "It would be a little expensive but much more agreeable," he wrote.

Back in Miamisburg, "Davie had a touch of the flux but I got it checked immediately…. Pap is still getting better," Elizabeth wrote on August eleventh. And the town was welcoming back the first of its Hundred Days' men: "The first Ohio boys returned home tonight they are going to have a reception I suppose they were glad to see old miamisburg again"

The men of the 132nd were among the last to get home, but Charles took advantage of the delay. He spent the next two weeks soaking up the southern charm of Norfolk, which had avoided widespread damage in 1862 by surrendering to Union forces without a fight. He found the city basking under a "genuine southern sun- but when in the shade there is a good breeze from the bay that makes it pleasant." He adored its "beautiful tropical shrubs & flowers" and enclosed some crape myrtle buds in his letter. "I am acquiring something of a liking for this southern country- the more I see of it the better I like it," he confessed in his August twenty-seventh letter. "I think you might be infatuated with this place."

The terms of the Hundred Days' regiments expired, and Lee surrendered his army at Appomattox Court House on April ninth, 1865, but scattered fighting went on. President Andrew Johnson finally declared the insurrection over on August 20, 1866.[146]

Meanwhile, Charles bade a fond farewell to a state where he had spent most of his time on the edge of a battlefield. September first found him back in Columbus, relieved to be in Ohio but anxious to see his family. "I feel very much concerned about home," he wrote in his last letter of the collection.

The final letter was a brief but news-filled missive from Elizabeth, dated September third.

> Ella has been quite sick with the flux but now is well
> and running around again he took so much waiting
> on that I think I over done myself … last fryday night
> I took very sick I had the Dr in about day light he
> gave me a dose of morphine which releive me of my
> misery I was in a stupor all most all day I have been
> very weak and not able to do any thing since

Perhaps sitting back and seeing the anxiety her words would bring to her husband, she closed on a more reassuring note: "You need not be uneasy about me I think I will get along well enough now."

Charles was soon back in Miamisburg, where he apparently recovered from his enchantment with Norfolk. In short order he and Elizabeth produced their third child and first daughter, Kate.

Charles applied his sutlering skills to a store at the north end of town until 1866, when he joined his father-in-law David Hoover and his brother-in-law Abel in their prosperous farm implement business. David Hoover died in 1870, but Abel and Charles continued the business as Hoover & Company.

Despite his federal service as a private, around town Charles would always be known as Major Allen, his old National Guard rank. He died in 1879 at age fifty. Abel carried on the business with another brother-in-law, William Gamble—he was married to Abel's younger sister Samantha—and the company's name changed again to Hoover & Gamble. The Allens' younger son, David, and the Gambles' son, William H., started the well-remembered Acme Folding Boat Company.

Elizabeth never remarried. She lived out her life with or near her children on North Main Street. She died at age seventy-nine In 1910.[147]

The lager beer brewery that William Nusz built, as depicted in the 1886 lithograph of Miamisburg when August Kuehn owned it.

CHAPTER NINE

New Brewery for New Beer

Whe hen the Civil War ended, the beer tax remained. But it did nothing to blunt beer's popularity. By the 1860s, a variety new to America was beginning to supercharge the U.S. brewing industry: lager beer. Most historical accounts and newspaper reports date Montgomery County's first lager beer brewery to 1852. In December that year, Beers wrote in *History of Montgomery County*, the brothers John and Michael Schiml, recent immigrants from Bavaria, started making lager beer in their new Dayton brewery.[148]

Before lager beer, what Americans called beer, ale and porter were all variations of ale. They were all brewed in much the same way. Lager was different. Brewers say it offers a lighter, crisper taste than ale, although today ales and lagers come in so many flavors it can be hard to tell them apart. What makes it different is the type of yeast used. Ale is the product of a species of yeast named *Saccharomyces cerevisiae*—good old brewer's yeast—while lager beer uses a hybrid species dubbed *Saccharomyces pastorianus.* Lager beer yeast does its work in a colder range than brewer's yeast: its fermentation and storage requires temperatures close to freezing. This cold fermentation period is where lager beer gets its name: "lagern" means "store" in German.[149]

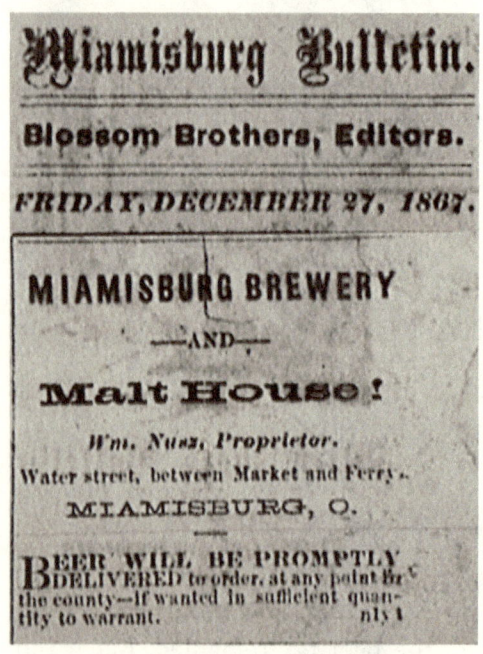

This ad from an 1867 *Miamisburg Bulletin* is the earliest one found for the Miamisburg Brewery.

By all accounts, Bavarian brewers developed lager beer as early as the fourteenth century, but it did not reach North America until the early 1800s. A historical marker in Philadelphia credits Bavarian immigrant John Wagner with bringing the first lager beer yeast to America in 1840 and brewing the first American lager beer. Once on the continent, brewers carried the special yeast inland, reaching the Schimls' brewery twelve years later. Theirs came "from stock brought from Boston, by a cousin of the Schimls who was a brewer," Beers wrote.

Ohioans quickly grew familiar with the new variety. "Lager beer is fast becoming naturalized among us," the *Newark* (Ohio) *Daily Advocate* noted in 1854. It even figured in political campaigns. "The *Dayton Daily Empire* says that there is a banner on Jefferson Street in that place which reads—'Fremont and Dayton and Lager Beer,' " reported the *Cadiz Democratic Sentinel* in 1856. It was an allusion to the three-way

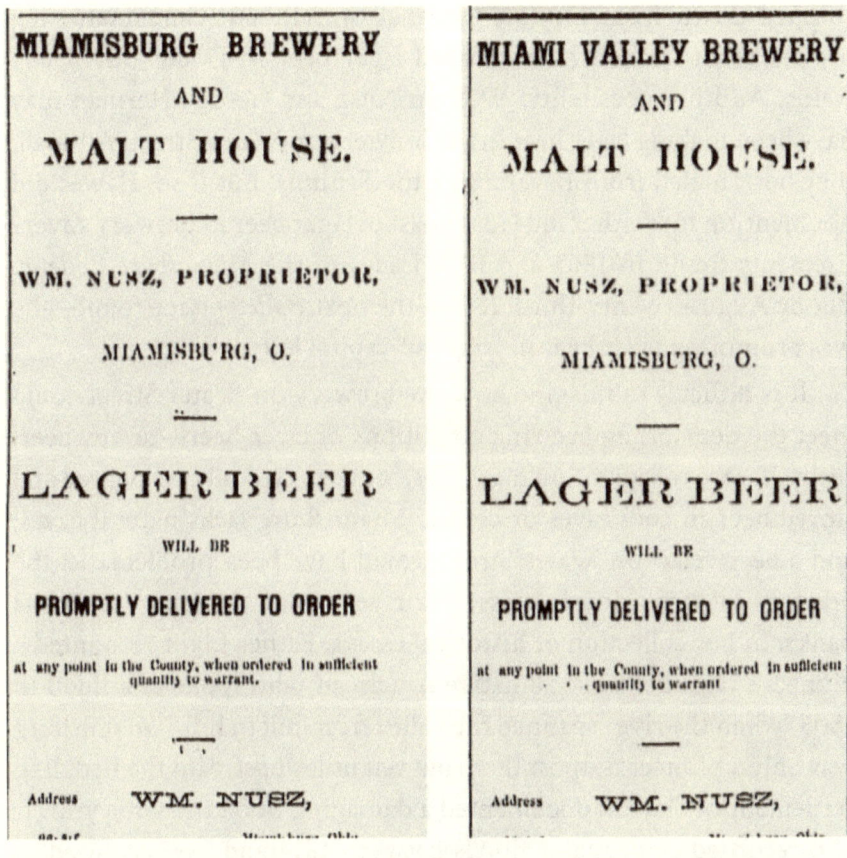

Nusz advertised lager beer at the Miamisburg Brewery as early as August 1872 but switched to the Miami Valley Brewery in November.

presidential contest in which Democrat James Buchanan defeated Republican John C. Fremont and "Know Nothing" Millard Fillmore. "We suppose," the *Sentinel*'s editors added, "that the getters up of that banner go in for Fremont and Dayton for President and Lager Beer for Vice President."[150]

It was only a matter of time before Miamisburgers were enjoying lager beer. Hawes' 1860 gazetteer listed a "lager beer saloon" on Market Street (Central Avenue) under the proprietorship of William "Dodd" (spelled "Dodds" in other records and on his gravestone.)[151]

Dodds might have stocked his saloon with Schiml's beer, having it shipped down from Dayton by canal or railroad. Cincinnati's big breweries also might have shipped lager beer to Dodds on CH&D trains. Another possibility: William Nusz and George Herman may have been making lager beer in the brewery on Water Street. After all, they both hailed from Bavaria like the Schimls. But if so, Hawes did not mention it. Neither did Nusz boast of lager beer in brewery advertisements found in 1867 and 1870 issues of the *Miamisburg Bulletin*. But by August twenty-third, 1872—the next *Bulletin* issue found—he was promoting lager beer in large, all-capital letters.[152]

It is difficult to imagine how the brewery on Water Street could meet the demanding brewing conditions of lager beer—or any beer, really. Before refrigeration machines, brewers typically fermented and stored beer in cool caves or cellars. Miamisburg lacks natural caves, and a beer cellar on Water Street would have been problematic: the brewery sat precariously close to a river prone to rising out of its banks. In her collection of historical essays, Esther Light recounted a pioneer's tale about a local native American who spoke of a flood in 1805 "when the river spanned the valley from hill to hill." Miamisburg was only a pioneer outpost then, but ten miles upstream the fledgling settlement of Dayton documented a damaging flood the same year. It also recorded eight major floods between 1814 and 1898. A flood in 1858 did not make Dayton's greatest hits list, but a June twelfth diary entry by Pastor Isaac H. Reiter gives a glimpse of the river's destructive power in Miamisburg:

> Rain for the last three days. The streams are much swollen. Was just down to the Miami river, which is unusually high; the banks are overflowing; fields of wheat, corn & tobacco are under water; much damage is being done. Bridgeport on the opposite side of the river from Miamisburg is inundated, and all the families have forsaken their dwelling. Skiff is running from the bridge to the railroad depot.

In any of these floods, a brewery near the river would have been vulnerable. Nusz's must have endured numerous floods. The structure even survived—barely—the ravages of the 1913 flood, whose angry waters cut away the riverbank right to its foundation.[153]

How was Nusz able to store his beer in such conditions? He may have done what architect Marlin Heist believed Daniel Gebhart did for Gebhart Tavern decades earlier: store his beer in a hand-dug cave in the side of the big hill.

On the first day of April, 1863, Nusz bought a bit more than five acres of what had been the sprawling estate of Daniel Gebhart's brother Phillip. The estate stretched from the river to the hill and from Mound Avenue southward for nearly half a mile. Today, Miamisburg Community Park covers just a portion of the northern end of the plat. Nusz's parcel started at a line about even with Sunset Street, on the west side of South Main, and extends northward roughly the length of two football fields to the south end of what is now Canal Run, the municipal dog park. The land was higher, and the foot of the hill offered a site for a beer cave.[154]

It is easy to imagine Phillip allowing his brother Daniel to dig a beer cave along the foot of his hill. If that were indeed the case, Nusz may have taken advantage of it decades later. If not, he may have dug his own.

Of course, Nusz did not need five acres for a beer cave. He likely farmed the rest of the tract, perhaps growing barley and hops for his brewery. But he clearly had something bigger in mind.

The Miamisburg Brewery seemed to thrive throughout the 1860s. The 1870 census showed four people working there, all living under William and Margaret's roof. They included Nusz as the brewer and three others as brewery workers: his fifteen-year-old son John; George Herman, and Jacob Alexander, another Bavarian immigrant who married William's and Margaret's daughter Wilhelmina in 1875. Nusz may have begun brewing lager beer there: the August 1872 advertisement in the *Bulletin* promoted it. But just three months later, Nusz replaced the brewery's name in newspaper ads with a new one: the Miami Valley Brewery.[155]

The change signaled that Nusz' beer was coming from a new brewery he had built on his tract south of the village. The Miami Valley Brewery was palatial compared to the Water Street works, and it was built for brewing lager beer. Major features of the new plant included spacious lagering cellars, an ice house, a bottling plant, a wagon shed and a horse stable. Altogether it was the biggest change in Miamisburg's beer scene since Henry Emde brought commercial brewing to town nearly a half-century earlier.[156]

The new brewery was one of many changes Miamisburg saw as it rolled into the new decade. After its population dipped a bit in the 1860s—it shrank by slightly more than two hundred residents to 1,425—the 1870s saw it rebound by more than five hundred, to 1,936 in the 1880 census.

Miamisburg was growing more sophisticated as well. It reflected America's accelerating pace of industrialization. One sign of it was Henry Groby's new house on the second block of East Market Street. Another transplant from Pennsylvania's Berks County, Groby was a prominent builder and contractor who had leveraged his growing wealth by co-founding a bank in 1866. With Groby eventually its president, the bank played its own role in the town's development. It held countless loans and mortgages over the years and eventually became the community's first national bank in 1888. Perhaps Groby's most enduring legacy is the tall-steepled St. Jacob's Evangelical Lutheran Church at First and Central. Groby designed and built it with his brother David in the early 1860s. Its melodic bells remain a familiar part of central Miamisburg's soundscape. In August 1876, Groby decided to build a new house for himself on the east side of St. Jacob's. It featured some of the latest advancements in home comfort. Long gone today, it was just nearing completion in June 1877 when the *Miamisburg Bulletin* marveled it would have "all the modern conveniences, including bath-rooms, water-closets, wardrobes, pantries, etc., hot and cold water in nearly every room, lighted with gas, heated by a furnace, and, above all (in Mr. Groby's estimation) 'a place to throw old boots.' "[157]

Having a place just for boots in the 1870s may not have been as trivial as it sounds. Despite its growing sophistication, Miamisburg was like many Miami Valley towns. Still dependent on horses for local transportation, it was years away from paving its streets and sidewalks. Anyone walking about town faced the prospect of boots covered with mud and manure.

The most conspicuous, consequential and enduring development of the decade was Miamisburg's second railroad. Rail transportation of people and goods was spreading across America, and railroad companies were creating the big-business model for U.S. corporations—one which in the decades ahead would extend to all sectors of the economy. Miamisburg's new railroad was a

Jeff Moore's clear, green-glass bottle is embossed with the words "John Nusz Miamisburg, O."

product of the Cincinnati and Springfield Railway. It was formed in September 1870 as a branch of the Cleveland, Columbus, Cincinnati and Indianapolis Railway, or CCC&I. It gave Miamisburg another quick connection with Dayton and Cincinnati. Work began in 1871, and the line opened on July first, 1872. Maps of the time show a single track squeezed between the east side of the canal and Nusz's new brewery.

Just north of the brewery it curved to the east, then turned north again into the village. It cut through the town and placed a depot at the corner of East Market and Buchner (East Central and North Fourth, now the home of the Dental Depot.) Eventually it became a part of the Cleveland, Cincinnati, Chicago and St. Louis Railway—the Big Four.[158]

Lager beer was not the only big innovation in local brewing. In May 1873, six months after Nusz began advertising his new brewery, a smaller notice appeared on the second page of the *Bulletin*:

"Bottled Beer.

I am prepared to furnish, for family use, bottled lager of the best quality. Orders solicited and promptly filled. Wm. Nusz"[159]

The modest announcement is the earliest word of bottled beer in Miamisburg. To be clear, the bottling house was a place for filling bottles, not making the bottles themselves. A report on U.S. manufacturing in the 1880 census rated Ohio fourth among the states in glass furnaces, but only ninth in the output of green glass—the category that included bottles. It found five Ohio furnaces turning out green glass products, none close to Montgomery County. With no local supplier, Nusz must have ordered bottles in batches from some distant source.[160]

Only one beer bottle has turned up from Nusz's time. A Nusz descendant possesses a clear, longneck bottle that stands twelve inches tall and holds twenty-four ounces. The maker's mark on the bottom—"C & Co"—suggests the bottle may have come from a Pittsburgh glassmaker known as "Cunningham & Co.," which was producing bottles in the 1870s. But what makes this bottle remarkable is the enigmatic label embossed on its side. Raised letters spell out the words "John Nusz Miamisburg, O."[161]

Why it was embossed with John's name instead of William's is a mystery to their descendants. It may be the case that William did not close his old brewery on Water Street when he opened his new one.

Instead, he may have handed it over to John, who turned eighteen the same year. This would have meant the Nusz family had two breweries going at the same time. The bottle may have come from a batch John ordered for his own beer, taking advantage of his father's bottling works. When the *Bulletin* ads began promoting the Miami Valley Brewery in November 1872, references to the Water Street brewery ended. But one can imagine John continuing to serve the old brewery's small, long-established clientele while William pursued a larger market with his big, new brewery south of town.

William, Margaret and their two daughters, Wilhelmina and Susanna, moved into an apartment above the new brewery sometime in the 1870s, likely as soon as it was finished. John stayed on Water Street with his wife Anna Marie and their three-year-old daughter Maggie. But William's estate papers show he and Margaret continued to own the Water Street property. Years later, the estate appraisal listed a frame house on Water Street valued at seven hundred dollars and a "brick brewery" valued at fifteen hundred (a small fraction of the eleven thousand dollars' value of the newer brewery.)[162]

Even if John kept the Water Street brewery going through the 1870s, its days were over by 1882. While the 1880 census listed William as a brewer, it showed John working as a "laborer" while still living on Water Street. The same year's business directory said he "wks brewery," but the Miami Valley Brewery was the only one listed. An 1880 *Bulletin* report also placed John at his father's brewery when he got into a fight—but more about that later. Altogether, the listings suggest that by 1880, John was living in town but working in his father's brewery. The Water Street brewery was certainly closed by 1882. A brief report in the March thirty-first *Bulletin* noted Jacob Zimmerman had changed his residence from South Main Street "to the old brewery property on Water Street." The next year, the paper mentioned that "The brick tenement of Mrs. Margaret Nusz, on Water street, has been nicely painted." The old brewery continued to stand for more than a century, but it only served as a dwelling.[163]

More details are available about Nusz and his brewery because of the advent of a regular weekly newspaper. From the time its press started in 1867, the four-page *Bulletin* gave townsfolk their first steady source of local news, and today most of its issues from August 1872 until the end of its run in 1895 survive on the Internet.

The weekly broadsheet was the enterprise of the three Blossom brothers: Albert, Charles and Miles. They were sons of Mathias (or Matthias) S. Blossom, who opened a saddle and harness shop on Main Street in 1827, served as mayor for one term and sat on the local school board. The two older boys were coming of age when the Civil War broke out. Both Albert and Charles, then about sixteen and fourteen respectively, joined the Squirrel Hunters militia in 1862. Two years later, Albert became a Hundred Days' man, serving as a musician in the 131st Regiment's Company D. After the war, all three started the newspaper and a commercial printing business. The paper's offices and print shop stood on the north side of Bridge Street between Water and Main (now Linden Avenue at the southeast corner of Riverfront Park's parking lot.) Reflecting the two elder brothers' military service, the paper nearly always identified other veterans with the honorific "comrade."[164]

It is difficult today to imagine the importance of a local newspaper to daily life in a time without television, radio or digital media. Every Friday, the *Bulletin* served up a mixture of news, entertainment and gossip. National or world stories could fill whole columns on the front page, but local news on the inside pages could be as short as a single paragraph. The paper rarely put writers' names on stories, so it is seldom clear who wrote any given article. But a single voice seemed to dominate—one at times witty or even brash. For example, a January 1874 article reported, "Miller kicked a three cent dog through a five dollar window glass in his meat store, a few days ago. The dog wasn't hurt." That was the whole story.[165]

The Blossoms' reporting always carried a tone of great authority and often confidently foretold important changes in the offing. They were usually wrong. So it was in May 1873, when their paper reported "A Big Find" in the basement of Nusz's new brewery—iron ore, it claimed. Workers digging a well had sunk a shaft about twenty-four feet when they "hit something hard" that picks and even blasting powder could not not get through. While the reporter who visited the brewery admitted not actually having seen any ore, the article assured readers the discovery would soon result in the production of iron pipe to supply gas works throughout the region. "Nusz will be rich, and he should be happy," the article declared. It is unclear if Nusz himself believed he had struck an iron deposit or if the reporter was writing tongue-in-cheek; either way, no iron mine ever came of it. The only other strike the reporter found noteworthy was when Nusz tapped a keg of his lager, "which we found strictly genuine, and were informed that he intends bottling it for families, during the summer. Nusz makes the best beer in the state." At least the bottling part was true: his ads for it had just started.[166]

However misinterpretive, embellished or invented, the *Bulletin*'s reporting offered glimpses of Nusz, his family and his brewery over time. For example, readers learned of a wagon incident in November 1873 that cost John Nusz a toe. In Dayton on some errand, Nusz tried to climb onto his heavily loaded wagon while it was moving, lost his footing and let a foot slip under a wheel. The wheel "severely" bruised his foot and cut off the small toe. "John pulled off his boot, and putting the toe in his pocket, continued his journey" home, the paper reported. Along the way, the horse's harness broke and the wagon tipped over, but Nusz and another person with him righted it and went on their way.[167]

William himself suffered a wagon accident with a brewery worker named Julius Young in July 1879 as they headed for Farmersville with a load of beer. They were crossing the canal at Mound street when one of the wagon's rear wheels broke, the paper reported, "hurling Nusz and Young down the west embankment of the bridge." Young was unscathed, but Nusz, by then nearly fifty-four, "was pelted with beer kegs in a most painful and alarming manner." His right hand and left leg were "severely injured," but he was back at work a week later.[168]

Equine-based transportation could be hazardous, but horses were vital to the nineteenth century economy. They carried riders and pulled wagons, streetcars and fire apparatus. Anything affecting horses affected nearly everything in daily life. What has been dubbed the Great Epizootic of 1872 widely afflicted horses across North America with flu-like symptoms, sometimes fatally. Running from September 1872 through the end of the year, the epizootic—an epidemic in an animal population—disrupted daily life across the country in countless ways, even sidelining city street cars and firefighting wagons. In Miami Township, farmers avoided taking their horses into the village, where stables and liveries raised the risk of exposure to infected animals. "Very few horses were seen on our streets, Saturday; farmers walked five or six miles to town ... fearing the horse plague," the November twenty-ninth *Bulletin* reported. By December sixth, few horses had died from the outbreak, but "a majority of animals in the city are suffering severely with the disease."[169]

The outbreak faded by the end of the year, but while it was running the epizootic raised fears of how it might impact people's lives. Nusz, for instance, needed horses not only to fetch supplies and deliver beer, but also to harvest ice from local ponds or streams during the winter. Nusz gathered tons of ice to chill his lager beer cellars throughout the warm months. Before the era of mechanical refrigeration, Nusz sawed ice by hand and used horses to cart or drag the heavy cakes to the brewery. With horses ill, "Considerable difficulty is apprehended in supplying ice houses this winter," the December sixth *Bulletin* reported. It did not single out Nusz's ice house, but the thought of facing hot summer days without cold lager beer may have weighed on the writer's mind.[170]

The Miami Valley Brewery stood in what is now Community Park, just south of the Canal Run Dog Park. Note part of the big hill in distance.

CHAPTER TEN

"Mr. Nusz was Largely Known"

Margaret Nusz was out visiting friends when people from Miamisburg, Franklin, Dayton and other surrounding towns began converging on the Nusz residence at the brewery on February seventh, 1879. Philip Herrmann went to fetch her.

When they returned, she found a crowd of well-wishers waiting to celebrate the silver anniversary of her marriage to William. "It was a complete surprise to Mrs. Nusz, planned and successfully executed by her daughters," the *Miamisburg Bulletin* reported. William and Margaret renewed their vows in a ceremony performed by the Reverend Christopher Albrecht, minister of Saint Jacob's Evangelical Lutheran Church. "A royal repast was served," the report continued, "and the host and hostess were the recipients of a large number of valuable presents, among which was a handsome, gold-headed cane, presented

to Mr. Nusz by his son-in-law, Mr. [Jacob] Alexander." Dancing followed, with music by a string band.[171]

Throughout the 1870s, William Nusz was the king of beer in Miamisburg. People around the area knew and respected the man who
made their lager.

Lager beer was driving phenomenal growth in the U.S. brewing
industry. As early as the 1860s, lager beer's growing popularity drew
the attention of corn farmers. "Lager beer instead of whisky has become the national drink, and of course to that extent decreases the
commercial demand for corn," *The Illinois Farmer* reported in 1861. In
his assessment of the brewing industry at the end of the 1870s, Frederick William Salem counted 2,520 breweries nationwide and observed "a great majority" of them "have been erected within the last
fifteen years." Much of what they turned out was lager, according to
numerous profiles of breweries published in the 1880s. "Lager beer
has become almost a national beverage," E. H. Bartley, chief chemist of
the Brooklyn Department of Health, wrote in an 1886 paper for the
Brooklyn Pathological Society. "Some of the breweries [in Brooklyn]
are sending out from 800 to 1,000 kegs of beer a day, and this is no
exceptional city in this respect."[172]

In the late 1870s, Salem found, Ohio had the fifth most breweries
(186,) following New York (365,) Pennsylvania (317,) Wisconsin (226)
and California (195.) But it earned third place in the amount of beer
sold, 965,480 barrels, or enough to pour more than 239 million pints.
Cincinnati dominated Ohio's industry with nineteen breweries, fifteen of them selling more than ten thousand barrels each in the twelve
months ending May first, 1879. Christian Moerlein's brewery dominated them all, selling 93,337 barrels in that period—nearly ten percent of the state's total sales volume. Dayton's eleven breweries included five that sold more than one thousand barrels, led by Coelestin
Schwind with nearly six thousand. In smaller towns around Miamisburg, Sebald in Middletown sold 5,866, Fastnacht & Rau in Eaton sold
424 and Katlein & Company in Franklin sold 113.[173]

Salem's tally included 949 barrels for Nusz's Miami Valley Brewery.

That was more than the Eaton and Franklin breweries combined but barely more than twice as much as Henry Emde was said to have brewed half a century earlier, while Miamisburg's population had grown fourfold since then. More worrying, its sales were down 225 barrels from the twelve months before—possibly a sign of trouble as Nusz's enterprise neared the end of its first decade.[174]

One reason for it might have been competition. Out-of-town breweries were encroaching on his market. Railroads gave Miamisburg saloons quick access to breweries between Dayton and Cincinnati. As noted earlier, William Dodds was serving lager beer in his saloon by 1860. He did not name the brand, but in October 1872 Burkhardt's Saloon, on the corner of Market and Canal (Central and First,) claimed to have the "best Cincinnati lager." Miamisburg saloonist Philip Schroeder bought at least some of his lager beer from elsewhere—a fact he publicized in a spectacular way in January 1875, when the *Bulletin* reported "about a dozen kegs of Hamilton lager" he had ordered "exploded at the C. H. & D. depot," across the river in Bridgeport. The likely culprit was carbon dioxide, the natural byproduct of fermentation that gives beer its suds. Some pressure in a vessel of beer is normal, but homebrewers are rightly wary of "bottle bombs"—over-carbonated brews that can cause their bottles to shatter or explode. Such may have been the case with Schroeder's order: too much fizzy gas may have turned them into foamy bottle bombs on a grand scale.[175]

Lagging sales amid growing competition might have been why, in March 1880, a new ad appeared in the *Bulletin*: "Brewery for Sale." The ad did not explain why Nusz had decided to sell his brewery, but it held a possible clue. It said the brewery "has capacity to manufacture twenty-five barrels of beer, daily," or up to 6,500 barrels yearly at five days per week. If Salem's figure was correct, after nearly a decade in business Nusz's sales were far short of the volume he must have envisioned when he built the place.[176]

The ad recorded the first detailed description of Nusz's brewery—or any Miamisburg brewery, for that matter. It was "a large three story brick brewery and malt house" with two ice houses and ice handling machinery, three beer cellars with room for three thousand barrels, a malt house and a banked-earth barn for eight horses. It also included a living area with seven rooms and a kitchen, a three hundred barrel cistern and "large springs" supplying "an abundance of pure water" to all parts of the building throughout the year.

The ad did not include an asking price, but either Nusz found no buyers willing to pay what he wanted, or else he had a change of heart: after running for four weeks, the ad disappeared.

Instead of selling, Nusz hired new help. In May the *Bulletin* reported, "Mr. Nicholas Martz, an experienced brewer of Cincinnati, has secured a situation as foreman at the Miamisburg brewery." It meant the Miami Valley Brewery, not the older one on Water Street. The county directory for the year listed Martz as working and boarding at the Miami Valley Brewery. And it was there a few months later that he and John Nusz clashed. In September, the *Bulletin* reported Nusz struck Martz "in an altercation" and knocked him to the floor. "In falling, Martz caught his foot in one of the gutters along the floor of the establishment, breaking his left leg in two places below the knee." Nusz fled to Franklin, but the authorities quickly caught up with him. The next February a common pleas court judge found him guilty of assault and battery. No more mention was found about Martz at the brewery, and his trouble with the proprietor's son may well have been all he wanted of it.[177]

A few months later, a one-sentence news note appeared in the *Bulletin*'s July twenty-second issue: "Mr. Wm. Nusz is prostrated with an affliction of the stomach." The eleven-word statement did not seem unusually alarming. The paper's "Sick List" column ran such reports all the time. Just the week before, it had reported Margaret Nusz "was taken with a severe attack of cholera morbus." William may have come down with the same gastrointestinal ailment that struck Margaret. She recovered, but the July twenty-ninth paper carried a grim update on William. It was his obituary.[178]

George Wilhelm Nusz died on July twenty-seventh, 1881. He was less than two weeks from his fifty-sixth birthday. His name is long forgotten, but he was a Miamisburg brewer for at least twenty-one years—the longest run of any local brewer to this writing.

His funeral took place at St. Jacob's. The service "was one of the largest witnessed here for some time. Mr. Nusz was largely known, and friends from Dayton, Salem and adjoining country, with the great

number of citizens who attended, filled the church completely," reported the *Dayton Journal*. Coverage by an out-of-town paper was another indication of how widely Nusz was known. The regionally popular Apollo Band of Hamilton "furnished music suitable to the occasion." Today, William Nusz and his wife rest under the Herrmann family monument, one of the tallest in Hillgrove Union Cemetery.[179]

After Nusz's death, an inventory of his estate found a variety of brewery and farm items, including 190 barrels of beer valued at three dollars per barrel. An appraisal set the

St. Jacob's Evangelical Lutheran Church in 2025.

brewery's value at eleven thousand dollars, with another five hundred dollars for the bottling house and an equal amount for the stable. Nusz's real estate on Water Street—again called "River Street" in the appraisal—included a frame house valued at seven hundred dollars and a brewery worth fifteen hundred.

But Nusz's estate papers also revealed a list of unpaid bills and IOUs—from seven dollars for bricks to 3,266 dollars and sixty-six cents in promissory notes to Margaret and sixteen hundred dollars in notes to his mother-in-law, Susanna. The notes were dated January seventeenth, 1880, and they were to have been repaid in one year. They added to signs of financial problems in Nusz's last years. Margaret, the estate's executor, petitioned the probate court to allow her to sell the brewery in order to pay off the debts William had left.

What followed for the brewery, hidden in county deed records, was a shadowy tale of mystery and deception. It involved members of a prominent family who apparently did not want it known their holdings included a brewery, at a time when determined women marching for temperance were bending public opinion against breweries, distilleries and saloons.

Temperance crusaders in an 1874 *Leslie's Illustrated Newspaper*.

CHAPTER ELEVEN

"These 'Tippling Houses' are a Sore Evil"

On the last day of November in 1882, a curious news article appeared in the *Eaton Democrat* of Preble County. It was short, sharp and sarcastic:

> Emanuel Shultz has purchased a Brewery in Miamisburg, and will go into the beer business extensively. He was the Republican candidate for Congress in this District, and the sham temperance Christians prayed unceasingly for his success. We suppose he has reformed.[180]

True to its name, the weekly paper stood firmly with the Democratic Party and seldom missed a chance to nettle the opposition. Shultz was a prominent local Republican from Miamisburg who was nearing the end of his first term in Congress. Born in Pennsylvania's Berks County in 1819, Shultz had been forced to make his own way at age eleven after his father's untimely death. He had learned bootmaking in Philadelphia and set up shop in Miamisburg at about age nineteen. He proved to have a talent for business and prospered in that work. He had numerous business interests but was perhaps best known locally as the senior partner of the Miami Valley Paper Mill, just north of the village. He was also active in politics. He held numerous local and state offices, and in October 1880 he won Ohio's Fourth District seat in Congress. He ran for re-election in 1882. The district then included Montgomery, Miami and Preble counties, but the Eaton paper's attempt to paint him as some kind of temperance hypocrite seems odd: Shultz was not a noted evangelist for prohibition, nor was he ever known as a brewer, and no public documents ever showed him owning a brewery—certainly not in Miamisburg. Yet the *Democrat*'s snarky note held a grain of truth.[181]

On October second, 1882, Margaret Nusz sold the Miami Valley Brewery to someone named S. A. Baxter for the appraised price, twelve thousand dollars. On October sixth, Baxter resold the brewery for the same amount to an M. E. Manning. It was all a bit mysterious: the deeds did not give either party's first name or place of residence. There was more: although the deed was recorded in Montgomery County, it was signed in Lima before an Allen County notary public.[182]

A few clues in the deed records prompted more research. S. A. Baxter turned out to be Samuel Alexander Baxter, a banker, industrialist and medical doctor in Lima. One of his many business interests was the Lima Car Company, a railway car factory that later became a part of the Lima Locomotive Works. Among those joining him in organizing the company were Shultz and William H. Manning, Shultz's paper-mill partner and son-in-law. The deed noted the property was going to "M. E. Manning, her heirs and assigns"—revealing the buyer to be a woman. When the brewery was sold later, the deed identified the owners as "M. E. Manning and William H. Manning, her husband." So the mysterious M. E. Manning proved to be Mary E. Manning, William's wife and Schultz's daughter.[183]

The *Democrat* was wrong: Emanuel Shultz did not buy a brewery—his daughter did, just four days before the election. The secretive nature of the deal seems meant to shield Shultz from any association with it.

The Eaton paper apparently did not learn about the deal until well after the election, and even then it only seemed to have an inkling of it. In the end, it made no difference: Shultz lost his re-election bid to Democrat Robert Maynard Murray of Piqua.[184]

Why did it matter if someone in Shultz's family owned a brewery? Possibly because the temperance movement had become a partisan issue. Reform-minded Republicans leaned toward some regulation of liquor sales, while business-friendly Democrats opposed it. The *Bulletin* supported temperance laws that would close saloons on Sunday and restrict alcohol sales in other ways. It endorsed Shultz as a "Christian gentleman" with "fine ability as a legislator" but stopped short of labeling him a temperance candidate. The *Democrat* claimed Shultz was "running for Congress on a temperance platform" but luring votes with free drink. In July it claimed "the bung hole of his 'bar'l' will be surrounded from now until the October election."[185]

The temperance movement dates to the earliest years of the nation. Laws to regulate alcoholic beverages were on the books of the Northwest Territory even before Ohio gained statehood. Efforts to license and regulate tavern keepers began in 1805. Temperance organizations sprouted in the 1820s and gained influence throughout the century.[186]

Miamisburg occasionally dragged liquor-law violators into court. In June 1855, Pastor Isaac H. Reiter wrote in his diary about a trial in Town Hall that resulted in a twenty-five dollar fine against an unnamed person for the illegal sale of intoxicating drinks. Reiter did not describe the specific violation, but Ohio had passed a law the year before that limited liquor sales, including a prohibition against selling alcohol to anyone who became intoxicated as a result. The avowed abstinent's diary entry reflected his feelings: "These 'tippling houses' are a sore evil in the community, & very ruinous to the peace, order & morals of Miamisburg. … It is to be hoped that the time is not far distant when intoxicating drinks of all kinds will be prohibited."[187]

The situation had not changed much six years later, at least in the eyes of an organizer for the Order of the Temple of Honor, a temperance group based in Cincinnati. Reporting on a visit to Miamisburg in the June 1860 issue of *Templar's Magazine*, the unnamed correspondent observed, "The liquor traffic here is in the hands of a few low, lager bier Dutch and bad whisky Irishmen, and the better class of community have resolved that it must and shall be crushed."[188]

Little crushing was evident through the early 1870s. Beer and liquor were available in saloons, restaurants and grocery stores around town. The *Bulletin*'s early issues had little to say about the temperance movement. One advertiser, at least, made a nod to the sensibilities of drinking men's wives. In his 1873 ads for his saloon and restaurant on what is now North Fourth Street, between East Central and Buckeye, John Voegle promised:

> Should there be any ladies in Miamisburg who have objections to their husbands drinking at my saloon, it will only be necessary for them to give me a notice and their requests will be strictly complied with. Minors will get nothing to drink."[189]

But in January 1874, the *Bulletin*'s mix of world, national, regional and local news included a small item that hinted more than beer was brewing in southern Ohio: "A temperance revival is in progress in Hillsboro, Ohio. The same is true of Washington C. H., and several other towns. Women are, if our information is correct, at the bottom of the movement."[190]

Ohio was feeling the first restive breezes of a coming storm. It had started the previous December in Fredonia and Jamestown, New York, where the traveling temperance speaker Dio Lewis had inspired hundreds of women to march on local saloons and hold prayer vigils. But the movement really started to take hold in Ohio's Hillsboro and Washington Court House. After hearing Lewis speak there, local women held their own marches. Remarkably, several saloons closed under their pressure. Galvanized by their success, women marched, prayed and organized across Ohio. They demonstrated in small Ohio towns at first, but later in larger cities and other states. The phenomenon became known as the Women's Crusade of 1873-1874. It galvanized the movements for temperance and women's suffrage, which would bring about constitutional amendments in the next century that instituted both Prohibition and a woman's right to vote.[191]

The *Bulletin* started to take notice. A report on the movement appeared in nearly every issue. "The women's war on the liquor traffic is still going on. At Xenia, Springfield, New Lexington, Sidney, Athens, London, Logan, Columbus, Mansfield, Ripley, Dayton, Franklin, Lebanon, Morrow, and other places throughout the state, the work is either in progress or about to commence," it reported on February thirteenth. It added, "All quiet here."[192]

Not for long. Three weeks later, three ministers—Reiter, Christopher Albrecht and "M. Dustin" (likely Mighill Dustin of Dayton, a Methodist leader of the budding state temperance movement)—called for a "mass meeting in the Town Hall in Miamisburg" on Monday, March ninth, to oppose "the evil of intemperance in our community."[193]

The *Bulletin*'s Friday, March thirteenth report on the meeting covered nearly two full columns in the middle of page one—an enormous spread for a local story in that paper. So many people jammed the room that a reporter, arriving late, had to perch in a window. The crowd included clergy from around the area, many women and—near the door—"many of the liquor dealers of the city, who seemed deeply interested in the proceedings." After several speakers, Albrecht read a resolution to form a committee of nine women to petition the village council for a law prohibiting anyone from keeping a place "for tippling

or intemperance, or in which intoxicating liquors of any kind are ha-
bitually sold or furnished to be drunk in or about the said places."[194]

Friday the Thirteenth was unlucky indeed for local saloonists.
The village council called a special meeting that night and swiftly
drafted an ordinance echoing Albrecht's resolution, with a final vote
to be taken on Wednesday. Such swift and stern action must have be-
mused many in a community that had harbored breweries, distilleries
and saloons from its earliest days. A *Bulletin* piece headlined "Charge
of the Light Brigade" in its March twenty-seventh issue seemed to
sum up the local reaction: "It is a matter of astonishment to many that
such interest and determination as have been manifested by the
friends of this measure, should be maintained in Miamisburg where
the population is largely German, and the liquor traffic has flourished
without restraint for so many years."[195]

A day before the council was to vote, local hoteliers, saloonists
and farmers staged their own "anti-temperance" rally at a downtown
hall. Organizers fired cannon salutes "to arouse the farmers" outside of
town, and a cornet band played in front of the hall. Of several speakers, the *Bulletin* only reported remarks by Daniel W. Young. A native
of Munichweiler when it was in Prussia's Rhine province, Young had
emigrated in 1853, arrived in Miamisburg in 1859 and married Elizabeth Jacobus, whose parents were also Rhine province immigrants.
He had worked for the Kauffman Carriage Company until 1870, when
he bought the Valley House hotel on the southeastern corner of Main
and Sycamore. He had sold it after a couple of years to take over a hotel in Dayton, then returned to buy the Arcade, a restaurant and saloon on the east side of Main south of Market. The *Bulletin* sometimes
called him "Captain" Young in recognition of his Civil War service in
three Ohio infantry regiments. At the anti-temperance rally, Young
complained the movement was already hurting farmers, brewers,
suppliers and business owners from Franklin to Dayton. "I don't
know a saloon keeper in Miamisburg who is not in debt. ... What will
farmers do with their barley and corn if this movement goes on? The
Franklin malt house can't sell a pound of malt." Young continued that

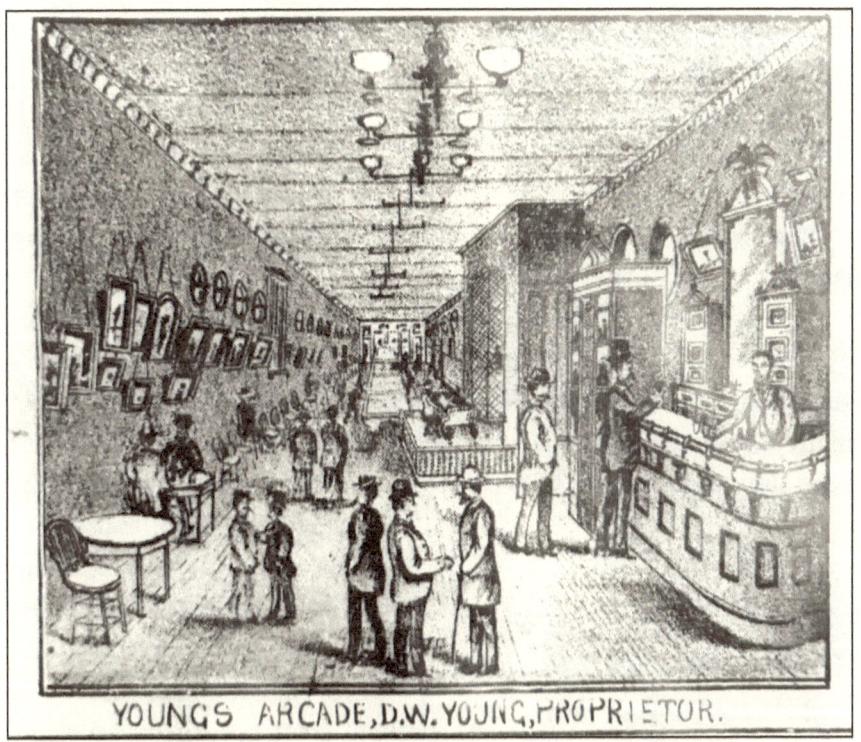

YOUNGS ARCADE,D.W.YOUNG,PROPRIETOR.

Young's Arcade, as depicted in the 1886 lithograph of Miamisburg.

Coelestin Schwind, the prominent Dayton brewer, "has discharged many of his workers, and his cellars are full of beer." Young urged a more moderate measure: "Let council close the saloons on Sunday, forbid the sale of whiskey by the drink, and to minors."[196]

The council met the next day and passed the ordinance, largely as originally proposed, by a vote of five to one. It rejected a proposal to let voters decide the issue. The audience sang a hymn and church bells rang. Another mass meeting on April thirtieth formed the Temperance Union of Miamisburg. Heading it were some of Miamisburg's most prominent business leaders, including wagon maker Daniel Bookwalter; manufacturer David Hetzel; local merchant William Hoff, and coal and lumber dealer Henry Wantz. At the same time, regular ads for saloons and the Miami Valley Brewery disappeared from the *Bulletin*'s pages, either because of a new advertising policy or as a general feeling in the alcohol trade that it would be best to lie low.[197]

The law seemed to have some impact. On the centennial anniversary of Independence Day two years later, the *Bulletin* found "less drunkenness ... than we have ever known on the Fourth of July in Miamisburg, and consequently there were no fights, no arrests, and less hideousness generally."[198]

Brewers across the nation sought to distinguish beer from liquor, even promoting it as a form of temperance in its own right. Salem's 1880 book echoed the view of the brewing industry, and very likely many members of Miamisburg's strongly German population: "It has been shown that beer is wholesome and so mildly alcoholic as to make drunkenness from its use very uncommon. ... A man who drinks in order to become intoxicated can no doubt accomplish his purpose with beer, but such men are almost unknown where beer is the common beverage. This abnormal impulse usually comes only in consequence to a course of ardent spirits." Miamisburg's law seemed to spare common and lager beer by specifying "ale, porter beer, wine or intoxicating liquors of any kind" as beverages prohibited from being consumed where they were sold. (A later change to the ordinance added "fermented liquors" to drinks forbidden to sell to "intoxicated persons or to persons who are in the habit of becoming intoxicated.")[199]

Buehner's saloon ad in an 1880-1881 directory.

Despite the disappearance of the weekly newspaper ads, the 1870s passed without the brewery or the saloons going extinct. Occasional reports of Nusz's ice-cutting indicated his brewery was still in business, as did the story about his 1879 accident with a beer wagon. His church-packing funeral showed the community still held him in high regard. The 1880 directory found three saloons clustered around the public square: Buehner's Restaurant and Beer Hall on the northwest

New To-day.

The Miami Valley Brewing Company

" Announce that they have purchased the

Miamisburg Brewery,

And commenced the manufacture of lager beer, and will be ready to deliver the same by December 1st, 1882. The Company will spare no expense or labor in refitting said brewery with the most modern machinery, and propose to offer to the public

SUPERIOR LAGER BEER

That will be equal in purity, quality and flavor to any beer in the country. They ask the patronage of the public, and guarantee satisfaction in every respect.

12v16tf   MIAMI VALLEY BREWING CO.

Advertising for the Miami Valley Brewery resumed with this announcement in the *Miamisburg Bulletin* on October 27, 1882.

corner of Canal (First) and Market; John Schneider's saloon on the northwest corner of Main and Market, and Young's Arcade just south of the corner. Not much farther away, Jacob Schwartztrauber had a saloon on Main north of Market, and the saloon of Lorenz Wieland stood on the northwest corner of Bridge (Linden) and Water. Few records survive to tell what they served, but Buehner placed a prominent ad in a local directory that declared, "Weyand and Jung's Cincinnati Lager Beer always on tap," and "pure liquors and best cigars."[200]

After years of absence, advertisements for breweries and saloons began creeping back into the *Bulletin*'s pages. In May 1882, ads for the Washington House, on the west side of Main just south of the Public Square, disclosed Wieland was now its proprietor. The very bottom of the ad included a note that Wieland was also the local agent for the Gambrinus Stock Company Brewery of Cincinnati. A native of Württemberg, Wieland ("Lawrence" in some records but "Lorenz" on his gravestone and in his obituary) would become more deeply connected to Miamisburg's brewing scene in years to come.[201]

The Miami Valley Brewery seems to have kept running until Nusz's death. As the estate inventory showed, he left it with 190 barrels of beer in the cellars. It may have ceased business at that point. But it, too, returned to the *Bulletin*'s advertising columns in 1882. In the October twenty-seventh issue, the brewery's secretive owners, Mary and William Manning, sponsored a large ad at the top of the second page. The Miami Valley Brewing Company, it announced, had started brewing "and will be ready to deliver the same by December first, 1882."[202]

The announcement was premature. December first came and went while the same ad continued to appear in the *Bulletin*. State records put Miami Valley Brewing's incorporation date as January twenty-fifth, 1883, with a capitalization of fifty thousand dollars. But notifications the company would offer stock for sale ran through February—sometimes right next to the outdated ad, which continued unchanged until June.[203]

On June eighth, the *Bulletin* announced yet another change in ownership. The buyer was the ex-brewery foreman of the big Jackson Brewing Company in Cincinnati, August Victor Kuehn.[204]

THE MIAMI VALLEY BREWERY!

AUGUST KUEHN, PROPRIETOR.

Having purchased the Miami Valley Brewery, announces that h
has commenced the manufacture of

PURE LAGER BEER!

and is prepared to deliver the same at any time. No expense
labor has been spared in refitting this establishment with mode
appliances and machinery for the manufacture of a superior ar
cle of beer, and the quality of the manufacture will at all tim
he guaranteed. The patronage of the public is solicited.
45v16tf   AUGUST KUEHN,

August Kuehn's first newspaper advertisements appeared in the June 15, 1883, *Miamisburg Bulletin*.

CHAPTER TWELVE

A. Kuehn's Brewery

August Kuehn was born in Ammerschwihr, a small village in northeastern France. A French immigrant brewing beer for a German community might seem odd, but Ammerschwihr lies close to Germany—just fourteen miles west of the upper Rhine River, in the Alsace region annexed by the German Empire in 1871. Kuehn emigrated the following year, which might explain why he gave France as his country of birth on the U.S. passport application he filed in 1900, while the same year's census said he was from Germany.[205]

The passport application offers a rare portrait of a nineteenth-century Miamisburg brewer. It did not include a photo, but its words would have satisfied a sketch artist: he stood five feet, nine inches tall with graying hair, beard and mustache. His florid face held hazel eyes, a grecian nose, a broad chin and a small mouth with full lips.

Once in the United States, Kuehn made his way to Cincinnati. By 1875 he was working as a brewer, and by 1876 he had taken a job in the Jackson Brewery. The following year he married Catherine Theureling, a Hamilton native. In 1883 he quit his brewing job and relocated to Miamisburg.[206]

The Cincinnati directory for 1882 listed him as the Jackson Brewery's foreman. Why leave such a job with a big brewery in bustling Cincinnati to take over a small, apparently idled brewery in a village up the valley? He may have been fed up with Jackson Brewing's dysfunctional management. A would-be tycoon named George Weber had bought the brewery on credit in 1874. He had failed to pay off his creditors, which quickly led to legal disputes. The big question was whether to settle debts by allowing the business to continue under an assignee, or by shutting it down and selling off its assets. Meanwhile, Weber triggered a long-running "beer war" of words by accusing competitors of tainting their products. "Chaos was the order of the day at the Jackson Brewery under George Weber's tenure," Michael D. Morgan wrote in *Cincinnati Beer*. Uncertainty about the

A brown glass bottle embossed with "A. Kuehn Miamisburg," with closure.

brewery's future might have prompted Kuehn's exit and sparked a desire to be his own boss.[207]

On June first, Kuehn bought the Miami Valley Brewery and the surrounding plat for twenty-one thousand dollars. The *Miamisburg Bulletin* announced the sale on page three of its June eighth issue. Meanwhile, the old ad continued to run, promising beer by the previous December. Kuehn replaced that ad in the next issue with a new one. It announced he had "commenced the manufacture of pure lager beer! and is prepared to deliver the same at any time. No expense or labor has been spared in refitting this establishment with modern appliances and machinery for the manufacture of a superior article of beer." The wording was not much different from before, except Kuehn's ad asserted he had beer on hand.[208]

The *Bulletin* exhorted local saloonists to stop buying beer from out-of-town breweries. Instead, they should rally around Miamisburg's new brewer—who also happened to be a new advertiser. Asked the paper rhetorically on June twenty-ninth: "Can anybody tell why thirty thousand dollars' worth of beer should be shipped to this city annually, with a first class brewery right at home?" The saloonists quickly responded, or perhaps they simply found Kuehn's beer better or cheaper. "Every saloon in the city except one now sells beer made by the Miami Valley Brewery. This is as it should be," the August seventeenth issue asserted. The *Bulletin* was still cheerleading for Kuehn the following June: "Capt. D. W. Young, one of the first to sell and first to abandon Cincinnati lager in the place, says the beer manufactured by the Miami Valley Brewery in this city is the purest and the best in the country. Dan knows what he is talking about."[209]

The Miami Valley Brewery returned to the stage just as Miamisburg was transforming from just one of many canal towns into a budding manufacturing center. As it did so, it was taking on the accoutrements of metropolitan life.

On Saturday night, January twenty-fourth, 1880, a crowd filled Charles Baum's office in the Baum House hotel on the southeast corner of the public square. A wire strung all the way from Farmersville via Germantown snaked into the office. All watched as it was hooked up to a boxy device on a table. The new Miamisburg and Farmersville Telephone Company had just wired up the town's first phone. The January thirtieth *Bulletin* reported what happened next:

> ... much lively conversation and badinage went back and forth between officers of the company, and others interested in the enterprise. The line was fully tested and found perfect in every respect. Voices were readily recognized, and the tones of musical instruments were carried with wonderful accuracy. The company is now ready for business.[210]

Near the Miami and Erie Canal's downtown lock, the old mills still "clacked and clattered away in rhythmic song," as the *Bulletin* put it in 1882. At least one miller, Uriah Engleman, upgraded his flour mill's machinery that year, and subsequent improvements more than doubled its output over the decade. But the power available from the Miami Valley's waterways had its limits, and modern mills—like factories in general—were shedding their nostalgic water wheels for steam engines. North of town, the new Ohio Paper Company's mills gulped water in their paper- and pulp-making processes, but most of their power came from four steam engines. Likewise, Hoover & Gamble— the company founded by early brewer David H. Hoover, now carried on by his son Abel and son-in-law William Gamble—converted its growing Excelsior Agriculture Works south of Bridge Street (Linden Avenue) to steam power in 1881.[211]

Hoover & Gamble's switch to steam coincided with another change that catapulted the company into an era of rapid growth. It had prospered with the production of reapers and mowers through the 1870s. In 1879 the company was one of the first to license the labor-saving twine binder invented by John F. Appleby in Beloit, Wisconsin. Attached to a horse-drawn reaper for cutting grain, the binder automatically gathered the grain into sheaves and bound them with

Hoover & Co. advertised its Excelsior Harvester & Binder with color illustrations in an 1882 company booklet.

twine made of hemp or sisal. It was a game-changer in the farm-machine industry: farmers were rejecting binders that used metal wire because they left bits of metal in the grain; the bits were lethal to livestock and damaged milling machines. Twine was a safer and cheaper alternative, making the twine binder an instant hit. Hoover & Gamble never matched Cyrus McCormick's huge harvester company in Chicago, but it licensed the new binder just ahead of McCormick and leaped into the booming twine-binder market. South of Bridge Street, its Excelsior works grew on Locust (South Second) and sprawled eastward to the railroad tracks. Close on its heels, the Miamisburg Binder Twine & Cordage Company organized to make twine and rope in a line of buildings along the west side of Locust. By the mid-1880s, Hoover & Gamble employed more than two hundred workers, and 120 more worked at Miamisburg Binder Twine.[212]

Another important economic driver—decades before medical science understood its danger—was tobacco. At least one source credits Thomas Pomeroy, in 1839, with establishing Miami Township as the Miami Valley's center for seedleaf tobacco, a type mainly used in cigars. Tobacco became a major crop in the region. The 1870s and later saw the Blossom brothers devote ever more space to tobacco news. Miles Blossom eventually became a tobacco dealer, and the brothers promoted their paper as a tobacco journal. They even offered subscribers their own brand of tobacco seeds: Zimmer Spanish, a Cuban variety they named for the same Jacob Zimmer who had briefly owned Hoover's old brewery and managed the Miami House. The tobacco trade was where Zimmer made his biggest mark. Tobacco supported farmers, warehouse owners, packers, shippers and traders like Zimmer. Tobacco warehouses dotted Miamisburg in the late nineteenth and early twentieth centuries.[213]

Charles Baum's Star City Opera House was new when it appeared on the 1886 lithograph of Miamisburg.

Perhaps the boldest sign of Miamisburg's vitality was the brick-walled, mansard-roofed Star City Opera House, erected by Charles Baum on the south side of his hotel. The Baum Opera House Association dates it to 1884, although the *Bulletin* reported finishing touches to the interior were still underway in late 1885. Opera houses were dressing up towns across the country in the 1880s, and Baum's ensured Miamisburg was not left behind. More than strictly a highbrow venue, it doubled as a community entertainment center. An 1886 map shows its first floor, below the opera hall, housed a roller skating rink, billiards room, bowling alley and shooting gallery.[214]

Miamisburgers must have been full of pride for their prosperous town. Signs of progress were everywhere. In the *Bulletin*, the Blossom

A framed print of the 1886 lithograph of Miamisburg hangs in the Miamisburg Historical Society's History Center.

brothers painted an imaginative word picture of the village as they saw it, perhaps over a pint of Kuehn's beer, in 1886:

> The streets of our thriving city are daily thronged with vehicles of patrons to our differents [sic] lines of businesses, comprising the farming community from near and remote. These with the teams from paper and pulp mills, twine factories, agricultural works, flouring mills, hub and spoke factory, lumber wagons, furniture delivery wagons, grocery delivery wagons, tobacco in transit to and from the packing houses, sash and blind factories' teams, freight and express wagons, and a host of others ... present an endless panorama

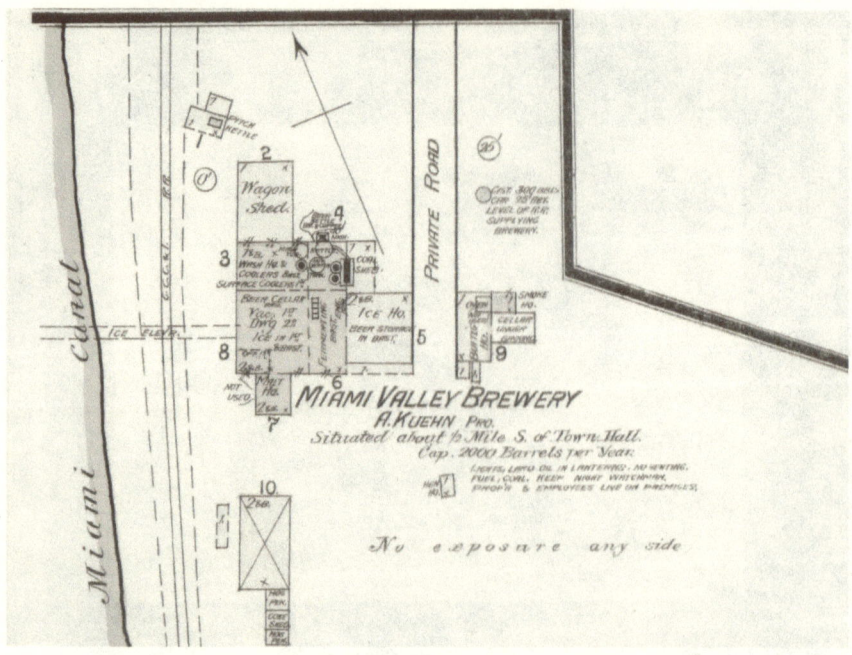

The 1886 Sanborn map included a plan view of Kuehn's brewery. Note brew house (center,) CCC & I Railroad (left) and bottling house (right.)

like the shifting views of a kaleidoscope. At night the
brilliantly illuminated business houses and long lines
of lamp lit streets crowded with their jostling throngs
of evening shoppers and gaily dressed promenaders,
make up an attractive and enlivening scene. We are
fast becoming a great people."[215]

About the same time, an artist for the O. H. Bailey Company of Boston
drew a panoramic view of the village as it looked from atop the ridge
west of the river. The resulting lithograph effectively froze 1886 Miamisburg in time, making it the defining image of the city's past. And
Miamisburg has preserved enough historical architecture for the broad outlines of the lithograph—even many of its details—to be recog-
nizable today. A border surrounding the main scene includes sketches
of individual businesses and homes, including one in the lower right

corner labeled "A. Kuehn's Brewery"—the earliest known picture of a Miamisburg brewing plant. Modern reprints of the lithograph hang in countless local businesses and homes.[216]

Also appearing in 1886 was Miamisburg's first Sanborn fire insurance map. It offered detailed plan views of many local buildings, including the brewery. Together, the lithograph's sketch and the Sanborn map show how the Miami Valley Brewery looked and worked. An ice elevator ran from the canal to a second-floor opening on the west end of the building, crossing over a road and the Big Four railroad tracks. The second floor enclosed a long corridor through which the ice passed to a large, frame ice house against the east wall. The brewing works occupied the northeast corner of the building with an office in the southwest corner. The Kuehns lived in apartments on the third, uppermost floor. The frame bottling house was a separate building east of the brew house. The map cited a brewing capacity of two thousand barrels per year—the same as Nusz advertised when he tried to sell the brewery in 1880.[217]

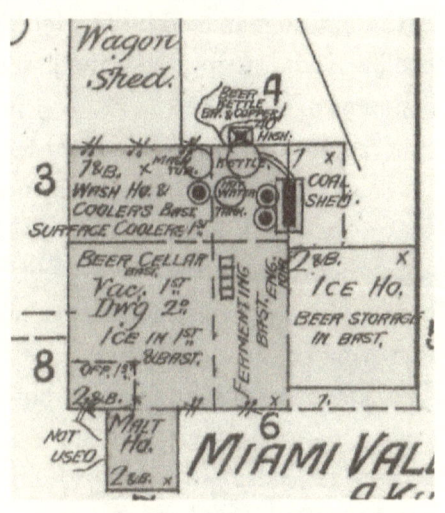

A closer view of the Sanborn map shows more brewery detail. Dark gray areas are brick structures.

More details emerged when a *Bulletin* correspondent toured the brewery in 1888. The newspaper described the brewery's cellars as "four great vaults, filled with huge casks, the largest of which holds 1167 gallons; these are surrounded with ice and kept at a temperature of 34 to 40" degrees. The beer itself followed the simple recipe of traditional lager, "made strictly from malt and hops" with "no corn or rice." Much of the article closely followed Kuehn's latest newspaper ad, which appeared on the next page of the same issue. Kuehn claimed his beer was "admirably adapted to general use, for families and invalids. Being chiefly nutritious and but mildly stimulated, it is prescribed by the medical fraternity with decided benefit in all cases of weakness and impaired nutrition." Kuehn's health claims reflected the defensive stance beer brewers were taking in the face of the temperance movement. But the ad also noted, "consumers will do well to compare the merits of Miamisburg beer with the boasted qualities of cheaper products manufactured abroad"—possibly a veiled reference to the Carling London Amber Ale available "for medicinal use" at the Arcade, now managed by Daniel W. Young's son, Daniel Junior. He had been advertising the Canadian brand since remodeling the establishment in late 1886.[218]

The 1886 lithograph etched Kuehn's name in Miamisburg's history, but it is surprising he is not remembered for his midnight shootout with a gang of safecrackers in January 1887. Newspapers around Ohio reported the dramatic robbery. The *Bulletin*'s report of January seventh was the most detailed, although the eyewitness-like reporting seems imaginative at best.

Close to midnight on a cold January second, so the paper reported, a gang of men emerged from a nearby tobacco shed and sneaked across the iced-over canal to the brewery, where they forced open a window. Two men entered the office and began drilling into the brewery's safe. Others stood guard around the building, including one at the door to the stairway leading up to the top floor where Kuehn, his wife Catherine and their two young children were sleeping. The safecrackers' noises roused Kuehn. He grabbed his revolver and opened the door at the top of the stairway, only to be met by the flash and roar of a pistol from below. Kuehn returned fire, slammed the door and hurried to a balcony at the west end of the brewery, where another robber posted outside fired up at him.

Kuehn alerted a neighbor to the robbery while Catherine threw open another window and called for help. "This performance was greeted with a volley of pistol shots, in such rapid succession as to sound like a pack of exploding firecrackers" as the robbers and Kuehn exchanged fire, the *Bulletin* reported. Down in the office, the robbers working on the safe forced it open. (The *Bulletin* only reported it "gutted," but other reports said they blew it open.) Mission accomplished, the robbers fled across the canal and the frozen Miami, where another gang member waited with a two-horse sleigh. (Other papers speculated they escaped on a midnight train.) However they got away, they seem to have left with empty pockets: the *Bulletin* and other papers reported Kuehn only used the safe to store documents, keeping the brewery's cash in Henry Groby's bank up in town.[219]

Kuehn was not the only Miamisburg business owner to face gunmen. Charles Baum had his own shootout thirteen months later.

Another Bavarian native, Baum emigrated in 1869 and arrived in Miamisburg in 1874. There he married Elizabeth Schneider and managed the Miami House until 1878, when he opened a new hotel of his own on the public square, and later the opera house. Conover's *Centennial Portrait* painted Baum as a widely known but reclusive soul who lived in his hotel and seldom left it except for a monthly trip to the bank.

Sunday night on February twenty-sixth, 1888, found him seated behind the counter of his hotel. The next Friday's *Bulletin* reported he was "awaiting the arrival of the midnight trains" before locking up for the night, when two masked robbers walked in. One pulled out a pistol and kept it aimed at Baum while the other went to the still-open safe and scooped out 140 dollars.

As they started to leave, Baum picked up his own pistol and went after them, firing once. But as he closed on the pair, one of the robbers "fired point blank in Baum's face," the *Bulletin* reported. The bullet hit at an angle above his right eye and flattened against his skull. A second round struck him in the abdomen. Neither bullet inflicted a life-threatening wound. Doctors removed the slug from his forehead the next day. Meanwhile, the *Bulletin* scolded town gossips and other newspapers for spreading the "absurd gabble" that Baum had attempted suicide. The dramatic story drew widespread coverage, and

A Jackson Brewery advertisement in the *Miamisburg Bulletin* promoting August Kuehn as its foreman.

some papers—the *River Falls Journal* of Wisconsin was one—claimed he died in the gunfight. Baum passed away at the young age of forty-three, but not until 1895, and then it was from natural causes unrelated to the shooting.[220]

Kuehn fared better than Baum: the only injury his robbers inflicted was to his safe. But fate had something else in store for him in 1889.

The brewery was already coming awake an hour before sunrise on Monday, March twenty-fifth. A worker lit a fire under the brew house boiler. About the same time, flames from an unexplained source appeared in the attached ice house at the east end of the building. One might expect an ice-house fire to put itself out as it melted the ice, but strong winds fanned the flames. They spread to the adjoining malt house, the nearby bottling house and "the whole upper floor of the establishment," the next Friday's *Bulletin* reported. The blaze swept through the Kuehns' apartments. "Some of the furniture including a piano, was saved, but most of it was destroyed," the paper reported, "and what was one of the most complete and substantial structures of its kind in the Miami Valley is now a blackened heap of ruins."[221]

The brewery stood just south of the town's boundary, but the village fire department turned out anyway, as did workers from the Hoover & Gamble foundry on Locust Street. Some neighbors also pitched in to fight the flames. Their efforts might have kept a bad fire from becoming tragic, although the *Bulletin* also credited lucky timing: "Had the fire broken out at midnight, the whole family might have perished." They relocated temporarily to Lorenz Wieland's Washington House on Main Street.

The fire also consumed the brewery's malt supply, but the brewing works and the underground vaults survived. Kuehn had a new supply of malt shipped up from Hamilton and was brewing again the same week. Despite its stark description of the brewery's damage, the paper was sanguine about its prospects: "As soon as the loss is adjusted by the insurance companies, the work of rebuilding will be commenced and hurried to completion. Meanwhile, Mr. Kuehn bears his misfortune with courage, and has made every arrangement to supply the rapidly increasing demand for the wholesome beverage, made at the Miami Valley Brewery, with usual regularity."

By April, local millwright Simon L. Schwytzer had a crew hard at work repairing the building, but Kuehn's career took another turn. Despite its upbeat assessment just two weeks earlier, the *Bulletin* tersely reported on April twelfth, "The Miami Valley Brewery ... is to be abandoned." Down in Cincinnati, the troubled Jackson Brewery was under new management. Either at Kuehn's request or by invitation from the new president, Leo Brigel, he quickly reclaimed the position of brewery foreman. Two weeks after announcing Kuehn's departure, the *Bulletin* published a correspondent's report on a tour of the "admirably equipped" Jackson brewery by its "courteous foreman," Kuehn. The fawning story coincided with the first of Jackson Brewing's advertisements in the paper.[222]

If only from a distance, Kuehn still served Miamisburg's palates. Jackson Brewing's ads ran regularly in the paper, promoting Kuehn's role in brewing the "pure old lager" coming up from Cincinnati. They noted one of Kuehn's former hands, Jacob Scheu, would be Jackson's local sales agent. A news brief in March 1890 hinted that Scheu was using the vaults of Kuehn's old brewery for local storage. The company "cut and packed ice last week," it reported, most likely to chill the still-intact cellars. Kuehn himself dropped in from time to time. But the odds on the old brewery becoming active again seemed slim.[223]

In 1892 a meeting in the Hotel de Young (originally Miami House, now Jayne's) organized a new company to revive Miamisburg's brewery.

CHAPTER THIRTEEN

"Order out of Chaos"

A ugust Kuehn continued to own the Miami Valley Brewery property during his Jackson Brewing tenure. The 1892 Sanborn fire insurance map showed the Miamisburg works still under his name, but marked "Closed." Gone were some key features visible on the 1886 map, including the upper-floor dwelling spaces and the bottling house east of the brewery. The ice house and malt house had been repaired or replaced.

Meanwhile, Kuehn relocated to Muskingum County. By late summer 1892, he was brewing beer for the Riverside Brewery in Zanesville. Although he was now 130 or more railroad miles from Miamisburg, he tried to keep his local customers. The September second *Miamisburg Bulletin* reported he had shipped twenty-six dozen bottles of Riverside beer to Lorenz Wieland's Washington House on consignment. The newspaper assured readers, "all who sampled it pronounced it first class," but it did not report whether Wieland ever ordered more.[224]

Kuehn stayed in Zanesville for less than six years. By 1898 he was co-owner of the Marietta Brewing Company, and eventually he became its president. Marietta was his final home, and he died there in 1913.[225]

Soon after Kuehn moved to Zanesville, a new name surfaced in Miamisburg: Henry P. Deuscher.

Deuscher was a business owner in Hamilton, twenty miles southeast of Miamisburg. While Kuehn and Nusz seemed to have been cut from the same cloth as lifelong brewers, Deuscher's history was closer to David Hoover's: his roots were in farming, and he had some experience as a distiller. His natural talents, though, seemed to lie in commerce and manufacturing. Born in the Grand Duchy of Baden in 1829, Deuscher emigrated as a child with his parents. They lived briefly near Lancaster, Pennsylvania, before buying a farm in Butler County between Hamilton and Trenton. He was living there when he married Ellen Ball in 1854. The Civil War brought him the lifelong title of "Captain" as commander of Company G in Ohio's Eighty-Third Infantry Regiment. He served for eight months and returned to his farm, but over the next several years he leased it while he worked as a store keeper in Trenton and operated distilleries in Hamilton and the tiny hamlet of Collinsville. He must have done well: in 1870 he erected a stately, Italianate home of stone and brick on his farm. (The house took its place on the National Register of Historic Places in 1984 and still stands at this writing.) Deuscher's business career really took off in 1874 when he started a malting and grain business in Hamilton. Later he founded the H. P. Deuscher Manufacturing Company, a maker of farm tools and machines.[226]

Deuscher's name was prominent in Hamilton, but he was not a newsmaker in Miamisburg until September twenty-sixth, 1892, when Hamilton attorney Eugene C. Poicey took a room in the Hotel de Young, the former Miami House. (D. W. Young had become the hotel's proprietor in 1887 and managed it under his own name.) Word got around that Poicey was on a scouting trip for Deuscher, who had his eye on Kuehn's old brewery. Poicey's mission was to gauge the local business community's interest in putting the brewery back on its feet. News coverage did not explain what had drawn Deuscher's attention to the long-idled works, but the *Bulletin*'s report on the fire had noted Kuehn's or-

der for more malt from Hamilton. It may have come from Deuscher's malt house. Deuscher may have seen the brewer's misfortune as a chance to establish a new outlet for his malt business and make more money on the end product.[227]

Whatever his motive, Deuscher set up a new company with fifty thousand dollars in capital. He had secured half the amount in Hamilton and looked to Miamisburg business owners for the rest. On October sixth, Deuscher held a meeting at Hotel Young to organize the Miamisburg

CAPTAIN HENRY P. DEUSCHER.

Portrait of Henry P. Deuscher.

Brewing Company. Officers included Deuscher, president; Young, who hosted the meeting, vice president; Lorenz Wieland of the Washington House, treasurer, and Poicey, Deuscher's attorney, secretary. Deuscher bought the brewery property from Kuehn and then resold it to the corporation.[228]

The effort to revive Miamisburg's brewery came at a time of dramatic growth and change across the country. America was becoming an industrial powerhouse, and technology was advancing at a breathtaking pace. It also saw the rise of big business, monopolies and the antitrust movement. Change was rippling through every corner of the nation, including Miamisburg. Jobs in its growing manufacturing and tobacco sectors helped the town's population swell by a third in the 1890s.

The most vivid sign of change literally came in a flash at the start of the century's last decade. At 8:30 on the evening of Saturday, May tenth, 1890, a worker in the new municipal electric plant threw a switch, and "forty arc lights suddenly blazed out and illuminated the streets," the *Bulletin* reported. The town had entered the age of electricity. Lights were only its most visible feature. For example, by July 1896 Young's hotel, on Main at Linden, boasted a stop on the new electric trolley line to Dayton.[229]

Miamisburg added to its manufacturing base in 1890 when business leaders organized a Board of Trade to lure the Enterprise Carriage Company away from Cincinnati. By February 1892, its new factory, north of Pearl Street and east of the railroad tracks, was running at "full capacity" with three hundred workers. At the same time, Hoover & Gamble formally incorporated with a new business focus: its twine binder works, south of East Bridge Street (Linden Avenue) between Locust (South Second) and the railroad tracks, switched to manufacturing the machines for making cordage and twine.[230]

Another sign of a thriving business climate included work to get Miamisburg Brewing back in business. By December Poicey was overseeing workers at the old Miami Valley Brewery. They were clearing debris, repairing stonework, whitewashing the cellars—generally "beginning to bring order out of chaos," the *Bulletin* reported. A closely related project was a new bottling plant, this time set up as a separate company.[231]

But before it started brewing, the company found itself facing an unexpected challenge: heading off a winter heating crisis.

January 1893 was a great month for harvesting ice. Miamisburg Brewing was filling its ice house in anticipation of chilling beer when summer came. The month was not so great if you were trying to heat your home or shop. "For many years the Miami Valley has not experienced such an extended period of zero weather as now prevails," the *Bulletin* observed on January twentieth.

Meanwhile, coal supplies dwindled. The February third issue reported local dealers had run out, and bad weather was blocking a coal train from making its scheduled delivery. But Miamisburg Brewing had two train cars full of coal sitting on a siding, and the brewery, not yet in operation, could spare them. Local business leaders appealed to Young, the brewing company's vice president, to consider the situation. " 'Take the coal,' " the *Bulletin* quoted Young as saying. " 'Take a carload and supply the people who need it, and if one is not enough, then take two. You can return it by the time the company are [sic] ready to use it.' " The brewery's largesse relieved the crisis until the coal train finally chugged into town the next week.[232]

As winter gave way to spring, Miamisburg Brewing started production with John Maurer as its brewer. On May twenty-sixth the *Bulletin* published a bit of puffery typical of stories about current or potential advertisers. It described Maurer as "a talented and experienced brewer" who "acquired a thorough knowledge of the arts and mysteries of his profession in his youth in famous breweries in the fatherland, and has since satisfactorily maintained responsible positions in leading breweries in the United States." It did not name any of those breweries or offer any other biographical details about Maurer. But it asserted he had started to deliver "properly toned and ripened" beer made with "none but the best and purest ingredients," including "pure spring water from the Company's famous springs on the hillside." The story finished with the same plea the *Bulletin* had made on behalf of Kuehn's brewery a decade earlier: with such a fine product available locally, "would it not be no more than fair to sustain home enterprise?"[233]

While a new day seemed to be dawning for the brewery, an economic storm was gathering. Big trusts began to fail, triggering the Panic of 1893 and a depression that would persist for years. Nearly half a century earlier, David Hoover had blamed such conditions for the loss of his brewery. This time around, the manufacturing company he had left to his heirs would be in the heart of the whirlwind.

By the 1890s, Hoover & Gamble was no doubt keeping a close eye on a shady new player in the twine market. The National Cordage Company of New Jersey was the creation of four large cordage companies. Ostensibly competitors, their real agenda was to take over the whole cordage industry "for the sake of exacting monopoly profits," as Harvard University professor Arthur Stone Dewing described it in *A History of the National Cordage Company*. It quickly became "a giant" with a voracious appetite for smaller mills, including the Victoria Cordage Company of Dayton, Kentucky. In 1891 it used Victoria Cordage to buy Miamisburg Binder Twine & Cordage, along with mills in Middletown and Xenia. This put the fortunes of locally important companies and their workers at the mercy of a Gilded Age trust.[234]

But National Cordage's scheme had a fatal flaw: it was buying cordage mills at inflated prices while neglecting to control the market for cordage-making machines. This meant a cordage company could sell its old mill to National Cordage at a lucrative price and then use its windfall to open a new factory outfitted with the latest machinery. "As rapidly as the officials of the company would 'buy up' the competing mills, the old owners either in their own name or as representatives of others, would start to build new mills," Dewing wrote.[235]

What happened in Miamisburg and Ohio "admirably illustrated" the problem, Dewing wrote. On October second, the *Bulletin* announced Victoria Cordage's acquisition of Miamisburg Binder Twine and the Middletown and Xenia mills. Just two weeks later, it reported Hoover & Gamble had organized a new cordage company, Miamisburg Cordage. It hired Fred Holstman, the old company's superintendent, to manage it. The new mill occupied an existing brick building on Excelsior (South Third) below Linden. The town greeted 1892 with a new plant turning out twine and cordage. In response, Victoria quickly bought Miamisburg Cordage. Unfazed, Hoover & Gamble organized the nearly identically named Miamisburg Twine and Cordage and commenced building a new mill on West Sycamore Street, just across the river at the north end of town. (Today newer buildings surround the original factory, which is remembered as the home of the Groendyke Company, a later owner. A number of small businesses now occupy the site.) This was also when Hoover & Gamble switched its manufacturing focus to cordage-making machinery. It supplied the machines for the new mill. National Cordage closed its two Miamisburg mills, but the *Bulletin* shrugged at the news. In July it reported, "… another large cordage mill is in process of erection by a company that is not controlled by the cordage trust, and the machinery is being manufactured in this place …" All signs pointed to a quick resumption in the local cordage industry: machinery was in place by the end of September, and Hoover & Gamble was already making machines for another new mill in St. Paul, Minnesota. More mills were going up around the country. As Dewing wrote, the would-be monopolists found that their ill-conceived scheme "actually resulted in stimulating competition."[236]

But the *Bulletin* was too optimistic. National Cordage's great scheme abruptly unraveled in the first week of May 1893, and the company fell into receivership. The financial world was already nervous over the state of credit and other failures, especially that of the Reading Railroad. National Cordage's collapse sparked a panic, which led to a grinding depression. Banks, factories and other businesses shut down, restricted hours or reduced pay. The unemployment rate rose above ten percent for "five or six years" and reshaped U.S. politics and economic policy, wrote David O. Whitten, Auburn University economics professor, in a 2001 paper. Whitten and others have pointed to many factors behind the crisis, but Dewing said National Cordage's downfall played a key role "as it tended more than any other, to create the feeling of uncertainty which led to the panic of 1893."[237]

In Miamisburg, two cordage mills with more than one hundred workers between them closed while the new one across the river had yet to open. The *Bulletin* did not report it in operation until October 1894.[238]

News of bank failures and mill closures peppered the paper's columns in the summer of 1893. Besides the cordage mills, other local mills and factories shut down for a time. The *Bulletin*'s September first issue carried an unusually graphic account about the plight of several jobless mill workers. They were boarders at the Highland House, a small hotel and saloon that Louis and Anna Highland kept on the southeast corner of East Lock and South First, across the canal from the idled mills.

> ... when the mills shut down, after looking for work elsewhere in this vicinity, [they] concluded to take a tramp abroad in search of employment. They were sleek and fat when they departed but returned in a short time lean and hungry, with woeful tales of disappointment. It was the same story everywhere they applied for work. No work—no money. They had been obliged to subsist a part of the time on uncooked, green corn, which they plucked from fields by the roadside. The country was alive with wayfarers, like themselves, seeking work and finding none. ... Highland took them in and fed them and after a rest they took up the line of march again.[239]

Things seemed to perk up for a time. Local mills and factories reopened late in the year. But 1894 proved to be even worse nationally. Miamisburg greeted Independence Day in a gloomy mood, and the annual celebration was subdued. "The general depression in business, the prevailing impression among people of moderate means that the dull times will continue—and that the coming winter will be a tough season to pull through—has made our people unusually conservative," the *Bulletin* reported.[240]

Against this dismal backdrop, Miamisburg Brewing's next steps are hazy. In May 1893 the *Bulletin* announced the brewery had started delivering beer, but it did not begin advertising until the end of March the next year. Somehow, it persevered through the hard times. It even moved forward on some capital improvements, including one that surely sent a chill down Jacob Schwartztrauber's spine.

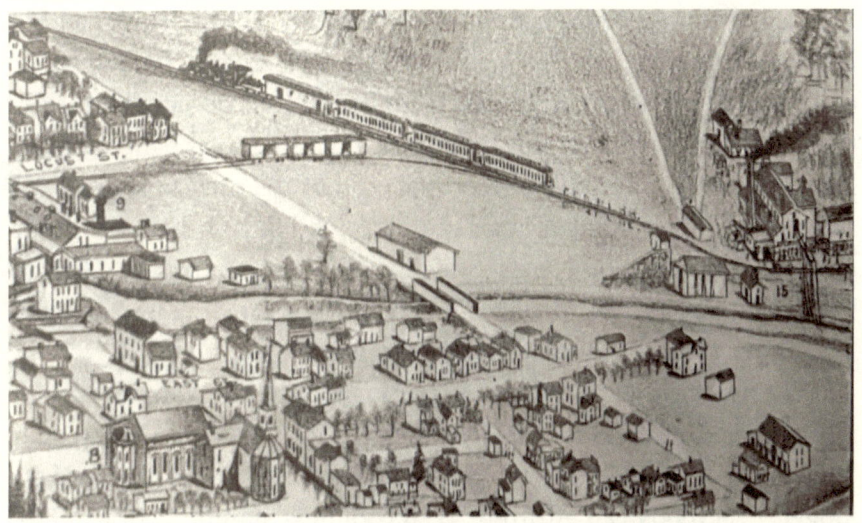

The 1886 lithograph of Miamisburg shows the location of Jacob Schwartztrauber's ice pond, between the canal and the railroad.

CHAPTER FOURTEEN

Miamisburg's "Ice War"

January 1874 was shaping up to be a mild winter. Relatively balmy temperatures made life easier for most people, but not for William Nusz. Brewing lager beer required near-freezing temperatures for fermentation and storage, and Nusz brewed lager beer. Even a mild Ohio winter was usually cold enough for brewing, but winter was also when Nusz harvested the mass of ice he would need to ferment and store his product when summer came. He could brew beer by the barrel, but only nature could make ice by the ton.

The prospects in mid-January did not look good. "The season thus far has been unfavorable to packing ice. The canals are frozen over, but there is no ice of consequence on the Miami," the January sixteenth *Miamisburg Bulletin* reported. "We were informed, yesterday, that Mr. Wm. Nusz would commence cutting ice on Bear Creek, in the afternoon."[241]

Ice harvesting could not have been an easy task for Nusz and his employees. It must have been an all-hands operation to float, drag or cart cakes of ice more than a mile from Bear Creek, across the river at the north end of town. It was hard work and sometimes dangerous. In December 1876, the *Bulletin* reported, one of the men unloading ice suffered an injury from another's mishap: "While unloading ice from a wagon in front of Nusz's brewery, Tuesday afternoon, George Dreher slipped and fell, the ice hook in his hand catching Lewis Highland above the right eye and inflicting a painful wound."[242]

The next few winters after 1874 brought colder temperatures. The ice on Bear Creek was four inches thick in early January 1875, the *Bulletin* reported. It added, "If the present cold snap holds out a few days longer, everybody can afford to keep cool next summer." In late December 1876 the paper found "Much skating during the week on the river and canal. ... Our ice merchants have secured a full supply of fine ice." But in February 1880, Nusz was only gleaning "a small supply" of two-inch ice off a reservoir at the north end of town. The cold, hard fact was this: he needed a better way to get ice.[243]

Harvesting and storing ice was nothing new. Farmers traditionally harvested ice from streams or ponds with simple hand tools. Even in the early 1800s, some American homes had "refrigerators"—which meant an insulated, zinc-lined cabinet for food storage with an iron ice chest in the top. At least from mid-century, Miamisburg possessed a number of ice houses, either for private use or commercial sales. When Jacob Zimmer sold the Miami House in 1857, the deal included a nearby ice house. In the mid-1870s, the H. Hoefer Co. of Dayton began advertising its ice-box refrigerators in the *Bulletin* "for Families, restaurants, saloons and meat storage."[244]

The ice trade was a nineteenth century innovation. It started in 1805, when Boston merchant Frederic Tudor exported the first shipload of ice to the West Indies in an effort to ease suffering there during a yellow fever outbreak. By 1880 the business of harvesting, shipping and storing ice was big enough for the U.S. Census Office to give it a special section in its report on American manufacturing.

Driving the ice industry's growth was the industrialization of food production, shipment and storage, from meats and fresh vegetables to dairy and other products—beer above all. "The brewers comprise the largest single class of consumers of ice in the United States," the report said. "They have found that the use of ice for cooling the wort and regulating the temperatures of the fermenting and storage rooms enable them to run their establishments the year round." Running a brewery through the summer months significantly boosted its annual capacity. "In fact," the report continued, "it is in large part due to the use of ice that the manufacture of beer has developed so rapidly in the United States during the last twenty years." In turn, the growth of breweries increased demand for ice. A large brewery consumed from fifteen thousand to forty thousand tons of ice in a year, while a small one needed from one thousand to ten thousand tons.[245]

The ice industry's evolution brought the construction of commercial operations with heavy equipment and barn-like ice houses to lakes, rivers and artificial ponds. In a typical ice harvesting operation, a crew cleared the surface of the ice, crosshatched it with grooves, then scored it ever more deeply with repeated runs of horse-drawn ice cutters. Finally, crews would saw the cakes loose and float them to the waiting ice houses on shore. Iron bars attached to chains grabbed the cakes and dragged them up inclined ramps called ice elevators, sometimes powered by steam engines.[246]

By 1880 Cincinnati was Ohio's "most important center of the ice trade, on account of the large number of its brewing and packing establishments," the study found. Cincinnati was consuming 200 to 225 thousand tons of ice annually by then. Because of waste, mainly from melting, ice producers had to harvest about 350 thousand tons to satisfy the demand. Three companies dominated Cincinnati's ice trade, but some sixty ice houses played lesser roles, and many more small businesses and individual farmers also supplied ice.

The Miami and Erie Canal was an important supply line in western Ohio's ice trade. In cold winters, brewers like Nusz used the canal itself as a source of ice. And by 1880, "a large number of ice ponds scattered

The Cullen Ice Works, south of Hamilton, as depicted in the 1875 Butler County atlas, illustrates the operation of a commercial ice pond.

along this canal" freely drew water from it, according to a state auditor's report. The state allowed it, reasoning it would see more revenue from toll payments as the ice merchants used the canal to ship their product. After mild winters, brewers and other consumers could turn to brokers who would have ice shipped down the canal from northern counties or beyond. For example, the Census Office study found that after 1880's meager harvest, "the Cincinnati men even bought [ice] largely from Lachine and Montreal, Canada."[247]

In December 1879, Jacob Schwartztrauber prepared to enter the ice trade. He had his own uses for ice as he now ran his father's saloon on the west side of Main Street, and a brief report in the May thirtieth *Bulletin* said he was building a "beer hall" somewhere outside of town. But he was gearing up to become a big ice merchant, at least for the Miamisburg area. He bought a large parcel of land just north of Nusz's brewery and dug a half-moon shaped pond whose flat side bordered the canal. The pond stretched almost up to Mound Avenue—nearly the length of three football fields. By November, millwright Simon Schwytzer was building a barn-size ice house at the south end of the pond with the capacity to store about fifteen hundred tons. The pond was meant for Schwartztrauber's business, but when it froze over, local residents found the vast sheet of ice also made a dandy skating rink.[248]

Schwartztrauber enlarged and improved his operation in 1885, prompting the *Bulletin* to give it a closer look. It described how a crew under Schwytzer's direction erected a massive framework on the east side of the ice house with five inclined elevators, each one leading to a different level of the building. As workers sliced the ice into cakes, they would float them to one of the elevators, where a steam-powered machine called a "Go Devil" pulled each cake up to the ice house. A supervisor oversaw the operation from a high perch. The new setup would allow Schwartztrauber to harvest the pond's ice "in mighty short order," and the paper declared Schwytzer "the best mechanic in all the Miami Valley." An 1887 article said Schwartztrauber's operation had grown to three ice houses that together covered forty by ninety feet—close to the size of a basketball court—and stood twenty-six feet tall. Another house under construction would increase its capacity by nearly a third.[249]

A commercial ice house next door to a brewery must have seemed like a match made in heaven. Schwartztrauber's operation gave Nusz—and later Kuehn—a ready supply of ice without all the back-breaking work. In turn, the brewery gave Schwartztrauber a large customer right next door. Nusz's brewery had two ice houses and its own elevator by March 1880, when his advertisement offering the brewery for sale described them. In December 1882, the paper noted Nusz's successor was remodeling the elevator.[250]

While Schwartztrauber was a merchant, his work in some ways was more like farming. He tended his large pond like a farm field, sowing it with water and waiting patiently for the ice to form. When cold winter days finally froze the pond's surface into a thick, white sheet, he hired crews to harvest it and fill his ice houses—the grain silos of his business.

Schwartztrauber maintained and improved his pond and ice houses throughout the 1880s. The first month of the next decade found

RANKIN'S
IMPROVED PATENT
Refrigerator and Condenser!
MANUFACTURED BY
H. HŒFER & CO.,
109 Commercial S reet.
DAYTON, OHIO.

For Families, Hotels. Meat Stores. Restaurants, Saloons. Groceries and Provision Stores. The best in use; takes less ice than any other; prices low as any, perfect satisfaction guaranteed; should be in every family   Don't purchase before examining the Rankin   "circulars free
    The Ice chest is above the preserving chamber, and is made of galvanized iron; cold always descends, hence the chamber is kept as cold at the bottom as on top. The top of the chamber has an incline of 45°, by which all moisture condensed upon it is carried off and the atmosphere is kept perfectly dry—the only kind of atmosphere in which meat, butter, milk, vegetables, etc., can be preserved from decomposition   37x9m3

An icebox-type refrigerator advertised in a June 1876 *Miamisburg Bulletin*.

Schwytzer upgrading the operation yet again. This time he added a new intake filter to the well that fed the pond, an upgrade that "guarantees pure ice," as a *Bulletin* headline put it. Schwartztrauber "has invested a large amount of capital in the ice trade," it went on, "and considering the limited territory to be supplied, deserves the good will of our citizens for his enterprise."[251]

It was hard work—hazardous, too. While supervising the annual ice harvest in January 1892, Schwartztrauber slipped from his perch high up on an elevator. The sixty-year-old landed on frozen ground—injured, but apparently with no broken bones. He gradually recovered over the next few weeks.[252]

Assuming Schwartztrauber supplied ice to the brewery, as seems likely, the fire of 1899 would have hurt his business. So in 1892, he surely would have welcomed the news that the brewery was to be rebuilt—until he read that its intended business included brewing beer, selling malt and "manufacturing and selling ice."[253]

After decades of quiet development, new technology had begun to disrupt the nation's ice trade. In 1834, the Census study found, Jacob Perkins, an American working in London, patented an ice-making process that froze water by compressing and then evaporating a volatile fluid. By 1880 artificial refrigeration had become a "regular industry." Brewers were early adopters, and they drove the transformation. In *One Hundred Years of Brewing*, John Ewald Siebel wrote that Christian Moerlein, the big Cincinnati brewer, installed a refrigeration plant in 1875. By the time Schwartztrauber built his ice pond in 1880, refrigeration technology had already taken root. The Census study found refrigeration machines "have been introduced to breweries in large numbers

Miamisburg Brewing advertised ice at least by January 1899, when this ad appeared in the *Miamisburg News*.

within the last five years. There are those who now predict their universal adoption by brewers within the next ten years, at least by all the large firms."[254]

A reliable refrigeration machine meant a brewery could dispense with the back-breaking work of stuffing cakes of ice into cellars or ice houses. It also solved the problem of unsanitary conditions in cellars packed with melting ice from ponds, streams and canals. "It does away with slop, rotting of timbers, foul air, dampness and mold," boasted an 1890 promotional book by the Frick Company of Waynesboro,

Pennsylvania. Frick produced the *Eclipse* line of refrigeration machines. Such a machine could keep a beer cellar cool and relatively dry, either indirectly by circulating ice-cold brine through the cellar, or directly by piping the ammonia refrigerant itself. But Deuscher, like other brewers, saw another advantage: a refrigeration plant with extra capacity could manufacture ice for commercial sale. Some systems made ice from distilled water, which they condensed from the exhaust steam of the machinery's cooling system. It was cleaner and more sanitary than pond ice. For Deuscher, it meant a whole new product line. For Schwartztrauber, it meant the business next door was not coming to him, but at him instead.[255]

In 1894 Miamisburg Brewing installed what the *Bulletin* described as a "cold storage and artificial ice plant" that drew its water from wells. Hoover & Gamble built the plant, but the refrigeration machinery was likely made elsewhere: the producer of twine-making machines never branched into the refrigeration market. The new plant was in operation by August. A plan view of the brewery in the 1896 Sanborn map showed the refrigeration plant had replaced the ice house on the east side of the brew house.[256]

The brewing company may not have started selling ice right away. No mention of it appeared in the *Bulletin* through 1895, its last year of publication, and most bound copies of the *Miamisburg News* from those years were too fragile to examine. Schwartztrauber, meanwhile, doubled down on his ice business. Just three months after the brewery's refrigeration plant went on line in 1894, the *Bulletin* reported, "Mr. Jacob Schwartztrauber is extending his artificial lake, and enlarging his already extensive ice house with a 28x40 foot addition, thus increasing the capacity to 3,000 tons."[257]

Miamisburg Brewing ordered another ice machine in March 1898 to double its output. It was a Frick machine, one of its smaller *Eclipse* models, but it was able to turn out twenty tons of ice in a day—enough to fill Schwartztrauber's ice house twice in less than a year. To him, the new machine must have seemed like a cannon aimed straight at his business. One account has it that a cold war of sorts broke out in the

A Frick Co. *Eclipse* refrigerating machine, from the cover of its 1890 catalog.

local ice trade. "Miamisburg has an ice war, which is raging between the Miamisburg Brewing Company and the Schwartztrauber Ice Company," the *Dayton Daily News* reported in January 1899. "The competition got so sharp that both concerns are supplying the trade free of cost. It is needless to say that the people hope it will continue." Another *Daily News* report in April claimed Miamisburg Brewing would deliver ice "free of charge" to brewery customers that summer. Whether either company actually resorted to giving away ice is unclear. The brewing company ran a year-long newspaper campaign advertising ice "as low as any other in the market." No competing ads by Schwartztrauber turned up, but he may have placed ads in issues of the *Miamisburg News* that were too fragile to examine.[258]

How much the new competition cut into Schwartztrauber's ice business is unknown, but the market potential must have looked promising to the brewery. In February 1900, it ordered an additional five-ton unit from the Triumph Ice Machine Company of Cincinnati.[259]

To Schwartztrauber, just beginning his seventieth year, the prospects for his company must have looked bleak. To Miamisburg Brewing, the future must have gleamed like the frost on a newly frozen lake.

But the destiny of Miamisburg's brewery lay in fire, not ice.

Miamisburg Mound, as seen from Mound Avenue in 2022.

CHAPTER FIFTEEN

End of an Era

When Miamisburg Brewing finally began advertising in March 1894, it revealed a new brand: its "Celebrated Indian Mound Beer." It was, the company promised, a "pure, wholesome beverage" brewed "strictly from hops and malt."[260]

"Mound" was the key word. At the time, anyone outside of Ohio who had heard of Miamisburg most likely knew it as home to either of two things: the widely advertised Acme Folding Boat Company at the north end of town, or the mysterious, conical earthwork to the south.

The folding boat company was the brainchild of David H. Allen and William H. Gamble, grandsons of David H. Hoover. They started making foldable canvas boats in 1890, if not earlier. Ads and articles describing them appeared at least by May 1890 in *Forest and Stream*, a

Acme Folding Boat's products on display in the Miamisburg Historical Society's History Center.

weekly outdoor magazine. Allen and Gamble even displayed them at the World's Columbian Exposition in Chicago in 1893, making Miamisburg widely known through their products. Their small, oddly shaped factory—a narrow, two-story brick building with five irregular sides—still stands along the east side of the railroad tracks just below East Pearl Street.[261]

The Miamisburg Mound rises sixty-five feet from the top of the big hill. It occupies one of the highest points in Montgomery County. A symmetrical cone, monumental in scale, it was among thousands of mounds and more complex earthen structures European Americans found as they moved into the Northwest Territory in the late 1700s. Today, eight large Ohio earthworks enjoy the status of world heritage sites. Archaeologists believe people of what they call the Hopewell Culture built them between sixteen hundred and two thousand years ago. But even those early people may have regarded the Miamisburg Mound as something ancient and mysterious. Archaeologists estimate its age between two thousand and twenty-eight hundred years. It is the work of an earlier culture they call the Adena, ancestors of the Hopewell.[262]

The Mound's enigmatic presence and its scenic views brought

Miamisburg more notice than a small, western village would have expected in the early nineteenth century. An 1837 directory for Ohio identified it as a noteworthy feature. And in 1843, the Mound put Miamisburg on the front page of the *New York Herald*. Writing mainly about Dayton and state politics, the correspondent digressed with a long paragraph about the Mound. It included a first-person description of the dramatic view from its summit:

> From the top of this mound you can see the whole valley for thirty or forty miles round, and the view is beautiful and grand beyond description. The landscape lies out before you like a chess-board, with its bright and its dark spots alternatively, and you may trace, as on a map, the beautiful meanderings of the Miami River, for miles and miles, up and down. The town of Miamisburg, of which it commands a full view, is right below, and is situated in the environs of one of those fortifications mentioned before. ... A view of these stupendous works of art, left as memorials of a bygone age, is calculated to fill the mind with feelings of awe. We are insensibly led back in imagination to the time when this great valley was peopled by a totally different race of people than those who now inhabit it—a people whose history has been entirely lost, leaving nothing but these monuments to tell what they were.

In recent years, the correspondent noted, at least one attempt had been made to reveal the Mound's secrets by digging a hole in the top, "from which human bones, it is said, were extracted."[263]

This may have been a reference to the same incident mentioned in a 1920 story in the *Miamisburg News*. It recounted earlier reports of excavations, including one in 1839 when a man by the name of Lewis tried digging a well in the mound and unearthed bones. A more ambitious project in 1869 dug a shaft from the top to its base. Eight feet down, the shaft revealed the burial of a "bark-covered skeleton." Twenty-eight feet lower lay an empty vault made of logs. Alternating layers of ash and stones indicated the Mound had been built up over a period of years. Besides disturbing a grave, the project lopped three feet off the Mound's previous height. Today the Miamisburg Mound is a state memorial owned by the Ohio History Connection. Visitors may climb 116 stone steps, added in the 1930s, to enjoy the view and ponder what the Mound meant to its builders, their successors and later people who may have rediscovered it time after time through the ages.[264]

THE CELEBRATED
Indian Mound Beer,
Manufactured by the
MIAMISBURG BREWING CO.,
Miamisburg, Ohio.
STRICTLY FROM HOPS AND MALT.
IS A PURE, WHOLESOME BEVERAGE.
For Sale By All Dealers. Ask For It. Bottled Beer, For Family Use, Can Be Obtained From All Our Customers.

LOOK OUT !
For Miamisburg Indian Mound Bock Beer. Will be on tap today. For sale by all of our customers. Ask for it. A pure and wholesome beverage. Manufactured strictly from Malt and Hops.
MIAMISBURG BREWING CO.

Ads for "Indian Mound" beer appeared in 1894 issues of the *Miamisburg Bulletin*.

The Indian Mound Beer brand took advantage of Miamisburg Brewing's location at the foot of the hill. One month after its original announcement, it extended the brand to its new bock beer—a stronger, maltier brew than traditional lager. "Look out! For Miamisburg Indian Mound Bock Beer. Will be on tap today. For sale by all of our customers," announced its April thirteenth, 1894 newspaper ad. Whether Miamisburg Brewing applied the brand to the brewery itself is not clear, but at least two *Bulletin* reports in July referred to it as "the Indian Mound Brewery."[265]

Prospects for Indian Mound Beer must have looked good to Henry Deuscher, Miamisburg Brewing's president. In July of 1894, he

Miamisburg Brewing's fire captured the top headline on page one of the May 10, 1900 *Miamisburg News*.

filed new incorporation papers for the closely related Star Bottling Company, of which he was president. Its original filing gave its purpose as making and mixing "mineral waters, ginger ales, fruit extracts, etc." The new one redefined its bottling business as "beer, wine and ale" and doubled its capitalization to twenty thousand dollars. In October, Deuscher bought a controlling interest in the bottling company and started work on two new buildings for it north of the brewery.[266]

The brewery seemed to be doing so well that a significant fire in 1898 did not knock it out of business, as the 1889 blaze had done. The June twentieth issue of the *Hamilton Daily Republican* reported an early-morning blaze on Saturday, June eighteenth, "burned nearly the entire upper part of the building." It set the loss at four thousand dollars, but the June twenty-third *Miamisburg News* estimated damage between five thousand and ten thousand dollars. Neither the damage nor the cost stopped Miamisburg Brewing from installing a new ice machine and rolling out its commercial ice business the following year. But the fire was just a preview of what was to come.[267]

The May tenth, 1900, issue of the *Miamisburg News* described what happened. Shortly before noon on Tuesday the eighth, a Big Four train rumbled past the brewery, its locomotive belching smoke and ash from its smokestack. Minutes later, a brewery worker spotted flames in the stable south of the brewery. He shouted an alarm, but strong winds fanned the blaze. "In ten minutes the stable was a solid mass of fire," the *News* reported, "and the terrific wind quickly communicated the fire to the frame addition of the brewery building." Armed with only a hose and buckets, brewery workers fought the wind-driven flames. It was perilous work. The paper reported Bernard Wieland, a brewery worker possibly related to Lorenz Wieland, was throwing water on the burning stable when "the wind blew a sheet of flame right into his face." The fiery gust left him "severely burned about the head and hands." (Wieland recovered and moved to Dayton, where the next year found him working in Adam Schantz's big Riverside Brewery.) Another brewery worker who fought the fire was William Herrmann, a son of William Nusz's brother-in-law Philip.[268]

Miamisburg's fire department turned out to help. Firefighters put out flames on a nearby tobacco shed. The blaze threatened Jacob Schwartztrauber's ice house, "but a good wetting down prevented its catching." The firefighters' efforts also spared the brewery's bottling plant and several nearby homes. No people died, but five horses in the stable perished, and the brewery itself was reduced to rubble. Deuscher, the *News* reported, estimated the damage at forty thousand dollars—five to ten times the damage of the earlier fire, and nearly three times the company's insurance on the plant.

The *Dayton Daily News* published a similar account just hours after the fire. Like the Miamisburg paper, it reported local suspicions that embers from the Big Four locomotive sparked the conflagration. The Dayton paper downplayed the idea as "mere supposition, but it is generally accepted in the 'Burg."

Whatever the cause, it looked like the end of the line for Miamisburg's only brewery. As if to extinguish all hope, a severe thunderstorm swept through Miamisburg the next month and collapsed what little of the brewery still stood. It was never rebuilt.[269]

In truth, a new brewery would have faced increasing headwinds as the twentieth century unfolded. National brands were moving into local markets, and the temperance movement evolved into the more powerful Prohibition campaign. Activists formed the National Anti-Saloon League in Oberlin, Ohio, in 1893. Two years later, it joined with a similar group in Washington, D.C, to form a national organization, and in 1913 it made nationwide Prohibition its goal. A massive, years-long campaign led to the Eighteenth Amendment, which made Prohibition law in 1920. Many local breweries went under, although some survived by selling soda, dairy or other products until another amendment ended Prohibition in 1933. In Dayton, for example, only a few local breweries resumed making beer, and the last disappeared in the 1960s. By and large, national brands seized the post-Prohibition beer market.[270]

Jacob Schwartztrauber's ice business outlived the brewery, but not by much. In 1902 local businessmen incorporated the Miamisburg Ice and Cold Storage Company, and by 1905 it had erected a new artificial ice plant at the north end of town, just south of Kercher Street on the west side of the railroad. The ice pond was eventually filled in, and the site today is a part of Miamisburg's Community Park.[271]

The loss of its hometown brewery and the ice pond were just two of many changes Miamisburg saw as it rolled through the nineteen hundreds. In 1909, the Big Four realigned and graded its railroad between Miamisburg and Middletown. The biggest part of the project was the path it carved across the flank of the big hill. The excavation left a steep wall that rises above the old brewery site. The tracks remain active, operated by Norfolk Southern.[272]

David H. Hoover's legacy, the Hoover & Gamble Company, passed its zenith around the turn of the century. William Gamble died in 1908, and Abel Hoover followed in 1916. The company itself went out of business about 1918, when Dayton businesses acquired its factory buildings south of Linden and its foundry on South Second.[273]

Two World Wars came and went, and the world entered the nuclear age. A nuclear weapons plant—the Department of Energy's Mound facility—grew on the hill high above the old brewery site, just across the road from the Adena mound. The secretive plant added its own arts and mysteries to its nearby namesake until the end of the Cold War, when a consolidation of America's nuclear weapons sites took away its missions. The site was cleaned up and converted into a quiet business park.

The Miami and Erie Canal was abandoned, the old canal bed was filled in through town and its rich history was largely forgotten. But a row of old buildings still stands on South Second Street, their backs to the path of the canal. Repurposed for modern times, they nevertheless reflect the legacy of Miamisburg's first manufacturing district.

More than a century would pass before Miamisburg saw another hometown brewery. As it happened, one of those old mill buildings was the scene of its rebirth.

In 2013, Star City Brewing resurrected hometown beer in the former Peerless Mill Inn. The building was originally a sawmill.

CHAPTER SIXTEEN

A New Century

On a recent visit to the Star City Brewing Company, its taproom seemed to reach out from the past. Underfoot lay a worn stone floor, and overhead stretched massive wooden beams. TV screens over each end of the long bar failed to overpower its old-time ambiance. Justin Kohnen, its owner at the time, said the room offered the cozy atmosphere of "an old English pub," while numerous adjoining rooms of the former restaurant hosted a variety of programs and events, including a dart league and a comedy show.[274]

Opened in 2013, Star City introduced Miamisburg to the craft beer movement that had begun sweeping the country. The building it occupies at 319 South Second Street once drew crowds as the home of a landmark restaurant, the Peerless Mill Inn. But its story includes earlier chapters that go back to the first days of the canal and possibly a bit earlier. Long before it housed a brewpub or a restaurant, it was a sawmill. Local history publications date it to 1828, and Kohnen counts that year as the building's first—the same year water first flowed in the canal. No exact year has surfaced in official records, but anecdotal evidence supports his view.

Several published accounts note that a sawmill stood at the canal lock in its earliest years. The lock included a channel called a "tumble," made of stone or wood, which routed excess water around the lock. Jacob Ruegger, Miamisburg's first lock keeper, used the tumble to drive a water wheel for a sawmill that he built there, according to a reminiscent story about Ruegger in an 1891 issue of the *Miamisburg Bulletin*. It said the mill had "the first circular saw operated in this city," whose whirling blade cut stove wood for canal boats and "occasionally sawed lath for plasterers." (Old plaster walls commonly used thin strips of wood called lath as a backing.) The story did not say when Ruegger built the sawmill. Esther Light wrote, "machinery for a saw mill was moved to the lot, about 1827," but elsewhere she asserted water did not flow into the canal until September 1828. She did not explain what powered the saw in the meantime.[275]

A proper mill race soon replaced the lock's tumble. The first official record of any kind of mill at the lock only dates to early 1832, when the brothers Chaning and Erwin Madison signed a contract to build a large, four-story flour mill on the race. The contract says nothing about a sawmill, but an old patent record offers an intriguing clue. In April 1831, Chaning Madison received a patent for "the application of the circular saw to the cutting of lath off slabs at sawmills." Since the story about Ruegger noted he cut lath with a circular saw, the patent raises the question of whether the Madisons collaborated with Ruegger on the sawmill before they built the flour mill.[276]

From the beginning, both mills shared a single parcel of land even as the parcel changed hands numerous times over the years. The flour mill was always the main operation until about 1929, by which time it was doing business as the Great Peerless Mills, turning out Peerless Flour. Light wrote that owner Elwood Waters converted the sawmill

U. ENGLEMAN'S FLOUR MILLS.

The sawmill (left) and Engleman's Flour Mill, as depicted in the 1886 lithograph of Miamisburg.

building into the Peerless Pantry restaurant in 1929 and tore down the old flour mill nine years later.[277]

In the 1960s, the restaurant took the name Peerless Mill Inn, and it enjoyed a regional reputation for fine dining. A fire in 2003 nearly gutted it. The owner rebuilt it, but then closed it again in 2008. The structure sat idle until 2012, when a father-son venture tried to resurrect the restaurant. After a year of work, it was nearly ready to open, but they put it up for sale instead. At the same time, Kohnen, his brother Brian and Brian Yavorsky were searching for a place to turn their home-brewing hobby into a business. They bought the site in June 2013 as Star City Brewing, LLC. Besides minor remodeling, Kohnen said, the building only needed some work on the air conditioning system, installation of brewing equipment and a new bar. They began tapping kegs a few months later. Brian Kohnen and Yavorsky left the business after a few years, and Justin Kohnen carried on as sole owner.[278]

In late 2025, Kohnen sold the business. The buyer was Chris N.

Lucky Star Brewery Cantina (above) occupies a part of what once was the Miamisburg Binder Twine and Cordage Co. (top)

Small, who grew up in neighboring Jefferson Township and recalled visiting the Peerless Mill Inn as a child. "I've always loved this place. When I saw it was for sale, I had to try to purchase it, to bring it back to its glory," Small said. At this writing, he was planning to renovate the building, add food to the menu and restore the well remembered brand as the Peerless Mill Inn and Brewery, with Brandon Warmoth of Carlisle as general manager.[279]

The Entropy Brewing Company occupied the Silberman building on South Main Street.

A block up the street at 219 South Second, the Lucky Star Brewery and Cantina opened the next year. It occupies another old mill built of stone and brick. It played a role in the great twine saga, first as one of several buildings comprising the Miamisburg Binder Twine & Cordage Company, and then as a part of Victoria Cordage. In the twentieth century, manufacturing in central Miamisburg faded, and the old cordage shops on South Second, were repurposed for tobacco processing and warehousing. Glenn and Ana Perrine returned one to manufacturing—brewing, that is—as the Lucky Star Brewery and Cantina, with food featuring tacos, burritos, burgers and other fare. The Perrines sold the business to Jason and Lara Freshwater in April 2025. They continue to operate it as the slightly renamed Lucky Star Brewery Cantina.

Another brewpub opened in 2024 in the heart of downtown at 26 South Main Street. Entropy Brewing occupies parts of the Silberman

Building, a three-story brick commercial structure built in 1900. It is remembered locally as the longtime home of Suttman's clothing store. Real estate developer Eric Joo bought the building after Suttman's closed and converted the upper two floors into apartments. Jordan and Brianna Joo, Eric's son and daughter-in-law, turned the ground floor and basement into a brewpub and restaurant.[280]

Choosing the name "Entropy," a scientific term for the state of disorder in a closed system, may have been prescient: on December 12, 2025, the brewery announced that it was closing. It ceased business a few days before end of the year.[281]

Collectively, the return of hometown brewing played a role in central Miamisburg's transformation from an aging retail district in decay to a thriving entertainment hub. The new wave of breweries ended a hiatus that spanned more than a century. By repurposing old buildings, they also helped to preserve the town's nineteenth century architecture. It seems especially fitting because their style of brewing—small, local, by brewers who know their customers—reflects how beer was brewed in the town's early years.

Miamisburg has grown up and out, but if the old brewers came back today, they would recognize much of the area where they practiced their craft. The new breweries are no more than a short stroll from any of the old sites. They allow one to sip a pint in the midst of two centuries of history, contemplate the lives and times of Emde, Hoover, Nusz, Kuehn and the others, and perhaps raise a glass to their memories.

Notes

Citations shortened here are fully cited in the bibliography.

[1] Beers, *History of Montgomery County*, Book III, 135, 144.
[2] "Council agrees to fund Tavern Museum work," *Miamisburg News*, March 11, 1981, 9.
[3] Light and Ransdell, *Miamisburg*, 160.
[4] Mary Sikora, "A Tavern in the town," *Dayton Daily News*, April 12, 1982, n. p.
[5] Williams, *American and English Encyclopedia of Law*, 4; Drury, *History*, Volume I, 111.
[6] *Williams' Dayton Directory for 1896-1897*, 1307.
[7] Elizabeth Emdee, grave marker, Union Chapel Cemetery, Saint Paul, Decatur County, Indiana, digital image, s. v. "Elizabeth Emdee," FindaGrave.com; marriage record for Henry Emde, Montgomery County, probate court, marriage record book A2, 80.

8 "Pioneer Reminiscences," *Miamisburg Bulletin*, Sept. 15, 1893, 3; Beers, *History of Montgomery County*, Book III, 140.

9 Montgomery County formed Miami Township from western Washington Township in 1829: Beers, *History of Montgomery County*, Book II, 347.

10 Beers, *History of Montgomery County*, Book III, 135-136, 140, 145; "Our History," St. John's Lutheran Church, stjohnsmiamisburg.org; Faust, *German Element*, 428-429.

11 Beers, *History of Montgomery County*, Book III, 28-29.

12 Jacob Kercher and Emanuel Gebhart, grave markers, Hillgrove Union Cemetery, Miamisburg; Brown, *Memoir of Dr. John Treon*, 13, 16.

13 "Beer Ingredients," American Homebrewers Association, homebrewersassociation.org; Salem, *Beer, Its History*, 60; Bishop, et. al., *American Manufactures*, 244-245.

14 National Park Service, "Brewing in the Seventeenth Century," *Historic Jamestowne*, nps.gov.; Dexter, *Mourt's Relation*, 64; Blakely, "Beer on Board in the Age of Sail," blog, Smithsonian Libraries and Archives, blog.library.si.edu.

15 "Our Forefather's Song," *Collections of the Massachusetts Historical Society*, Volume VII, 30.

16 Commissioners of Patents, *Abridgements Relating to Brewing*, 238-239.

17 "Washington's Love of Beer," *George Washington's Mount Vernon*, mountvernon.org.

18 Winthrop, "On the Culture, and Use of Maize," *Philosophical Transactions*, 469.

19 Drake, *Discourses*, 34-35; Herndon, *Outline*, 21-22.

20 Bishop, et. al., *American Manufactures*, 245; Wiebe, "Introduction of Barley into the New World," *Barley*, 4; Hop Growers of America, "We're not New to This," *USA Hops*, usahops.org.

21 Ehret, *Twenty-five Years of Brewing*, 7, 18, 26.

22 Thomas, "An Historical and Geographical Account of Pensilvania and of West-New-Jersey," in Myers, *Narratives of Early Pennsylvania*, Volume 12, 331; Bishop, et. al., *American Manufactures*, 261.

23 Bishop, et. al., *American Manufactures*, 258; Nelson, *Documents*, Volume XX, 109-110.

24 Coxe, *Arts and Manufactures for 1810*, tabular statements by states, 22; by counties, 42, 59.

[25] Beers, *History of Warren County*, 510; Eve is identified as Henry's wife in Montgomery County, deed book V, 136. The 1850 census for Miamisburg lists her age, her birth state and Henry Junior as her eldest child.

[26] Bond, *Correspondence of John Cleves Symmes*, 2-3, 5-6.

[27] Bond, *Symmes*, 9, 14, 21.

[28] W. H. Shinn, "Settlement of the Miami Valley," in Hover, et. al., *Memoirs*, Volume I, 77-78.

[29] Warren County, deed book 4, 244; Everts, "Franklin and Springboro," map, *Combination Atlas Map of Warren County*, 34; Beers, *History of Warren County*, 520.

[30] Huntington, *History of Banking*, 42.

[31] Browning, *Panic of 1819*, 4.

[32] Warren County Deed Book 4, 246; Huntington, *History of Banking*, 57-58.

[33] Huntington, *History of Banking*, 59, 60, 102-104.

[34] Beers, *History of Montgomery County*, Book II, 569, 578; Chase, "An Act to Encourage the Killing of Wolves and Panthers," *Statutes of Ohio*, Volume I, 335-336; Drury, *History*, Volume I, 132-133; Browning, *Panic of 1819*, 14, 72.

[35] Beers, *History of Warren County*, 520-521, 813; Warren County, deed book 9, 60 and book 11, 438; Warren County Common Pleas Court, case book 7B, 160.

[36] Warren County Common Pleas Court, case book 7B, 463.

[37] Warren County Common Pleas Court, case book 3, 373; "Sheriff's Sales," *Western Star* (Lebanon, Ohio,) Oct. 20, 1821, 3, and Feb. 16, 1822, 3; Warren County, deed book 10, 326.

[38] Warren County, deed book 11, 438; Montgomery County, deed book P, 34.

[39] Huntington, *History of Banking*, 107.

[40] Montgomery County, deed book H4, 356; Titus, "Miamisburg," *Titus' Map of Montgomery County*; Proudfoot & Urquhart, *Directory*, 570; "Died," *Miamisburg News*, Nov. 24, 1898, 1.

[41] Montgomery County, tax duplicates for 1832, Miami Township town lots, n. p.; Montgomery County, deed book S, 370, 372; Ohio General Assembly, *Acts of a General Nature*, XXIX, 272, 280.

[42] Jacobs, *Plant Guide for Common Barley*, USDA; W. C. Culkins, "The Story of Hamilton County," in Hover, *Memoirs*, Volume II, 534; Drake, *Picture of Cincinnati*, 147.

43 "Barley Wanted," *Western Star*, Oct. 8, 1817, 4; Morgan, *Cincinnati Beer*, 17-18.

44 "Lebanon Brewery," *Western Star & Lebanon Gazette*, Dec. 28, 1822, 3; Beers, *History of Warren County*, 287.

45 Drake, *Picture of Cincinnati*, 85; B. Day, "Records of a Past Generation," *Bulletin*, July 27, 1883, 1, and Aug. 3, 1883, 1.

46 Huntington and McClelland, *History of the Ohio Canals*, 8, 12, 16, 18, 20-21.

47 Huntington and McClelland, *Canals*, 24, 31-32.

48 Canal Commission, *Miami and Erie Canal through Miamisburg*, map.

49 Kilbourn, *Ohio Gazetteer*, 310-311.

50 Montgomery County, tax duplicates for 1836, Miami Township town lots, n. p.; no headline, *Bulletin*, June 20, 1890, 2.

51 *Heritage Village*, historical marker, Miamisburg Historical Society and the Ohio Historical Society; Beers, *History of Montgomery County*, Book III, 135.

52 Montgomery County, deed book L, 502.

53 National Archives, "Case File of Elias Murray," *War of 1812 Pension and Bounty Land Warrant Application Files*, catalog.archives.gov.

54 Schmidt, et. al., "Elias Murray," *Hoosier Packet*, 6; Buckingham, *Moses Byxbe*, 27-29.

55 Leggett, *History of Marion County*, 338, 489; Perrin, *History of Delaware County*, 213; Kilbourn, *Public Documents Concerning the Ohio Canals*, 166; Ohio General Assembly, *Journal of the Senate*, Volume 29, 191, 193, 208, 209.

56 Schmidt, et. al., "Elias Murray," *Hoosier Packet*, 7; marriage record for Elias Murray, Montgomery County Probate Court, Marriage Record book A & B: *1803-1837*, 168.

57 Montgomery County, tax duplicates for 1827, Washington Township Personal Property, n. p.

58 Canal Commission, *Miami and Erie Canal through Miamisburg*, map.

59 Montgomery County, mortgage book M, 182 and 431; deed book L, 401.

60 Montgomery County, deed book S, 222; Burrell, *Complete List of the Members*, 24, 49, 64; Hunter, *Forced from our Homes*, blog, Aacimotaatiiyankwi.org; Rafert, *Miami Indians of Indiana*, 111-112.

61 Montgomery County, deed books D2, 390, 393 and E2, 197, 201.

62 Grave markers for David H., Fred. A. and Magdalena Hoover, Hillgrove Union Cemetery; Drury, *History*, Volume II, 802-803; Montgomery County, deed book F, 132.; Montgomery County, tax duplicates for 1832, Miami Township Real Estate, n. p.

63 Marriage record for David H. Hoover, Montgomery County, marriage records book A&B, 1803-1837, 15; Drury, *History*, Volume II, 803; Miami Township, "Demographics," miamitownship.com.

64 Montgomery County, deed books D2, 176; E2, 201 and 197; mortgage book A5, 591.

65 Montgomery County, tax duplicate for 1836, Miami Township Town Property, n. p.; Montgomery County, mortgage book C5, 109.

66 Beers, *History of Montgomery County*, Book III, 141; Jenkins, *Ohio Gazetteer*, 296.

67 Montgomery County, mortgage book J6, 170.

68 Beers, *History of Montgomery County*, Book III, 141; "Died," *Bulletin*, March 16, 1877, 2.

69 No headline, *Bulletin*, June 10, 1887, 3. "Loaf sugar": refined sugar in the nineteenth century was commonly sold in solid, cone-shaped blocks called loaves.

70 Montgomery County, deed book E2, 478.

71 Joseph Watson, 1850 U.S. census record, Center Township, Marion County, Indiana, digital image, s. v. "Joseph Watson," FamilySearch.org; "Died," *Bulletin*, Oct. 25, 1889, 3; marriage record for Joseph Watson, Montgomery County, marriage records book A&B, 1803-1837, 11; Montgomery County, tax duplicates for 1836, Miami Township Town Property, n. p.; Beers, *History of Montgomery County*, Book III, 142.

72 Huntington, *History of Banking*, 124, 127; Roberts, *America's First Great Depression*, 32, 34.

73 Montgomery County, mortgage book A5, 478 and 591, on microfilm; Montgomery County, deed book U-583 (recorded as mortgage); Montgomery County, common pleas court records, book G, 487.

74 Montgomery County, deed books D2, 176 and E2,197, 478, 480.

75 Montgomery County Common Pleas Court, book G, 487; Montgomery County, mortgage book B5, 334, on microfilm.

76 Roberts, *America's First Great Depression*, 43, 47, 53.

77 Conover, *Centennial Portrait*, 57, 158; *Cleveland Herald*, in "Mississippi," *Western Star* (Lebanon, Ohio,) May 31, 1839, 3; "Hard times—worse coming," *Clermont Courier*, Batavia, Sept. 21, 1839, 3, Ohio Memory.

78 "Maumee City Cash Store," *Maumee City Express*, Ohio, Jan. 4, 1840, 3; Ohio Memory; "Stoves! Stoves!!" *Hamilton Intelligencer*, Jan. 14, 1842, 3; Ohio Memory; "Notice," two advertisements by Wm Russell, *Western Star*, May 13, 1842, 4.

[79] Joseph Nutt, "Washington Township," in Beers, *History of Montgomery County*, Book III, 15-16, 17; Stanton, *Reports of Cases Argued and Determined in the Supreme Court of Ohio*, Vol. XL, 96-99; Ohio General Assembly, *Acts of a Local Nature*, 1840, 197-198.

[80] Montgomery County, mortgage book B5, 420, on microfilm.

[81] "The Late Col. Gebhart," *Dayton Journal*, Jan. 1, 1868, 3, LOC.

[82] "Died," *Bulletin*, Sept. 28, 1877, 2; "Sawyer, William," *Biographical Directory*, congress.gov.

[83] Knapp, *History of the Maumee Valley*, 310.

[84] "Rumors and Humors at Washington," *New York Daily Tribune*, Feb. 27, 1846, 1, LOC.

[85] "Expulsion of the Tribune Reporter," *New Bedford Mercury*, in *New York Daily Tribune*, March 16, 1846, 1, LOC; "The Saga of 'Sausage' Sawyer," *Whereas*, history.house.gov.

[86] Montgomery County, deed book O2, 387, 388.

[87] John Swartztrauber's obituary in the July 30, 1880 *Miamisburg Bulletin* said he had lived in Miamisburg for "thirty-eight years," while Catharine's on June 15, 1888, said she had arrived on November 25, 1843—later than the date on Swartztrauber's deed. While this leaves the exact date of their arrival in doubt, it seems clear they were very recent arrivals when John bought the brewery.

[88] Montgomery County, common pleas court book U-1, 203.

[89] Montgomery County, deed book O2, 196; Beers, *History of Montgomery County*, Book III, 132, 425; "Jacob Zimmer Called Above," *Dayton Daily News*, April 30, 1901, 9; Montgomery County, deed book O2, 390, 391.

[90] Montgomery County, deed book P2, 9.

[91] *Reilly & Co.'s Ohio State Business Directory for 1853-4*, 102; Charles Shroider, 1850 U.S. census record, Miami Township, Ohio, digital image, s. v. "Charles Shroider," FamilySearch.org.

[92] Aetna, *Aetna Guide to Fire Insurance*, 355; Montgomery County, deed books V2, 259 and Q4, 575.

[93] Beers, *History of Montgomery County*, Book III, 142.

[94] Ellsworth, *A Digest of Patents*, 3, 72; no headline, *Daily Union* (Washington, D.C.,) November 22, 1853, 1, LOC.

[95] Montgomery County, deed books Y, 532 and A2, 299; Montgomery County, tax duplicates for Miami Township, 1839, Personal Property, 928 and 1840, Personal Property, 744.

[96] Montgomery County, deed book S2, 281, 282.

[97] George McElwee, 1850 U.S. census record, Miami Township, Ohio, digital image, s. v. "George McElwee," FamilySearch.org; *Reilly & Co.'s Ohio State Business Directory for 1853-54,* 231.

[98] Ohio Senate, *Journal of the Senate,* 275; Beers, *History of Montgomery County,* Book II, 469, and Book III, 141.

[99] Beers, *History of Montgomery County,* Book III, 141.

[100] Reiter, *Diary,* Volume 1, 1-2, 5, 294 and Volume 2, 136-137; "Cary, Samuel Fenton," *Biographical Directory,* Congress.gov. Reiter mentioned stomach or undefined ailments throughout his diary.

[101] Sheridan, "Town Patents the Lattice Truss Bridge," *Today in CT History,* CTHumanities.org; Beers, *History of Montgomery County,* Book III, 140.

[102] "Destruction of the Miamisburg Bridge," *Dayton Daily Empire,* April 19, 1859, 1, LOC.

[103] "Miamisburg," *Empire,* June 23, 1859, 1, LOC.

[104] "Miamisburg Brewery and Malt House," *Bulletin,* Dec. 27, 1867, n. p.; Hawes, *Gazetteer,* 437; Montgomery County, deed book I3, 537; *Sanborn Fire Insurance Map,* 1911, 5; *Sanborn Fire Insurance Map,* March 1919, 5.

[105] George Herman, Philip Herrmann, William Nusz, 1860 U.S. census record, Miamisburg, Ohio, digital images, s. v. "George Haman," "Philip Harman," "William Nuiest," FamilySearch.org and 1870, s. v. "George Harman," "Philip Herman," "William Nusz," FamilySearch.org.

[106] "Pioneer Woman Gone Above," *Dayton Daily News,* Aug. 22, 1901, 5; Montgomery County, deed book P2, 356.

[107] "Nusz," *Bulletin,* July 29, 1881, 3; "Died," *Bulletin,* Dec. 24, 1880, 2; no headline, *Bulletin,* Dec. 19, 1879, 2.

[108] George Herman, 1860 U.S. census record, Miamisburg, Ohio, digital image, s. v. "George Haman," FamilySearch.org; "Miamisburg Brewery and Malt House!" advertisement, *Bulletin,* Dec. 27, 1867, microfilm, Dayton Metro Library.

[109] "A Notable Event," *Bulletin,* Feb. 14, 1879, 2; Montgomery County, deed books A3, 407 and H3, 344.

[110] Montgomery County, deed books I3, 537 and F4, 29; Montgomery County, 1860 tax duplicates for Miami Township, Miamisburg Real Property, n. p.

[111] Drury, *History,* Volume I, 406-407, 834; Reiter, *Diary,* Volume 1, 154; Beers, *History of Montgomery County,* Book III, 151. Beers and others said the *Miamisburg Union* started in 1856, but Reiter noted it in his diary on November 29, 1855.

[112] Reid, *Ohio in the War*, Volume II, 4; "Civil War (1861 to 1865)," Miamisburg Historical Society, *Miamisburg Veterans Honor Roll*, historicalmiamisburg.org.

[113] Middleton, *Black Laws*, 3, 49-50, 51, 52.

[114] Sawyer, *Speech of Hon. William Sawyer*, 3; U.S. Congress, *An Act of April 16, 1862.*.

[115] Smith, *Report of the Debates and Proceedings*, 56.

[116] Kilbourn, *Ohio Gazetteer*, 311; Debow, *Seventh Census: 1850*, 840; U.S. Census Office, *Population of the United States in 1860: Ohio*, 388..

[117] Vallandigham, *Speeches*, 118.

[118] "Miamisburg Meeting," *Empire*, July 14, 1860, 2, LOC; Conover, *Centennial Portrait*, 1015.

[119] " 'Never Sleeps' Attention," *Empire*, Sept. 5, 1860, 2, LOC; "Movements of the Burg-o'-Master," *Empire*, July 31, 1860, 1, LOC.

[120] "Ground swell in Miami!" *Empire*, Sept. 12, 1860, 2, LOC.

[121] Russel, "Report of the Secretary of State," *Messages and Reports*, 294; "Congressional Vote of Ohio—Official," *Holmes County Republican*, November 8, 1860, 2, LOC.

[122] Conover, *Centennial Portrait*, 171; "Representative Clement Vallandigham of Ohio," *History, Art & Archives*, history.house.gov; Gottlieb, *Lincoln's Northern Nemesis*, 191; "Official Vote of Montgomery County," *Empire*, Oct. 17, 1863, 2, LOC.

[123] Ohio Roster Commission, *Official Roster*, Vol. IV, 85, 104, 118 and Vol. VIII, 563; Conover, *Centennial Portrait*, 980.

[124] Reid, *Ohio in the War*, Volume I, 84-88.

[125] Reid, *Ohio in the War*, Volume I, 73 and Volume II, 518; "The Gallant 93rd," *Bulletin*, June 12, 1891, 2.

[126] Reid, *Ohio in the War*, Volume I, 88-90.

[127] Reid, *Ohio in the War*, Volume I, 92-94.

[128] *Squirrel Hunters from Dayton & Montgomery County, Ohio*; Philip Swartztrauber, 1860 U.S. census record, Miamisburg, Ohio, digital image, s. v. "Philip Schwartztrauber," FamilySearch.org. Philip Swartztrauber's relationship to John is inferred from the 1860 census.

[129] Ohio Roster Commission, *Official Roster*, Vol. VII, 196-199; Sultana Association of Descendants and Friends, *The Disaster*, thesultanaassociation.com.

[130] Reid, *Ohio in the War*, Volume I, 208- 210.

[131] Reid, *Ohio in the War*, Volume II, 4.

132 Ohio Roster Commission, *Official Roster*, Vol. VIII, 563; *Consolidated Enrollment Lists*, draft records for Philip Hermann and William Nusz, Volume 1, image 531 and Volume 3, 397; Meier, "Civil War Draft Records," *Prologue*.

133 Hogeland, *Whiskey Rebellion*, 64, 239, 272; U.S. Congress, "Revenue Act of 1862," *Fraser*, fraser.stlouisfed.org.

134 Montgomery County, deed books F3, 570; L3, 282-284; P3, 82. Marisha Doan, ed., *Letters of Charles R. Allen and Elizabeth Allen During the Civil War*.

135 Reid, *Ohio in the War*, Volume I, 130.

136 Although Charles never mentioned it, Camp Chase was also a large prison camp, holding up to eight thousand captured rebel soldiers in 1863. Later it became Camp Chase Confederate Cemetery, a national cemetery overseen by the Dayton National Cemetery. More than two thousand confederate soldiers are interred there. National Cemetery Administration, *Camp Chase Confederate Cemetery*, cem.va.gov.

137 Ohio Roster Commission, *Official Roster*, Vol. VIII, 572.

138 Perrin, et. al., *History of Logan County*, 634; Haines, *Correspondence to the Governor*.

139 Hogan, *Overland Campaign*, 70.

140 George J. Grove, grave marker, Hillgrove Union Cemetery, Miamisburg; Ohio Roster Commission, *Official Roster*, Vol. II, 16, 726 and Vol. VII, 197.

141 Allen, *Intelligence in the Civil War*, 43.

142 Reilly, "Medical and Surgical Care," *Baylor University Medical Care Proceedings*, tandfonline.com; Hagen, *Toxin-Based Diseases*, asm.org.

143 "Cholera Morbus," *MedGen*, ncbi.nlm.nih.gov.

144 Reiter, *Diary*, Volume 2, n. p.

145 Griffing, *Spared and Shared 23*, sparedshared23.com.

146 Johnson, *End to Insurrection*, University of Virginia.

147 Conover, *Centennial Portrait*, 927; "Charles R. Allen," *Bulletin*, June 13, 1879, 2; *Williams' Dayton Directory for 1896-97*, 1305.

148 Beers, *History of Montgomery County*, Book III, 238.

149 Carpenter, "Difference between Ale and Lager," *Craft Beer & Brewing*, beerandbrewing.com.

150 *Newark Daily Advocate*, in *Gallipolis Journal*, Sept. 14, 1854, 1, LOC; *Cadiz Democratic Sentinel*, Aug. 20, 1856, 1, LOC.

151 Hawes, *Gazetteer*, 436.

152 "Miamisburg Brewery and Malt House!" advertisement, *Bulletin*, Dec. 27, 1867, 1; "Miamisburg Brewery and Malt House," advertisement, *Bulletin*, Aug. 26, 1870, 1, and Aug. 23, 1872, 4.

153 Light and Ransdell, *Miamisburg*, 83; Morgan and Bock, *Ohio Archaeological and Historical Publications*, Volume XXXIV, 477-478; Reiter, *Diary*, Volume 1, 366; "1913 Flood Damage Near River," photo, Miamisburg Historical Society.

154 Montgomery County, deed book B, 425 and P3, 186; Montgomery County, plat book A2, 126.

155 Advertisements, *Bulletin*, Aug. 23, 1872, 4, and Nov. 8, 1872, 4.

156 Montgomery County, plat book A4, 317; Sanborn Fire Insurance Map, 1886, 5.

157 National Register of Historic Places, registration form, St. Jacob's Evangelical Lutheran Church, Catalog.archives.gov.; "Died," *Bulletin*, April 24, 1891, 3; no headlines, *Bulletin*, Aug. 25, 1876, 3, and June 15, 1877, 2.

158 Poor, *Manual of the Railroads*, 427-428.

159 "Bottled Beer," *Bulletin*, May 9, 1873, 2.

160 Weeks, "Report on the Manufacture of Glass," in *Manufactures of the United States*, 10, 17.

161 Lockhart, et. al., "Cunningham Family Glass Holdings," *Historic Glass Bottle*, secure-sha.org, 625-626.

162 Montgomery County, probate court, estate records for William Nusz, Appraisal Schedule "G"—Real Estate, 1882.

163 Proudfoot & Urquhart, *Directory*, 577-578; "Removals," *Bulletin*, March 31, 1882, 3; no headline, *Bulletin*, June 22, 1883, 3.

164 Beers, *History of Montgomery County*, Book III, 144, 414; *Squirrel Hunters from Dayton & Montgomery County, Ohio*, n. p.; Ohio Roster Commission, *Official Roster*, Vol. VIII, 563; Drury, *History of the City of Dayton and Montgomery County*, Volume I, 834; Sanborn Fire Insurance Map, 1886, 3.

165 *Bulletin*, Jan. 16, 1874, 3.

166 "A Big Find," *Bulletin*, May 9, 1873, 2.

167 No headline, *Bulletin*, Nov. 14, 1873, 3.

168 "Sick List," *Bulletin*, Aug. 1, 1879, 3.

169 Law, "Influenza in Horses," *Report of the Commissioner of Agriculture*, 206-209; no headline, *Bulletin*, Nov. 29, 1872, 3.

[170] No headline, *Bulletin*, Dec. 6, 1872, 3, and Dec. 27, 1872, 2.

[171] "A Notable Event," *Bulletin*, Feb. 14, 1879, 2.

[172] Dunlap, "Corn vs. Wheat," *The Illinois Farmer*, 232; Salem, *Beer, Its History*, 79, 189-190; Bartley, "Modern Adulterations in Foods, and their Relations to Disease," *Transactions*, 101.

[173] Salem, *Beer, Its History*, 189, 240-246.

[174] Salem, *Beer*, 244.

[175] Burkhardt's Saloon," advertisement, *Bulletin*, Oct. 18, 1872, 2; no headline, *Bulletin*, Jan. 29, 1875, 3.

[176] "Brewery for Sale," *Bulletin*, March 26, 1880, 2.

[177] Proudfoot & Urquhart, *Directory of Dayton and Montgomery County for 1880-81*, 577; no headline, *Bulletin*, May 21, 1880, 3, Sept. 17, 1880, 1, and Feb. 11, 1881, 3.

[178] "Sick List," *Bulletin*, July 22, 1881, 3; no headline, *Bulletin*, July 15, 1881, 1; "Died," *Bulletin*, July 29, 1881, 3.

[179] "Miamisburg," *Dayton Daily Journal*, Aug. 3, 1881, 4.

[180] No headline, *The Eaton Democrat*, Nov. 30, 1882, 2, LOC.

[181] Conover, *Centennial Portrait*, 1053-1054; "OH District 04," *ourcampaigns. com*.

[182] Montgomery County, deed book 130, 4-7.

[183] Warner, Beers, *History of Allen County*, 509; Rusler, *A Standard History*, 16; Drury, *History*, Volume II, 340-341; Montgomery County, deed book 131, 520.

[184] U.S. Congress, "Robert Maynard Murray," *Biographical Directory*, Congress.gov.

[185] "Last Words," *Bulletin*, Oct. 6, 1882, 2; no headlines, *Eaton Democrat*, July 6, 1882, 2, and Aug. 24, 1882, 2, LOC.

[186] Galbreath, *History of Ohio*, Volume II, 316-318.

[187] Reiter, *Diary*, Volume 1, 88.

[188] "Sketches of Travel," *Templar's Magazine*, 195.

[189] "John Voegle's Saloon and Restaurant," advertisement, *Bulletin*, June 27, 1873, 3.

[190] No headline, *Bulletin*, Jan. 16, 1874, 2.

[191] Galbreath, *History*, 318-319; Chused, *The Temperance Movement's Impact*, 385, digitalcommons.nyls.edu.

[192] No headline, *Bulletin*, Feb. 13, 1874, 2.

[193] "Temperance Mass Meeting," *Bulletin*, March 6, 1874, 2; Ohio Synod, *Acts and Proceedings*, 4.

[194] "The Tomahawk Dug Up!" *Bulletin*, March 13, 1874, 1.

[195] No headline, *Bulletin*, March 20, 1874, 2; "An Ordinance" and "Charge of the Light Brigade," *Bulletin*, March 27, 1874, 2.

[196] No headline, *Bulletin*, March 20, 1874, 2; "An Ordinance" and "Charge of the Light Brigade," *Bulletin*, March 27, 1874, 2; Conover, *Centennial Portrait*, 1080.

[197] No headline, *Bulletin*, May 8, 1874, 2.

[198] No headline, *Bulletin*, July 7, 1876, 3.

[199] Salem, *Beer, Its History*, 151; "An Ordinance," *Bulletin*, May 9, 1879, 2.

[200] Proudfoot & Urquhart, *Directory*, 562, 566, 580, 581, 584, 585.

[201] Lorenz Wieland, grave marker, Miamisburg Catholic Cemetery; "Lorenz Wieland Dead," *Miamisburg News*, Sept. 29, 1898, 5.

[202] "The Miami Valley Brewing Company," advertisement, *Bulletin*, Oct. 27, 1882, 2.

[203] Newman, *Annual Report of the Secretary of State*, 165; "Notice," *Bulletin*, Feb. 16, 1883, 2.

[204] No headline, *Bulletin*, June 8, 1883, 3.

[205] August Victor Kuehn, U.S. Passport application, Cincinnati, Hamilton County, Ohio, digital image, s. v. "August V Kuehn," FamilySearch.org; August Victor Kuehn, 1900 U.S. Census record, Marietta, Washington County, Ohio, s. v. "August Kachn," FamilySearch.org.

[206] *Williams' Cincinnati Directory* issues for 1875, 551; 1876, 572, and 1883, 694; marriage record for August Kuehn, Hamilton County, s. v. "August Kuhn," FamilySearch.org.

[207] *Williams' Cincinnati Directory*, 1882, 692; "The Beer War!" *Cincinnati Daily Star*, June 7, 1877, 4; Morgan, *Cincinnati Beer*, 86-97.

[208] Montgomery County, deed book 131, 520; "Miami Valley Brewery," advertisement, *Bulletin*, June 8, 1883, 2 and no headline, 3; "The Miami Valley Brewery!" advertisement, *Bulletin*, June 15, 1883, 2.

[209] No headline, *Bulletin*, June 29, 1883, 2, Aug. 17, 1883, 3, and June 27, 1884, 3.

[210] No headline, *Bulletin*, Jan. 30, 1880, 2.

[211] No headline, *Bulletin*, June 2, 1882, page 1; Committee on Finance, U.S. Senate, "Reply of Uriah Engleman," *Bulletin No. 36. Replies to Tariff Inquiries*, 89; Bryan, et. al., *Paper Mill Directory*, 102; no headline, *Bulletin*, Aug. 26, 1881, 3.

[212] Swingle, "Invention of the Twine Binder," *Wisconsin Magazine*, September 1926, 36, 38, 40; *Sanborn Fire Insurance Map*, 1886, 4.

213 Selby and Houser, "Tobacco Culture in Ohio," *Bulletin of the Ohio Agricultural Experiment Station*, 266-268, 340-343; "Tobacco Planters!" advertisement, *Bulletin*, April 6, 1883, 3.

214 Baum Opera House Association, "History," baumoperahouse.org; no headline, *Bulletin*, Oct. 16, 1885, 3.

215 No headline, *Bulletin*, May 7, 1886, 3.

216 "Fine View of Miamisburg," *Bulletin*, April 16, 1886, 3; Bailey & Company, *Miamisburg*, lithograph.

217 *Sanborn Fire Insurance Map*, 1886, 5.

218 No headline, *Bulletin*, July 13, 1888, 3 and "Miami Valley Brewery," advertisement, 4; "Grand Opening of the Oyster Season!" advertisement, *Bulletin*, Nov. 5, 1886, 2.

219 "Anarchy," *Bulletin*, Jan. 7, 1887, 2; "Safe Blowers," *Hamilton Daily Democrat*, Jan. 4, 1887, 2, Newspaperarchive.com.

220 Conover, *Centennial Portrait*, 930; "Masked Robbers at the Baum House," *Bulletin*, March 2, 1888, 3; Montgomery County, probate court, death record for Charles Baum, 1893-1901, 12.

221 "Miami Valley Brewery Fire," *Bulletin*, March 29, 1889, 3.

222 No headline, *Bulletin*, April 12, 1889, 3, and April 26, 1889, 3; "Drink the Best!" advertisement, *Bulletin*, April 26, 1889, 3.

223 No headline, *Bulletin*, March 14, 1890, 3, and May 30, 1890, 3.

224 *Sanborn Fire Insurance Map*, 1892, 5; no headline, *Bulletin*, Sept. 2, 1892, 3.

225 "Brewing company on Front Street remembered," *Parkersburg News and Sentinel*, Feb. 2, 2014, newsandsentinel.com.

226 Cone, *Biographical and Historical Sketches*, Volume II, 406-407; Everts, "Henry P. Deuscher," *Combination Atlas Map of Butler County*, 28, and "H. P. Deuscher & Co.," lithograph, 71; National Park Service, "Deuscher, Henry P., House."

227 No headline, *Bulletin*, July 22, 1887, 3; "Movement to Establish a Brewing Company in this City," *Bulletin*, Sept. 30, 1892, 2.

228 "The Miamisburg Brewing company," *Bulletin*, Oct. 21, 1892, 2; Montgomery County, deed books 187, 295 and 188, 78.

229 "Electric Light," *Bulletin*, May 16, 1890, 3; "New Line in Ohio," *Street Railway Journal*, Volume XII, No. 7, 429; "Hotel Young," advertisement, *Williams' Dayton Directory for 1896-1897*, 1305.

[230] "Board of Trade Meeting," *Bulletin*, May 16, 1890, 2; "Enterprise Carriage Works," *Bulletin*, Aug. 1, 1890, 3; "Business Booming at the Enterprise" and "A New Industry," *Bulletin*, Feb. 19, 1892, 3.

[231] No headline, *Bulletin*, Nov. 11, 1892, 2; Moses, "Corporation Record," *National Corporation Reporter*, 508; Taylor, *Annual Report of the Secretary of State*, 470.

[232] No headline, *Bulletin*, Jan. 13, 1893, 3, and Jan. 20, 1893, 2; "A Coal Famine Narrowly Averted," *Bulletin*, Feb. 3, 1893, 3.

[233] "Encourage Home Enterprise," *Bulletin*, May 26, 1893, 3.

[234] Dewing, *National Cordage*, 3, 4, 11; No headline, *Bulletin*, Oct. 2, 1891, 3.

[235] Dewing, *National Cordage*, 24-25.

[236] No headline, *Bulletin*, Oct. 2, 1891, 3, and Oct. 16, 1891, 3; "Industrial Notes," *Bulletin*, No. 27, 1891, 3; "Manufacturing," *The Iron Age*, 72; "The Hoover & Gamble Manufacturing Co.," *Bulletin*, June 24, 1892, 2; "Dismantling the Cordage Mills," *Bulletin*, July 29, 1892, 2; no headline, *Bulletin*, Sept. 30, 1892, 3; "The Latest Factory," *St. Paul Daily Globe* (Minnesota,) Sept. 10, 1892, 1-2, LOC; Dewing, *National Cordage*, 25.

[237] Whitten, "Depression of 1893," *EH.Net Encyclopedia*, EH.net; Dewing, *National Cordage*, 2, 31-32.

[238] No headline, *Bulletin*, Oct. 12, 1894, 3.

[239] "The Good Times Promised," *Bulletin*, September 1, 1893, 2; *Williams Dayton Directory for 1896-1897*, 1311; *Sanborn Fire Insurance Map*, 1896, 4.

[240] "The Dawn of Prosperity," *Bulletin*, Nov. 17, 1893, 3; "The Fourth," *Bulletin*, July 6, 1894, 3.

[241] No headline, *Bulletin*, Jan. 16, 1874, 2.

[242] No headline, *Bulletin*, Dec. 15, 1876, 3.

[243] No headline, *Bulletin*, Jan. 8, 1875, 2, Dec. 22, 1876, 3, and Feb. 13, 1880, 3.

[244] Montgomery County, deed book C3, 503; Hawes, *Gazetteer*, 436; "Rankin's Improved Patent Refrigerator and Condenser," *Bulletin*, July 23, 1875, 2.

[245] Hall, "Ice Industry," *Census Reports*, 2-5, 9-10, 31-32.

[246] Hall, "Ice Industry," *Census Reports*, 9-10.

[247] Williams, "Annual Report," *Annual Reports for 1879*, 410.

[248] Proudfoot & Urquhart, *Directory*, 581; no headline, *Bulletin*, May 30, 1879, 3; Canal Commission, *Miami and Erie Canal through Miamisburg*, map; no headline, *Bulletin*, Feb. 20, 1880, 3; "Personal," *Bulletin*, Nov. 12, 1880, 3, and Jan. 14, 1881, 3.

[249] "A 'Go-Devil!'" *Bulletin*, Dec. 11, 1885, 2; no headline, *Bulletin*, Jan. 14, 1887, 2.

250 "Brewery for Sale," *Bulletin*, March 26, 1880, 2; no headline, *Bulletin*, Dec. 15, 1882, 3.

251 "Pure water Guarantees Pure Ice," *Bulletin*, Nov. 14, 1890, 3.

252 "A Narrow Escape," *Bulletin*, Jan. 14, 1892, 3; "Sick List," *Bulletin*, Feb. 12, 1892, 3.

253 "Movement to Establish a Brewing Company in this City," *Bulletin*, Sept. 30, 1892, 2.

254 Hall, "Ice Industry," *Census Reports*, 5, 19, 20; Siebel, *One Hundred Years*, 125.

255 Frick, *"Eclipse" Refrigerating Machines*, 18, 31-32, 184.

256 No headlines, *Bulletin*, July 20, 1894, 3, and Aug. 3, 1894, 2; *Sanborn Fire Insurance Map*, 1896, 6.

257 No headline, *Bulletin*, Nov. 9, 1894, 3. Copies of the *Miamisburg News* from the nineteenth century survive, but they are so fragile that only some issues from 1898 and 1899 were examined for this book.

258 Rich, "Frigiferous Particulars," *Ice and Refrigeration*, 193; "Ice Gratis," *Dayton Daily News*, Jan. 13, 1899, 5; "Miamisburg," *Dayton Daily News*, April 15, 1899, 2; "Artificial Ice," advertisement, *Miamisburg News*, Jan. 19, 1899, 4.

259 Rich, "New Plants and Improvements," *Ice and Refrigeration*, 129.

260 "Celebrated Indian Mound Beer," *Miamisburg Bulletin*, March 23, 1894, 2.

261 Conover, *Centennial Portrait*, 927-928; "The Nessmuks," *Forest and Stream*, Volume XXXIV, 384; "At the World's Fair," *Bulletin*, April 14, 1893, 2.

262 National Park Service, *Hopewell Ceremonial Earthworks*, nps.gov; Ohio History Connection, *Miamisburg Mound*, ohiohistory.org.

263 Jenkins, *Ohio Gazetteer*, 296; "Dayton," *New York Herald*, Jan. 23, 1843, 1, LOC.

264 "The Indian Mound, Mammoth Relic of a Vanished Race!" *Miamisburg News*, April 29, 1920, 1; "Miamisburg Mound," historical marker, Ohio Historical Society.

265 "Look out!" advertisement, *Bulletin*, April 13, 1894, 3; "Accidents," *Bulletin*, July 13, 1894, 3; no headline, *Bulletin*, July 20, 1894, 3.

266 Taylor, *Annual Report of the Secretary of State*, 470; no headline, *Bulletin*, Oct. 5, 1894, 3, and Oct. 19, 1894, 3.

267 "Loss to H. P. Deuscher," *Hamilton Daily Republican*, June 20, 1898, 4; "Fire," *Miamisburg News*, June 23, 1898.

268 "A Big Fire," *Miamisburg News*, May 10, 1900, 1; no headline, *Dayton Daily News*, January 14, 1901, 2; William Herman, Ohio death certificate, Miamisburg, Montgomery County, digital image, s. v. "William Herman," FamilySearch.org.

269 "Disastrous fire in Miamisburg," *Dayton Daily News*, May 8, 1900, 1; "Miamisburg," *Dayton Daily News*, June 27, 1900, 7.

270 "History of the Movement," *Anti-Saloon League*, Westerville Public Library, Westervillelibrary.org; Gaffney, *Dayton Beer*, 155-156.

271 "William Gamble," *Farm Implements*, Oct. 17, 1908, 15, Google.com; "Ice and Refrigeration," *The National Provisioner*, Vol. XXVII, 25; *Sanborn Fire Insurance Map*, 1905, 8.

272 "Miamisburg's Big Engineering Job," *Dayton Daily News*, June 30, 1910, 2.

273 "Financial Crop Ends," *Iron Trade Review*, June 13, 1918, 1515.

274 Author interview with Justin Kohnen, April 23, 2024.

275 "Jacob Ruegger," *Miamisburg Bulletin*, June 9, 1891, 2; Light and Ransdell, *Miamisburg*, 31, 148.

276 Montgomery County, deed book Q, 219; Jones, *Journal of the Franklin Institute*, 109.

277 Light and Ransdell, *Miamisburg*, 229.

278 "Peerless Mill Inn to Close April 30," *Dayton Daily News*, Feb. 26, 2008, daytondailynews.com; Montgomery County, deed 2013-00045181; "Star City Brewing opens today in Miamisburg," *Akron Beacon Journal*, Nov. 15, 2013, beaconjournal.com.

279 Natalie Jones, "Star City Brewing in Miamisburg is for Sale," DaytonDailyNews.com, Sept. 3, 2025; author interview with Chris N. Small, Nov. 18, 2025; "Meet our Staff," Star City Brewing, https://www.starcitybrewing.com/about-us/meet-our-staff

280 Natalie Jones, "Check out Entropy Brewing in Miamisburg," DaytonDailyNews.com, July 8, 2024; "Location & Building Details," Entropy Brewing Co., entropybrewingco.com.

281 Entropy Brew Co., "Entropy Brew Co.'s Post," Facebook.com.

Bibliography

Books

Aetna Fire Insurance Company. *Aetna Guide to Fire Insurance for the Representatives of the Aetna Fire Insurance Co. Hartford, Conn. Branch, Cincinnati.* Cincinnati: author, 1867. Google.com. https://www.google.com/books/edition/%C3%86tna_Guide_to_Fire_Insurance_for_the_Re/WcoiAAAAMAAJ

Allen, Thomas. *Intelligence in the Civil War.* Washington, D.C.: Central Intelligence Agency, 2007. https://www.cia.gov/static/Intelligence-in-the-Civil-War.pdf

Beers, W. H. & Company. *The History of Montgomery County.* Chicago: author, 1882. Google.com. https://www.google.com/books/edition/The_History_of_Montgomery_County_Ohio_Co/mkLgWuNANpECJ

Beers, W. H. & Company. *The History of Warren County, Ohio*. Chicago: author, 1882. Google.com. https://www.google.com/books/edition/The_History_of_Warren_County_Ohio/tyJEAQAAMAA

Bishop, John Leander, Edwin Troxell Freedley and Edward Young. *A History of American Manufactures from 1608 to 1860*, Volume I. Philadelphia: Edward Young & Company, 1864. Google.com. https://www.google.com/books/edition/_/eukJAAAAIAAJ

Bond, Beverley W., Jr., ed. *Correspondence of John Cleves Symmes*. New York: Macmillan, 1926. Google.com. https://www.google.com/books/edition/The_Correspondence_of_John_Cleves_Symmes/XE15AAAAMAAJ

Brown, W. M. *A Memoir of Dr. John Treon*. Dayton: United Brethren Publishing House, 1887. Google.com. https://www.google.com/books/edition/A_Memoir_of_Dr_John_Treon/ZJsyAQAAMAAJ

Browning, Andrew H. *The Panic of 1819: the First Great Depression*. Columbia: University of Missouri Press, 2019.

Buckingham, Ray E. *Moses Byxbe - His Impact and Image*. Delaware, Ohio: Historybook Inc., 1979, Five Colleges of Ohio. https://ohio5.contentdm.oclc.org/digital/collection/p15963coll29/id/6573

Chase, Salmon P., ed. *Statutes of Ohio and of the Northwestern Territory, Adopted or Enacted from 1788 to 1833 Inclusive*, Volume I. Cincinnati: Corey & Fairbank, 1833. Google.com. https://www.google.com/books/edition/The_Statutes_of_Ohio_and_of_the_Northwes/uGhMAAAAYAAJ

Commissioners of Patents, *Abridgements or Specifications Relating to Brewing, Wine-making, and Distilling Alcoholic Liquids*. London: Commissioners of Patents' Sale Department, 1881. Google.com. https://www.google.com/books/edition/Abridgements_of_Specifications_Relating/2b5BAQAAMAAJ

Cone, Stephen Decatur. *Biographical and Historical Sketches: A Concise History of Hamilton, Ohio*, Volume II. Middletown, Ohio: Republican Publishing, 1901. Google.com. https://www.google.com/books/edition/Biographical_and_Historical_Sketches/HjsVAAAAYAAJ

Conover, Frank, ed. *Centennial Portrait and Biographical Record of the City of Dayton and Montgomery County, Ohio.* Dayton: A. W. Bowen & Company, 1897. Google.com. https://www.google.com/books/edition/Centennial_Portrait_and_Biographical_Rec/2NsyAQAAMAAJ

Cox, E. T. *Twelfth Annual Report of the Indiana State Board of Agriculture.* Indianapolis: Alexander H. Connor, state printer, 1870. Google.com. https://books.google.com/books?id=GuFMAAAAYAAJ

Coxe, Tench. *A Statement of the Arts and Manufactures of the United States of America for the year 1810.* Philadelphia: A. Cornman, 1814. Google.com. https://www.google.com/books/edition/_/a8ZLAQAAMAAJ

Dewing, Arthur Stone. *History of the National Cordage Company.* Cambridge: Harvard University Press, 1913. Google.com. https://books.google.com/books?id=JjIZAAAAYAAJ

Dexter, Henry Martyn, ed. *Mourt's Relation, or Journal of the Plantation at Plymouth, with an Introduction and Notes.* Boston: John Kimball Wiggin, 1865. Google.com. https://www.google.com/books/edition/Mourt_s_Relation_Or_Journal_of_the_Plant/mQB1lN0cIpUC

Drake, Daniel. *Natural and Statistical View, or Picture of Cincinnati and the Miami Country, Illustrated by Maps.* Cincinnati: Looker and Wallace, 1815. Google.com. https://www.google.com/books/edition/Natural_and_Statistical_View_or_Picture/m7BgAAAAcAAJ

Drury, Augustus Waldro. *History of the City of Dayton and Montgomery County, Ohio*, Volumes I and II. Chicago and Dayton: S. J. Clarke Publishing Company, 1909. *Google.com.*
Volume I: https://www.google.com/books/edition/History_of_the_City_of_Dayton_and_Montgo/hhObs4HhLlEC
Volume II: https://www.google.com/books/edition/History_of_the_City_of_Dayton_and_Montgo/Y4AUAAAAYAAJ

Ehret, George. *Twenty-five Years of Brewing.* New York: Gast Lithograph and Engraving Company, 1891. Google.com. https://www.google.com/books/edition/Twenty_five_Years_of_Brewing/5BMZAAAAYAAJ

Ellsworth, Henry L. *A Digest of Patents, issued by the United States, Including the Years 1839, 1840, and 1841.* Washington, D.C.: William Greer, 1842. Google.com. https://www.google.com/books/edition/A_Digest_of_Patents_Issued_by_the_United/5uCwWO1AmKAC

Faust, Albert Bernhardt. *The German Element in the United States*, Volume I. Boston and New York: Houghton Mifflin, 1909. Google.com. https://www.google.com/books/edition/_/iO1mZiNife8C

Frick Company, Engineers. *"Eclipse" Refrigerating Machines for Use in Cold Storage Depots, Packing Houses, Breweries, Ice Factories, Etc.* Waynesboro, Pa.: author, 1890. Google.com. https://www.google.com/books/edition/_/CVkIAAAAIAAJ

Galbreath, Charles E. *History of Ohio*, Volume II. Chicago and New York: American Historical Society, 1925. Google.com. https://www.google.com/books/edition/History_of_Ohio/r_9YAAAAMAAJ

Gottlieb, Martin. *Lincoln's Northern Nemesis: The War Opposition and Exile of Ohio's Clement Vallandigham.* Jefferson, N.C.: McFarland & Company, 2021.

Herndon, Dallas T. *Outline of Executive and Legislative History of Arkansas.* Little Rock: Arkansas History Commission, 1922. Google.com. https://www.google.com/books/edition/Outline_of_Executive_and_Legislative_His/YKVCAAAAIAAJ

Hogan, David W., Jr. *The Overland Campaign: 4 May-15 June 1864.* Washington, D.C.: Center of Military History, United States Army. https://history.army.mil/Publications/Publications-Catalog/Overland-Campaign/

Hogeland, William. *The Whiskey Rebellion: George Washington, Alexander Hamilton, and the Frontier Rebels Who Challenged America's Newfound Sovereignty.* New York: Simon & Schuster, 2006.

Howe, Henry. *Historical Collections of Ohio.* Cincinnati: Bradley & Anthony, 1850. Google.com. https://www.google.com/books/edition/Historical_Collections_of_Ohio/FC4WAAAAYAAJ

Hover, John C., et. al., eds. *Memoirs of the Miami Valley*, Volumes I and II. Chicago: Robert O. Law Company, 1919. Google.com.
Volume I: https://www.google.com/books/edition/Memoirs_of_the_Miami_Valley/STwVAAAAYAAJ
Volume II: https://www.google.com/books/edition/Memoirs_of_the_Miami_Valley/pWJAAAAAYAAJ

Huntington, Charles Clifford. *A History of Banking and Currency in Ohio Before the Civil War: A Thesis Presented to the Faculty of the Graduate School of Cornell University for the Degree of Doctor of Philosophy.* Columbus, Ohio: Ohio Archaeological and Historical Quarterly, Volume 24, No. 3, 1915. Internet Archive. https://archive.org/details/cu31924060241514

Huntington, Charles Clifford and Cloys Peter McClelland. *History of the Ohio Canals: Their Construction, Cost, Use and Partial Abandonment.* Columbus, Ohio: Ohio State Archaeological and Historical Society, 1905. Google.com. https://www.google.com/books/edition/History_of_the_Ohio_Canals_Their_Constru/UC9AAAAAIAAJ

Kilbourn, John. *Public Documents Concerning the Ohio Canals.* Columbus, Ohio: I. N. Whiting, 1832. Google.com. https://books.google.com/books?id=EiMxAQAAMAAJ

Knapp, Horace G. *History of the Maumee Valley, Commencing with its Occupation by the French in 1680.* Toledo: author, 1877. Google.com. https://www.google.com/books/edition/History_of_the_Maumee_Valley/3ao-AAAAYAAJ

Leggett, Conaway, *History of Marion County, Ohio.* Chicago: Leggett, Conaway & Co., 1883. Google.com. https://www.google.com/books/edition/The_History_of_Marion_County_Ohio/ECFEAQAAMAAJ

Light, Esther and Mady Ransdell. *Miamisburg, Ohio: The Story of Our Town.* Miamisburg: Miamisburg Lions Club, 1993.

Middleton, Stephen. *The Black Laws: Race and the Legal Process in early Ohio.* Athens: Ohio University Press, 2005.

Morgan, Michael D. *Cincinnati Beer.* Charleston, S.C.: History Press, 2019.

Myers, Albert Cook, ed. *Narratives of Early Pennsylvania, West New Jersey and Delaware, 1630-1707*, Volume 12. New York: Charles Scribner's Sons, 1912. Google.com. https://www.google.com/books/edition/Narratives_of_Early_Pennsylvania_West_Ne/HNMLAAAAYAAJ

Nelson, William, ed. *Documents Relating to the Colonial History of the State of New Jersey*, Volume XX. Patterson, N.J.: The Call Printing and Publishing Company, 1898. Google.com. https://www.google.com/books/edition/Documents_Relating_to_the_Colonial_Histo/mw4bAAAAYAAJ

"Our Forefather's Song," in *Collections of the Massachusetts Historical Society*, Volume VII. Boston: Charles C. Little and James Brown, 1838. Google.com. https://www.google.com/books/edition/Collections_of_the_Massachusetts_Histori/P5JIAAAAYAAJ

Perrin, William Henry. *History of Delaware County and Ohio*. Chicago: O. L. Baskin & Co., 1880. Google.com. https://books.google.com/books?id=wRAVAAAAYAAJ

Perrin, William Henry and J. H. Battle. *History of Logan County and Ohio*. Chicago: O. L. Baskin & Co., 1880. Google.com. https://www.google.com/books/edition/History_of_Logan_County_and_Ohio/HREVAAAAYAAJ

Poor, Henry V. *Manual of the Railroads of the United States for 1877-78*. New York: H. V. & H. W. Poor, 1877. Google.com. https://www.google.com/books/edition/Poor_s_Manual_of_Railroads/SDibrfRbSsIC

Rafert, Stewart. *The Miami Indians of Indiana: A Persistent People, 1654-1994*. Indianapolis: Indiana Historical Society Press, 1996.

Reid, Whitelaw. *Ohio in the War: Her Statesmen, Generals and Soldiers*. Volumes I and II. Cincinnati: Moore, Wilstach & Baldwin, 1868. Internet Archive. Volume I: https://archive.org/details/ohiointhewar01reidrich/ Volume II: https://archive.org/details/ohioinwarherstat01reid/page/n7/

Roberts, Alasdair. *America's First Great Depression: Economic Crisis and Political Disorder after the Panic of 1837*. New York: Cornell University Press, 2012.

Rusler, William. *A Standard History of Allen County, Ohio.* Chicago and New York: American Historical Society, 1921. Google.com. https://www.google.com/books/edition/A_Standard_History_of_Allen_County_Ohio/FteOx8FKuDMC

Salem, Frederick William. *Beer, Its History and its Economic Value as a National Beverage.* Hartford: F. W. Salem & Company, 1880. Google.com. https://www.google.com/books/edition/Beer_Its_History_and_Its_Economic_Value/bLlBAQAAMAAJ

Sawyer, William. *Speech of Hon. William Sawyer of Ohio, on the Slave Trade in the District of Columbia.* Washington, D.C.: Congressional Globe Office, 1849. Google.com. https://www.google.com/books/edition/Speech_of_Hon_William_Sawyer_of_Ohio_on/ldBWgZMuIzsC

Siebel, John Ewald, contrib. *One Hundred Years of Brewing: A Complete History of the Progress Made in the Art, Science and Industry of Brewing in the World, Particularly During the Nineteenth Century.* Chicago and New York: H. S. Rich & Co., 1903. Google.com. https://www.google.com/books/edition/One_Hundred_Years_of_Brewing/1JFOAQAAMAAJ

Stanton, Edwin M. *Reports of Cases Argued and Determined in the Supreme Court of Ohio,* Volume XI. Cincinnati: Robert Clarke & Co., 1873. Google.com. https://www.google.com/books/edition/Reports_of_Cases_Argued_and_Determined_i/yycMAAAAYAAJ

Clement Vallandigham, *Speeches, Arguments, Addresses and Letters of Clement L. Vallandigham.* New York: J. Walter & Co., 1864. Google.com. https://www.google.com/books/edition/Speeches_Arguments_Addresses_and_Letters/wDHeXrEp3EcC

Warner, Beers & Co. *History of Allen County, Ohio.* Chicago: Warner, Beers & Co., 1885. Google.com. https://books.google.com/books?id=cjcWAAAAYAAJ

Whitten, David. "Depression of 1893," Robert Whaples, ed., *EH.Net Encyclopedia.* August 14, 2001. EH.net. https://eh.net/encyclopedia/the-depression-of-1893/

Williams, Charles F., ed. *The American and English Encyclopedia of Law*, Volume XXV. New York: Edward Thompson Company, 1894. Google.com. https://www.google.com/books/edition/The_American_and_English_Encyclopedia_of/TXQOn1s2-rAC

Winthrop, John. "On the Culture, and Use of Maize," in Hutton, Charles, George Shaw and Richard Pearson, *The Philosophical Transactions of the Royal Society of London*, Volume II. London: C. and R. Baldwin, 1809. Google.com. https://www.google.com/books/edition/Philosophical_Transactions_0of_the_Royal/HtAF42LnXx4C

County Records

Montgomery County, Ohio. Common pleas and probate court, land and county tax records in bound volumes and microfilm. Montgomery County Records Center and Archives, 117 South Main St., Sixth Floor, Reibold Building, Dayton, Ohio.

Warren County, Ohio. Common pleas and probate court and land records in bound volumes. Warren County Records Center and Archives, County Administration Building, 406 Justice Drive, Lebanon, Ohio.

Directories

Bryan, Clark W. & Co. *Paper Mill Directory of the World*. Holyoke, Mass., and New York: author, 1884. Google.com. https://books.google.com/books?id=0-xFAQAAMAAJ

Hawes, George W. *George W. Hawes' Ohio State Gazetteer for 1860-'61*. Indianapolis: Author, 1860. Google.com. https://www.google.com/books/edition/George_W_Hawes_Ohio_State_Gazetteer_and/yyBEAQAAMAAJ

Jenkins, Warren. *Ohio Gazetteer and Traveler's Guide*. Columbus, Ohio: Isaac N. Whiting, 1837. Google.com. https://www.google.com/books/edition/The_Ohio_Gazetteer_and_Traveler_s_Guide/5GgTAAAAYAAJ

Kilburn, John. *Ohio Gazetteer or Topographical Dictionary*. Columbus, Ohio: Scott and Wright, 1833. Google.com. https://www.google.com/books/edition/The_Ohio_Gazetteer_Or_a_Topographical_Di/dt48AAAAYAAJ

Proudfoot & Urquhart's Directory of Dayton and Montgomery County for 1880-81.
Dayton: Christian Publishing House, 1880. FamilySearch.org. https://www.
familysearch.org/ark:/61903/3:1:3QHV-V3DF-GBW3?cc=3754697

W. W. Reilly & Co's. Ohio State Business Directory for 1853-4. Cincinnati: Morgan
& Overend, 1853. google.com. https://www.google.com/books/edition/W_
W_Reilly_Co_s_Ohio_State_Business_Dire/XVF0AoZrSsQC

Williams' Ohio State Directory for 1872. Cincinnati: Williams & Co., 1872.
Cincinnati & Hamilton County Public Library. digital.cincinnatilibrary.org.
https://apps.cincinnatilibrary.org/citydirectory/
WilliamsCincinnatiDirectory_1872.pdf

Williams' Cincinnati Directory. Cincinnati: Williams & Co., 1875. Cincinnati &
Hamilton County Public Library. digital.cincinnatilibrary.org. http://apps.
cincinnatilibrary.org/citydirectory/WilliamsCincinnatiDirectory_1875.pdf
———for 1876. http://apps.cincinnatilibrary.org/citydirectory/
WilliamsCincinnatiDirectory_1876.pdf
———for 1882. https://apps.cincinnatilibrary.org/citydirectory/
WilliamsCincinnatiDirectory_1882_Pt01.pdf
———for 1883. http://apps.cincinnatilibrary.org/citydirectory/
WilliamsCincinnatiDirectory_1883.pdf

Williams' Dayton Directory for 1896-1897. Cincinnati: Williams & Co., 1897.
Familysearch.org. https://www.familysearch.org/ark:/61903/3:1:3QHV-J3DF-
L9KY?i=524&cc=3754697

National Archives. Record Group 15, Records of the Department of Veterans
Affairs, Series: *War of 1812 Pension and Bounty Land Warrant Application Files.*
catalog.archives.gov. https://catalog.archives.gov/id/187080808.

National Archives. National Register of Historic Places registration form,
Henry P. Deuscher House. https://National Archives Catalog. catalog.
archives.gov/id/71986965

National Park Service. "Deuscher, Henry P., House." National Register dataset
20230801. Excel spreadsheet. https://www.nps.gov/subjects/nationalregister/
database-research.htm#table

Internet Content

American Homebrewers Association. "How to Make Beer." https://omebrewersassociation.org

Baum Opera House Association. "History." baumoperahouse.org. https://baumoperahouse.org/history

Blakely, Julia. "Beer on Board in the Age of Sail." Blog. *Smithsonian Libraries and Archives*, https://blog.library.si.edu/blog/2017/08/02/beer-board-age-sail/

Carpenter, Dave. "What is the difference between Ale and Lager?" *Craft Beer & Brewing*. beerandbrewing.com. https://beerandbrewing.com/what-is-the-difference-between-ale-and-lager/

Chused, Richard H. *The Temperance Movement's Impact on Adoption of Women's Suffrage*. New York Law School, Digital Commons. digitalcommons.nyls.edu. https://digitalcommons.nyls.edu

Griffing, William, ed. "1864: John Evans Kinder to Elizabeth Ford Kinder," Civil War letters. *Spared and Shared 23*. https://sparedshared23.com/2024/08/29/1864-john-evans-kinder-to-elizabeth-ford-kinder/

Hagen, Ashley. *The Toxin-Based Diseases Common in North America during the 1600-1700s*. American Society for Microbiology. asm.org. https://asm.org/articles/2019/july/the-toxin-based-diseases-common-in-north-america-d

Hop Growers of America. "We're not New to This," *USA Hops*. usahops.org. https://www.usahops.org/enthusiasts

Hunter, Diane. "Forced from our Homes," *Aacimotaatiiyankwi*, October 1, 2021. Blog. aacimotaatiiyankwi.org. https://aacimotaatiiyankwi.org/2021/10/01/forced-from-our-homes.

Lockhart, Bill, Beau Schriever, Bill Lindsey and Carol Serr. "Cunningham Family Glass Holdings." PDF document, in Bill Lindsey, *Historic Glass Bottle Identification and Information Website*. Society for Historical Architecture. secure-sha.org. https://secure-sha.org/bottle/pdffiles/Cunningham.pdf

Miamisburg Historical Society. *Miamisburg Veterans Honor Roll.* historicalmiamisburg.org. https://www.historicalmiamisburg.org/veterans-honor-roll

Miami Township. "Demographics." Miamitownship.com. https://miamitownship.com/163/Demographics

National Cemetery Administration. *Camp Chase Confederate Cemetery.* cem.va.gov. https://www.cem.va.gov/cems/lots/campchase.asp

National Library of Medicine. "Cholera Morbus," *MedGen.* National Center for Biotechnology Information. ncbi.nlm.nih.gov. https://www.ncbi.nlm.nih.gov/medgen/64524

National Park Service. "Brewing in the Seventeenth Century," *Historic Jamestowne.* nps.gov. https://www.nps.gov/jame/learn/historyculture/brewing-in-the-seventeenth-century.htm

National Park Service. *Hopewell Ceremonial Earthworks.* Hopewell Culture National Historical Park. nps.gov. https://www.nps.gov/hocu/learn/historyculture/hopewell-ceremonial-earthworks.htm

Ohio History Connection. *Miamisburg Mound.* ohiohistory.org. https://www.ohiohistory.org/visit/browse-historical-sites/miamisburg-mound/

Office of the Historian. U.S. House of Representatives. "Representative Clement Vallandigham of Ohio," *History, Art & Archives.* history.house.gov. https://history.house.gov/Historical-Highlights/1800-1850/Representative-Clement-Vallandigham-of-Ohio/

———"The Saga of 'Sausage' Sawyer," *Whereas: Stories from the People's House.* blog. history.house.gov. https://history.house.gov/Blog/2015/August/8-11-Sausage-Sawyer/

Our Campaigns. "OH District 04." ourcampaigns.com. https://www.ourcampaigns.com/RaceDetail.html?RaceID=440732

Reilly, Robert F. "Medical and Surgical Care During the American Civil War, 1861-1865," in *Baylor University Medical Center Proceedings.* Tandfonline.com. https://www.tandfonline.com/doi/pdf/10.1080/08998280.2016.11929390

St. John's Lutheran Church. "Our History," stjohnsmiamisburg.com. https://stjohnsmiamisburg.org/wp/our-history

Sultana Association of Descendants and Friends. *The Disaster.* thesultanaassociation.com. https://www.thesultanaassociation.com/the-disaster

U.S. Congress. *Biographical Directory of the United States Congress.* Congress.gov. https://bioguide.congress.gov

"Washington's Love of Beer," *George Washington's Mount Vernon.* mountvernon.org. https://www.mountvernon.org/the-estate-gardens/food-culture/beer

Westerville Public Library. "History of the Movement," *Anti-Saloon League.* Westervillelibrary.org. https://westervillelibrary.org/antisaloon-history

Maps, Atlases, Lithographs

Schenck, W. C. and D. B. Cooper. *Town of Franklin.* Plat map, 1802. Warren County Recorder's Office. Warren County, records Center and Archives.

O. H. Bailey & Company. *Miamisburg, Ohio.* Lithograph. Boston: O. H. Bailey & Company, 1886. Framed copy, Miamisburg Historical Society, 35 S. Fifth St., Miamisburg.

Canal Commission of Ohio. *Miami and Erie Canal through Miamisburg.* Map. Columbus: author, 1915. Ohio History Connection. https://ohiomemory.org/digital/collection/p16007coll93/id/451

Everts, L. H. *Combination Atlas Map of Butler County Ohio, 1875.* Philadelphia: Hunter, 1875.
———*of Montgomery County, Ohio, 1875.*
———*of Warren County, Ohio, 1875.*
Maps and Atlases Collection, Cincinnati & Hamilton County Public Library. https://digital.cincinnatilibrary.org/digital/collection/p16998coll9

Heins, Gustavus. *Map of Montgomery County, Ohio.* Cincinnati: Lithography by Klauprech & Menzel, 1851. Library of Congress. https://www.loc.gov/item/2012592381

Titus, C. O. *Titus' map of Montgomery County, Ohio.* Philadelphia: author, 1869. Library of Congress. https: www.loc.gov/item/2012592383

Sanborn Map Company. *Sanborn Fire Insurance Maps from Miamisburg, Montgomery County, Ohio,* 1886-1919. Sanborn Collection, Library of Congress. https://www.loc.gov/collections/sanborn-maps

Van Cleve, John W. *Revised Map of Miamisburg.* Map, 1848. Miamisburg Historical Society Collection.

Newspapers (except where otherwise cited in notes)

LOC: Library of Congress. LOC's Chronicling America includes a database of digitized newspapers. All cited news articles referencing "LOC" may be found by searching the database. https://chroniclingamerica.loc.gov/

Miamisburg Bulletin. Google Newspapers. Google.com https://news.google.com/newspapers?nid=H1FpnsQ9v50C

Newspaper Archive. Digital database of newspapers. Newspaperarchive.com. https://newspaperarchive.com

Ohio Memory: Collaborative program of the Ohio History Connection, Ohio State Library and Library of Congress. https://ohiomemory.ohiohistory.org/newspapers

Western Star (also *Western Star and Lebanon Gazette*): Warren County (Ohio) Genealogical Society maintains a subset of Ohio Memory's newspaper collection. https://ohiomemory.org/digital/collection/p16007coll84

Periodicals

Bartley, E. H., M.D. "Modern Adulterations in Foods, and their Relations to Disease," *Transactions of the Brooklyn Pathological Society,* Volume I. New York: D. Appleton and Company, 1887. Google.com. https://www.google.com/books/edition/Transactions_of_the_Brooklyn_Pathologica/wexPAAAAIAAJ

Dunlap, M. L., ed. "Corn vs. Wheat," *The Illinois Farmer*. August 1861. Google. com. https://www.google.com/books/edition/The_Illinois_Farmer/-_ cjAQAAMAAJ

"Financial Crop Ends," *Iron Trade Review*, Volume LXII. Cleveland: Penton Publishing Co., 1918. Google.com. https://www.google.com/books/edition/ Iron_Trade_Review/2BtKAQAAMAAJ

Forest and Stream, a Weekly Journal of the Rod and Gun, Volume XXXIV. New York: Forest and Stream, 1890. Google.com. https://www.google.com/books/ edition/Forest_and_Stream/hEchAQAAMAAJ

"William Gamble," *Farm Implements*, Oct. 17, 1908. Google.com. https://www. google.com/books/edition/Farm_Implements/N8E7AQAAMAAJ

"Ice and Refrigeration," *The National Provisioner*, Vol. XXVII. New York: Floor A. Produce Exchange, 1902. Google.com. https://www.google.com/books/ edition/The_National_Provisioner/7NPmAAAAMAAJ

Jones, Thomas P., M.D., ed. *Journal of the Franklin Institute of the State of Pennsylvania*, Vol. VIII. Philadelphia: Franklin Institute, 1831. Google.com. https://www.google.com/books/edition/Journal_of_the_Franklin_Institute/ ok9SICJHn-sC

"Manufacturing," *The Iron Age*, Volume 49. New York: David Williams, 1892. Google.com. https://www.google.com/books/edition/The_Iron_Age/aJU-AQAAMAAJ

Meier, Michael T. "Civil War Draft Records: Exemptions and Enrollments," *Prologue* magazine, Winter 1994, n. p. Archived online at National Archives and Records Administration. https://www.archives.gov/publications/ prologue/1994/winter/civil-war-draft-records.html

Morgan, Arthur E. and C. A. Bock. "A History of Flood Control in Ohio," *Ohio Archaeological and Historical Publications*, Volume XXXIV. Columbus: Ohio State Archaeological and Historical Society, 1926. Google.com. https://www. google.com/books/edition/Ohio_Archaeological_and_Historical_Quart/ jrY1AAAAIAAJ

Moses, Adolph, ed. "Corporation Record," *National Corporation Reporter*, Volume V. Chicago: United States Corporation Bureau, 1893. Google.com. https://www.google.com/books/edition/The_National_Corporation_Reporter/cpNDAQAAMAAJ

"A New Line in Ohio," *Street Railway Journal*, Volume XII, No. 7. New York: Street Railway Publishing Co., 1896. Google.com. https://www.google.com/books/edition/Transit_Journal/0kw_AQAAMAAJ

"New Plants and Improvements," *Industrial Refrigeration*, Volume 18, February 1900. Google.com. https://www.google.com/books/edition/Host_Bibliographic_Record_for_Boundwith/FhdGAQAAMAAJ

Rich, H. S. & Co. "Frigiferous Particulars," *Ice and Refrigeration Illustrated*, Volume 14. Chicago and New York: H. S. Rich & Co., March 1898. Google.com. https://books.google.com/books?id=SuFBAQAAMAAJ

Schmidt, Robert and Carolyn Schmidt. "Elias Murray," *The Hoosier Packet*. Terre Haute: Canal Society of Indiana, October 2010. indcanal.org. https://indcanal.org/wp-content/uploads/2016/10/elias-murray.pdf

Selby, A. D., and True Houser. "Tobacco Culture in Ohio," *Bulletin of the Ohio Agricultural Experiment Station*, No. 238. Wooster: Ohio Agricultural Experiment Station, March 1912. Google.com. https://www.google.com/books/edition/Tobacco_Culture_in_Ohio/TMhPAQAAMAAJ

Sheridan, Kim. "Town Patents the Lattice Truss Bridge," *Today in CT History*. cthumanities.org. https://connecticuthistory.org/town-patents-the-lattice-truss-bridge-today-in-history

"Sketches of Travel," *Templar's Magazine*, Volume X. Cincinnati: Marshall & Hefley, June 1860. Google.com. https://www.google.com/books/edition/The_Templar_s_Magazine/nIIT0NttMgAC

Swingle, F. B. "The Invention of the Twine Binder," *Wisconsin Magazine of History*, Volume X. Cleveland: Evangelical Publishing House, September 1926. Google.com. https://www.google.com/books/edition/Wisconsin_Magazine_of_History/7MoyAQAAIAAJ

State Government Reports

Burrell, Richard T., ed. *Complete List of the Members of the Senate and House of Representatives of Indiana.* Indianapolis: William B. Burford, 1903. Google.com. https://www.google.com/books/edition/Complete_List_of_the_Members_of_the_Sena/bGIvAAAAYAAJ

Newman, James A. *Annual Report of the Secretary of State to the Governor of Ohio for the Year 1883.* Columbus: Myers Brothers, 1884. Google.com. https://www.google.com/books/edition/Annual_Report_of_the_Secretary_of_State/NBlHAQAAMAAJ

Ohio General Assembly. *Acts of a General Nature, Enacted, Revised and Ordered to be Reprinted, at the First Session of the Twenty-Ninth General Assembly of the State of Ohio*, Vol. XXIX. Columbus: Olmsted & Bailhache, 1831. Google.com. https://www.google.com/books/edition/Acts_of_the_State_of_Ohio/M2kqAAAAYAAJ

Ohio General Assembly. *Journal of the Senate of the State of Ohio*, Volume 29. Columbus: Olmsted & Bailhache, 1830. Google.com. https://books.google.com/books?id=b31DAQAAMAAJ

Ohio General Assembly. *Acts of a Local Nature, Passed by the Thirty-Eighth General Assembly of the State of Ohio.* Columbus: Samuel Medary, 1840. Google.com. https://books.google.com/books?id=DvJQAQAAMAAJ

Ohio Roster Commission. *Official Roster of the Soldiers of the State of Ohio in the War of the Rebellion, 1861-1865*, Vol. II, 1st-20th Regiments—Infantry. Cincinnati: Wilstach Baldwin & Co., 1886. Google.com. https://www.google.com/books/edition/Official_Roster_of_the_Soldiers_of_the_S/keRFAQAAMAAJ

———Vol. IV, 37th to 53rd Regiments—Infantry. Akron: Werner Printing and Manufacturing, 1887. Internet Archive. https://archive.org/details/ohiowarroster04howerich
———Vol. VII, 87th to 108th Regiments—Infantry. Cincinnati: Ohio Valley Press, 1888. Internet Archive. https://archive.org/details/officialrosterof07ohio
———Vol. VIII, 110th to 140th Regiments—Infantry. Cincinnati: Ohio Valley Press, 1888. Internet Archive. https://archive.org/details/officialrosterof08ohio

Ohio Senate. *Journal of the Senate, of the State of Ohio; Being the First Session of the Thirteenth General Assembly*. Columbus, Ohio: David Smith, 1831. Google.com. https://www.google.com/books/edition/Journal_of_the_Senate_of_the_State_of_Oh/a1kAR6WPhaQC

Russel, Addison P. "Report of the Secretary of State," in *Message and Reports to the General Assembly and Governor of the State of Ohio: For the year 1861*, Part I. Columbus: Richard Nevins, 1861. Google.com. https://www.google.com/books/edition/_/70eEkPwpfiMC

Smith, J. V. *Report of the Debates and Proceedings of the Convention for the Revision of the Constitution of the State of Ohio, 1850-51*, Volume I. Columbus: S. Medary, 1851. Google.com. https://www.google.com/books/edition/_/tDDKD5RJwJcC

Taylor, Samuel M. *Annual Report of the Secretary of State to the Governor of the State of Ohio for the Year Ending November 15, 1894*. Columbus: Westbote Co., 1895. Google.com. https://www.google.com/books/edition/Annual_Report_of_the_Secretary_of_State/TfInAAAAYAAJ

Williams, James. "Annual Report of the Auditor of State," *Annual Reports for 1879, Made to the Sixty-Fourth General Assembly of the State of Ohio*, Part I. Columbus: Nevins & Myers, 1880. Google.com. https://www.google.com/books/edition/Documents_Including_Messages_and_Other_C/O6kiAy1oD8wC

U.S. Government Reports

Committee on Finance, United States Senate. *Bulletin No. 36. Replies to tariff inquiries.* Washington, D.C.: June 2, 1894. loc.gov. https://www.loc.gov/item/2024771497/

Debow, J. D. B. *Seventh Census of the United States: 1850. An Appendix*. Washington, D.C.: U.S. Census Office. archive.org. https://archive.org/details/cu31924096440890

Hall, Henry. "Ice Industry of the United States, with a Brief Sketch of its History and Estimates of Production in the Different States," in W. P. Trowbridge, *Census Reports: Tenth Census. June 1, 1880: Report on Power and Machinery Employed in Manufactures*. Washington, D.C.: Government Printing Office, 1888. Google.com. https://www.google.com/books/edition/Census_Reports_Tenth_Census_June_1_1880/LvMqAAAAMAAJ

Jacobs, A. A. *Plant Guide for Common Barley (Hordeum vulgare I.)* Coffeeville, Mississippi: USDA-Natural Resources Conservation Service, Jamie L. Whitten Plant Materials Center, 2016. https://plants.usda.gov/DocumentLibrary/plantguide/pdf/pg_hovu.pdf

Johnson, Andrew. "Message Proclaiming End to Insurrection in the United States." Transcript. *Presidential Speeches*. University of Virginia Miller Center. Millercenter.org. https://millercenter.org/the-presidency/presidential-speeches

Law, James. "Influenza in Horses," *Report of the Commissioner of Agriculture for the Year 1872*. Washington, D.C.: Government Printing Office, 1874. Google.com. https://www.google.com/books/edition/Report_of_the_Commissioner_of_Agricultur/AWdhAAAAcAAJ

National Archives. *Bounty-Land Warrants for Military Service, 1775–1855*. Fact sheet. Washington, D.C: NARA, 2010. https://www.archives.gov/files/research/military/bounty-land-1775-1855.pdf

National Archives. Record Group 15. *Consolidated Enrollment Lists, 1863-1865*. Records of the Provost Marshal General's Bureau (Civil War,) 1861 – 1907. Ohio, 3rd Congressional District, Class No. 1, A-K (Volume 1 of 3): https://catalog.archives.gov/id/109519771
Ohio, 3rd Congressional District, Class No. 2, A-Z (Volume 3 of 3): https://catalog.archives.gov/id/226378312

U.S. Census Office. "Population of the United States in 1860: Ohio." Census.gov. https://www2.census.gov/library/publications/decennial/1860/population/1860a-28.pdf

U.S. Congress. "Revenue Act of 1862," *Fraser*. St. Louis: Federal Reserve Bank of St. Louis. fraser.stlouisfed.org. https://fraser.stlouisfed.org/title/revenue-act-1862-6137/fulltext

U.S. Congress. *An Act for the Release of Certain Persons Held in Service or Labor in the District of Columbia*. National Archives. https://www.archives.gov/exhibits/featured-documents/dc-emancipation-act

Wiebe, G. A., contrib. "Introduction of Barley into the New World," in *Barley: Origin, Botany, Culture, Winter Hardiness, Genetics, Utilization, Pests*. Washington, D.C: U.S. Department of Agriculture, Rev. 1979. https://search.nal.usda.gov/permalink/01NAL_INST/178fopj/alma9916346367507426

Weeks, Joseph D. "Report on the Manufacture of Glass," in U.S. Census Office, *Report on the Manufactures of the United States at the Tenth Census.* Washington, D.C.: Government Printing Office, 1883. Google.com. https://www.google.com/books/edition/Census_Reports_Tenth_Census_Report_of_th/hr5NAQAAMAAJ

Other Documents and Reports

Ohio Synod of the Reformed Church in the United States, *Acts and Proceedings of the Ohio Synod of the Reformed Church in the United States at Miamisburg, Ohio, April 21, 1875.* Miamisburg: Blossom Brothers, 1875. Google.com. https://books.google.com/books?id=_n0QAAAAIAAJ

Doan, Marisha, ed. *Letters of Charles R. Allen and Elizabeth Allen During the Civil War.* Transcript. Veterans collection, Miamisburg Historical Society.

Drake, Daniel, M.D. *Discourses Delivered by Appointment, Before the Cincinnati Medical Library Association.* Cincinnati: Moore & Anderson, 1852. Google.com. https://www.google.com/books/edition/Discourses_Delivered_by_Appointment_Befo/WBYgAQAAMAAJ

Haines, Captain Joel. *Correspondence to the Governor and Adjutant General of Ohio, 1861-1898, State Archives Series 147.* Letter to Governor David Tod, May 6, 1862. Abstract. https://resources.ohiohistory.org/onlinedoc/civilwar/sa0147/new/33_07.php

Heritage Village. Historical marker. Miamisburg: Miamisburg Historical Society and the Ohio Historical Society, 2012.

Squirrel Hunters from Dayton & Montgomery County, Ohio. Bound volume. Veterans Collection, Miamisburg Historical Society.

Reiter, Isaac H. *Diary of Isaac H. Reiter,* Volumes I and 2. Unpublished. Local History Collection, Dayton Metro Library.

BIBLIOGRAPHY

Picture Credits

For items not fully cited, see bibliography.

Cover: Nusz bottle photograph—author; Miami Valley Brewery, Young's Arcade illustrations—Bailey & Co., *Miamisburg, Ohio*, courtesy of Miamisburg Historical Society.

11, 12, 13, 27, 38, 41, 42, 48, 51, 107, 113, 117, 130, 143, 161, 162, 169, 172, 173—author.
15—Howe, *Historical Collections of Ohio*, 375.
16, 103, 127, 129, 140, 156, 164—*Miamisburg Bulletin*. Google.com.
19—Stauffer, David McNeely. *Wm Penn's old Brew-House*. Courtesy of Free Library of Philadelphia, Print and Picture Collection. https://libwww.freelibrary.org/digital/item/40615
21—*Plat of Miamisburgh*. Montgomery County, Plat Book 001, 23.
28—*Town of Franklin*. Plat map. Warren County Recorder's Office, provided by Warren County Records Center and Archives.

35, 39, 43—Van Cleve, *Revised Map of Miamisburg*, courtesy of Miamisburg Historical Society.

39, 65, 84, 98, 133—Courtesy of Miamisburg Historical Society.

55, 69—Titus, *Titus' map of Montgomery County.*

61—Cox, *Twelfth Annual Report of the Indiana State Board of Agriculture*, xii. Google.com.

63, 101, 125, 134, 135, 151, 171, 172—Bailey & Co., *Miamisburg, Ohio*, courtesy of Miamisburg Historical Society.

73—Mathews, A. E. *The Pontoon Bridge at Cincinnati.* Cincinnati: Middleton, Strobridge & Co., 1861-1865. Library of Congress. https://www.loc.gov/item/91721226/

76—*Hon. Clement Laird Vallandigham of Ohio.* Brady-Handy photograph collection, Library of Congress.

80—80 Reid, *Ohio in the War*, Volume I, 96. https://www.loc.gov/pictures/item/2017895906/

83—*White House Landing, Va.* Civil War photographs, 1861-1865, Library of Congress.

86—Ruger, A. *Bird's eye view of Camp Chase near Columbus, Ohio.* Cincinnati: Ehrgott, Forbriger & Co. Library of Congress. http://hdl.loc.gov/loc.gmd/g4084c.pm006831

91—*Petersburg, Va. Sutler's tent, 2d Division, 9th Corps.*Civil War photographs, 1861-1865, Library of Congress. https://www.loc.gov/pictures/item/2018666693/

102—*Miamisburg Bulletin*, Dayton Metro Library, microfilm collection.

119—Morton, S. B. "The Ohio whiskey war - the ladies of Logan singing hymns in front of barrooms in aid of the temperance movement." *Leslie's Illustrated Newspaper*, Feb. 21, 1874, 392. Library of Congress. https://www.loc.gov/pictures/item/96516943/

126—*Proudfoot & Urquhart*, 562.

136, 137—Sanborn, *Miamisburg, 1886*, 5.

145—Cone, *Biographical and Historical Sketches*, 406.

154—Everts, *Combination Atlas Map of Butler County*, 50.

157, 165—Courtesy Gina and Donald Miller, Miami Valley Newspapers.

159—Frick,*"Eclipse" Refrigerating Machines*, cover.

Digital alterations disclosure: author's pictures of St. Jacob's, Lucky Star Brewery and Entropy Brewing (pages 117, 172 and 173) were digitally altered to reduce the "leaning building" effect caused by perspective.

Index

A

Acme Folding Boat Company 100, 161–162, *162*

ale 22, 101, 126, 138. *See Also* beer

Alexander, Jacob 105, 114

Alexander, Wilhelmina Nusz 105, 109

Allen letters, Charles and Elizabeth 84–85

Allen Watson Allen 62–63

Allen, Charles R. 83–84, *84,* 100. *See Also* Allen letters, Charles and Elizabeth; Civil War, 132nd Regiment, Ohio; Civil War, Camp Chase; Civil War, disease among soldiers; Civil War, sutler

Allen, David 88, 92–93, 96, 98–99, *98. See Also* Acme Folding Boat Co.

Allen, Elizabeth Hoover 83, 100. *See Also* Allen letters, Charles and Elizabeth; Miamisburg, illness in

Allen, Ellwood 88, 93, 97, 100

Allen, George 63

Allen, Samuel S. *See* Allen Watson Allen

B

barley 22–23, 36, 125. *See Also* beer, brewing, maize, malt

Baum, Charles 131, 139–140. *See Also* Star City Opera House

Beachler, John R. and Sophia 15

beer 22–23. *See Also* breweries, lager beer

   bottles and bottling 106, *107,* 108, 111, 117, *130,* 136, 141, 143, 146, 164–166

   brewing 22–25, 115, 151, 161, 164

brewing industry 25-26, 36, 101, 114, 126, 153, 157, 167
caves and cellars 13-14, 104, 106, 112, 116, 137, 142, 157–158. *See Also* ice
craft beer 17, 169, 174
Berks County, Pa. *See* Pennsylvania, Berks County
Blossom brothers 17, 81, 110, 134
   Albert H. 81, 110
   Charles E. 81, 110
   Mathias (or Matthias) S. 110, 134
   Miles 81, 110, 134
breweries
   B. Day's brewery, 1822 37
   craft beer. *See* beer, craft beer
   Fastnacht & Rau Brewery, Eaton 114
   in Cincinnati 36, 104, 114, 127, 131, 141–142. *See Also* Christian Moerlein Brewing Company, Jackson Brewing Company
   in Dayton 14, 101–102, 114, 167
   in Miamisburg *See* Emde's brewery, Entropy Brewing, Gebhart Tavern, Hoover's brewery, Lucky Star Brewery and Cantina, Miami Valley Brewery, Miami Valley Brewing Company (Manning's), Miamisburg Brewery (Water Street), Miamisburg Brewing Inc., Schrauder's brewery, Star City Brewing Company, Swartztrauber's brewery, Wenzes' brewery
   Katlein & Company, Franklin 114
   Sebald Brewery, Middletown 114
brewing. *See* beer, brewing
Bridgeport, Ohio 16, 65, 67, 77, 104, 115
Buehner, J. F. *126*, 127
Burlington, N. J. *See* New Jersey, Burlington
Butler County, Ohio 76, 78, 144

C

canals 38, 43, 51, 157
   aqueducts 39, 44, 47, *48*
   basins 44. *See Also* Murray's basin
   boats *38*, 44–45, 47, 49
   Erie Canal 34, 38
   locks 37, *39*, 44, *55*, 132, 170
   Miami & Erie 37, *39*, 44–45, 47-49, 66, 153–154, 168, 169–170
   Ohio and Erie 38
   Wabash & Erie 42, 45
Carlisle, Ohio 28
cellars. *See* beer, caves and cellars
Christian Moerlein Brewing Company 114, 157
Cincinnati 13, 20, 27, 36, 47, 115. *See Also* breweries, in Cincinnati; ice, industry, in Cincinnati
Civil War 72, *73*, 81, *83*, 84, 99, 101
   1st Regiment, Ohio 90
   17th Regiment, Ohio 87
   39th Regiment, Ohio 79
   83rd Regiment, Ohio 144
   93rd Regiment, Ohio 79, 80, 81, 90
   131st Regiment, Ohio 79, 82, 85, 97, 110
   132nd Regiment, Ohio 85–87, 89, 92–93, 94, 95, 98, 99
   Camp Chase 83, 85–87, *86*, 92, 185
   disease among soldiers 91, 95, 98. *See Also* Miamisburg, illness in
   Hundred Days' Men 81-83, 85, 87, 90, 95, 99, 110
   Ohio National Guard 83, 85, 87–88, 100
   Squirrel Hunters *80*, 110
   sutler 88, *91*, 92, 100
Clay, Adam 81
Coleman, Nelson 81, 90

Copperheads 76, 78, 90
corn 22–25, 36, 104, 114, 124, 125, 137. *See Also* maize

D
Deuscher, Henry P. 144, *145*, 158, 164–166
disease and illness. *See* Civil War, disease among soldiers; Miamisburg, illness in
distilleries 35, 45–46, 49, 66, 118, 124, 144
Dodds, William 103, 104, 115
Donnellan, Joseph E. 86, 89-90, 93, 99
Dreher, George 152
Duetch, Erhard 59

E
Eagle, Bill 96–97
Emde, Eve 19, 22, 27, 29, 30, 40
Emde, Henry 17–18, 19–22, 27–40, 45. *See Also* Emde's brewery
  in Franklin 17, 27–33, *28*
  in New Jersey 20, 22, 25, 26
Emde, Sophia. *See* Beachler, John R. and Sophia
Emde's brewery 17, 22, *27*, *35*, 35–37, 40
Emdee, Elizabeth Longsdorff 15
Emdee, Henry Jr. 15–17, 19, 27, 30, 33, 40
Engleman, Uriah 132, 171. *See Also* mills, flour
Entropy Brewing 46, *173*
Excelsior farm machinery. *See* Hoover & Gamble

F
fires, brewery 60, 140–141, 156, 165–166
floods 12–13, 69, 104–105. *See Also* Great Miami River

foundry, iron 39, *55*, 55–56, 64, 141, 167. *See Also* Sawyer, William
Fox, Frederick 33
Franklin, Ohio 17, *28*, 28–30, 113–114, 116, 123–124. *See Also* Emde, Henry, in Franklin
Freshwater, Jason and Lara 173. *See Also* Lucky Star Brewery and Cantina

G
Gamble, Samantha Ann Hoover 100
Gamble, William 100, 132, 167. *See Also* Hoover & Gamble
Gamble, William H. 100, 161-162. *See Also* Acme Folding Boat Company
Gebhart Tavern *11*, *12*, 11-14, 17, 19, 41. *See Also* taverns
Gebhart, Daniel 11, 13–14, 20, 33, 105
Gebhart, Ellen 34-35
Gebhart, Emanuel 55
Gebhart, Phillip (also Philip) 13, 105
Gebhart, Valentine 12
German Township 20
Germantown, Ohio 16–17,20, 86, 132
Great Miami River 11, 19–20, 28, 38, 49, 104, 163. *See Also* floods
Groby, Henry 106, 139
Groendyke Company 149
Grove, George 90
Gunckel, Philip 20

H
Haines, Joel 86–88
Hall, Jeremiah 79
Hall, John A. 79
Hamilton, Ohio 115, 117, 130, 141, 144 145, 165
Heist, Marlin 13, 105
Heritage Village *11*, *12*, *13*, 41, *42*
Herman, George 69, 71, 104–105
Herrmann, John and Susanna 70–71, 118

Herrmann, Margaret. *See* Nusz, Margaret Herrmann
Herrmann, Philip 69–71, 80-81, 82, 113
Herrmann, William 166
Highland, Louis and Anna 150
Hoff, Clara. *See* Hoover, Clara Hoff
Hoff, William 125
Hoover & Co. *61. Also see* Hoover & Gamble
Hoover & Gamble 61–64, *63*, 100, 132–133, *133*, 141, 146, 148–149, 158, 167. *See Also* Allen Watson Allen; Gamble, William; Hoover, David H.
Hoover, Abel 96, 100, 132, 167. *See Also* Hoover & Gamble
Hoover, Catharine Houtz 46, 49
Hoover, Clara Hoff 96
Hoover, David H. 45–47, 49–50, 52, 55, 58–59, 61, 63-64, 96-97, 100, 174
Hoover, Elizabeth. *See* Allen, Elizabeth Hoover
Hoover, Frederick Adam 45, 52
Hoover, Martin 46, 49, 52, 58
Hoover, Samantha Ann. *See* Gamble, Samantha Ann Hoover
Hoover's brewery 45–47, 49–50, *51*, 52-53, 54–55, 58–59, 147
hops 22–25, 36–37, 105, 137, 161
horse power 37, 62, 63
Houtz, Catharine. *See* Hoover, Catharine Houtz
Houtz, John and Elizabeth 46
Houtz, Nancy. *See* Watson, Nancy Houtz

I
ice. *See* beer, caves and cellars; Schwartztrauber, Jacob
    boxes 152, *156*
    harvesting 152–154, *154*

houses 112, 116, 137, 140, 143, 152–153, 155-158
industry 152–154, 156–157, 160, 165, 167
    in Cincinnati 153–154, 157, 160
ponds 112, *151*, 152–154, *154*, 156–158, 167
refrigeration *156, 157,* 157–158, *159*
Indian Mound Beer. *See* Miamisburg Brewing Inc.

J
Jackson Brewing Company 128, 130, *140*, 141–142, 143
Joo, Jordan and Brianna 173. *See Also* Entropy Brewing

K
Keelboat Park 47–48, *48*
Kercher, Anna Margaret Gebhart 41
Kercher, Jacob 20, 41–42, 44
Kercher House *11*, 41, *42*
Kinder, John Evans 97
Kohnen, Justin 168, 169, 171. *See Also* Star City Brewing Company
Kuehn, August Victor 128, 129–131, 137–139, *140*, 141–142, 143–145, 174. *See Also* Jackson Brewing Company, Miami Valley Brewery under Kuehn
Kuehn, Catherine Theureling 130, 138

L
lager beer 101–104, 106, 114, 151
Lancaster County, Pa. *See* Pennsylvania, Lancaster County
Lebanon County, Pa. *See* Pennsylvania, Lebanon County
Lebanon, Ohio 33, 36, 54, 123
Light, Esther 12–13, 104, 170
Longsdorff, Elizabeth. *See* Emdee, Elizabeth Longsdorff
Lucky Star Brewery Cantina *172*, 173

M

Madison, Chaning and Erwin 170

maize 24. *See Also* corn

malt 22–24, 37, 124, 141, 145

Manning, Mary Shultz 120–121, 128. *See Also* Miami Valley Brewing Company (Manning's)

Manning, William. *See* Manning, Mary Shultz

Mays, Samuel 77

Mays, William A. 81

McElwee, George 55–56, 64. *See Also* foundry, iron

Miami House 15, 59, 68, 134, 139, *143*, 146, 152

Miami Tribe *41*, 44-45

Miami River. *See* Great Miami River

Miami Township 19, 132

Miami Valley Brewery *101, 113*

   Under Kuehn *129*, 129–131, *130*, 136–138, *136, 137*, 140–142, 143

   Under Nusz *103*, 103–104, 106, *107*, 109, 111–112, 114–117, 126, 128, 151, 155. *See Also* beer, bottles and bottling; Nusz, William

Miami Valley Brewing Company (Manning's) 119–121, *127*, 127–128

Miamisburg 19–21, 40, 61, 66, 106, 131, 134–135, *135*, 145, 148, 161, 167, 173

   illness in 96–97, 99–100. *See Also* Civil War, disease among soldiers

Miamisburg Binder Twine & Cordage 133, 148, 172, *172. See Also* mills, twine mills, twine and cordage

Miamisburg Brewery (Water Street) *65*, 68, *69*, 72, *102*, 102–105, 116, 117

Miamisburg Brewing Inc. 145–147, 150, 158, 161, *164*, 164–165, *164, 165. See Also* ice, refrigeration

Miamisburg Bulletin 17-18, 72, 109–111, 121, 133. *See Also* Blossom brothers

Miamisburg News 72, 97, 158, 160, *165*

Miamisburg Twine and Cordage 148. *See Also* Miamisburg Binder Twine & Cordage

Miamisburgh 20, *21*

Middletown, Ohio 38, 114, 148, 167.

mills *27, 39*, 39-40, 46, 55, 132, 135, 150, 168, 170. *See Also* foundry, iron

   flour 39, 49, 132, 169–171, *171*

   paper 120, 132

   sawmill *39*, 49, *169*, 170, *171*

   twine 133, 135, 148-150, 172

Mound nuclear weapons plant 167-168

Mound, Miamisburg 13–14, *161*, 161–164, 167

Mullison, John D. 52, 58

Murray, Dolly Byxbe Messenger 43

Murray, Elias 42–45. *See Also* Murray's basin

Murray, Henrietta Pond 44

Murray's basin *43*, 44–45, 48., 49, 52, 54. *See Also* canals, basins

N

national guard. *See* Civil War, Ohio National Guard

New Jersey 25–26, 28. *See Also* Symmes, John Cleves

   Burlington 22, 25–26, 27–28

Nusz, John (brother) 70

Nusz, John (son) 105, 108-109, 111, 116

Nusz, Margaret Herrmann 69–71, 109, 113, 116–118

Nusz, Peter 70

Nusz, Susanna 109

Nusz, Wilhelmina. *See* Alexander, Wilhelmina Nusz

Nusz, William 69–71, 82, 112, 113–114, 116-117. *See Also* Miami Valley Brewery, Under Nusz; Miamisburg Brewery (Water Street)

O

opera house. *See* Star City Opera House

P

panics
    Panic of 1819 30–32, 34, 37, 51
    Panic of 1837 31, 51-54
    Panic of 1893 147–150
Peerless Mill Inn 169, 171. *See Also* mills, sawmill
Pennsylvania 26
    Berks County 12, 20, 66, 106, 120
    Lancaster County 20, 46
    Lebanon County 45
    Pennsylvania Dutch 20, 46
    Philadelphia 26, 102, 120
    Pittsburgh 20, 27, 108
Poicey, Eugene C. 144–145, 146
Prohibition. *See* temperance

R

railroads 20, 51, 59, 93, 104, 115, 149
    CCCI "Big Four" Railway (east of river) 107–108, 137, *131*, *151*, 165–167
    CH&D Railway (west of river) 65,-66 77-78, 104, 115
Reiter, Isaac H. "I. H." 66, 72, 96–97, 104, 121-122, 123
Richard, Peter 46. *See Also* Hoover's brewery
Riverfront Park 69, 110
Rossman, Philip 32–33
Ruegger, Jacob 170

S

saloons 66, 103, 115, 118, *119*, 121–127, *125*, *126*, 131, 138, 150, 152, 154, 167. *See Also* temperance
Sawyer, William 52–53, 55–59, 64, 75
Schenck, Robert C. 78
Schenck, William C. 29–30
Scheu, Jacob 142
Schiml, John and Michael 101–102
Schneider, John 137. *See Also* saloons
Schrauder, Charles. *See* Schrauder's brewery
Schrauder's brewery 59-60
Schroeder, Philip 115. *See Also* Schrauder's brewery
Schwartztrauber, Jacob 58, 127, 154–160, 166–167. *See Also* Swartztrauber, John
Schwind, Coelestin 114, 125
Schwytzer, Simon L. 141, 155–156
Sharrits, Zebulon 81
Shoup, Henry 81
Shultz, Emanuel 119–121. *See Also* Manning, Mary Shultz
Shultz, Mary E.. *See* Manning, Mary Shultz
slavery 73–76, 79
Snyder, John T. 81
squirrel hunters. *See* Civil War, Squirrel Hunters
St. Jacob's Evangelical Lutheran Church 106, *117*
St. Marys, Ohio 57
Star City Brewing Company 56, *169*, 171–172
Star City Opera House 16, *134*, 139
Swartztrauber, Catharine Albrecht 58
Swartztrauber, John 58. *See Also* Schwartztrauber, Jacob
Swartztrauber, Philip 81
Swartztrauber's brewery 58–59
Symmes, Daniel 36

Symmes, John Cleves 29, 36

T

taverns 31, 121. *See Also* Gebhart
Tavern
temperance 66, 118, *119*, 119–126, 138,
167
Tobacco 88, 91, 133–134, 146, 173
  Zimmer Spanish 59, 134
Treon, Dr. John 20
twine and cordage 61-62, 132–133,
135, 146, 148-149, 158, 172. *See Also*
Hoover & Gamble, mills, twine mills,
panics, Panic of 1893

V

Vallandigham *76*, 76–79, 91
Vickroy, Edwin A. 44, 48. *See Also*
Murray's basin
Voegle, John 122

W

warrants, land 28
Warren County, Ohio 20, 27, 33, 36,
49
Washington Bank 54
Washington Township 19, 44
Waters, Elwood 170
Watson, Joseph 49-50, 52–53, 58, 61–
63. *See Also* Allen Watson Allen
Watson, Nancy Houtz 49
Wenz, William and Jacob. *See*
Wenzes' brewery
Wenzes' brewery 60–61, 68
Wieland, Bernard 166
Wieland, Lorenz (or Lawrence) 127,
144–145, 166

Y

yeast 22–24, 101–102
Young, Daniel Junior 138
Young, Daniel W. 124–125, 131, 144–
147

Young, Julius 111

Z

Zimmer, Jacob 59, 62, 65, 134, 152.
See Also Tobacco, Zimmer Spanish

About the Author

Timothy R. Gaffney was born in Dayton, Ohio, and has lived most of his life in Ohio's Miami Valley, more than half of it in Miamisburg. He attended Dayton public schools and studied journalism at The Ohio State University. He worked at the *Piqua Daily Call* and the *Kettering Oakwood Times* before settling at the *Dayton Daily News*, where he mainly covered military affairs, aviation and space. He retired at the end of 2006 and worked additional years in communications and marketing for nonprofits. He holds a private pilot's license. His wife Jean is retired from the Dayton Metro Library, where she was both branch manager and children's librarian for more than thirty years, and later assistant director of collection development for the library system. They have four grown children, two grandchildren and two dogs. This is his seventeenth book.